The
Master's Perspective
on
DIFFICULT
PASSAGES

The Master's Perspective Series
Volume 1

The

Master's Perspective on

DIFFICULT PASSAGES

ROBERT L. THOMAS
general editor

kregel
PUBLICATIONS

Grand Rapids, MI 49501

For more information about Kregel Publications, visit our web site at www.kregel.com.

Cover design: Alan G. Hartman

Library of Congress Cataloging-in-Publication Data
Thomas, Robert L.
  The Master's perspective on difficult passages / by Robert L. Thomas, editor.
      p.   cm. — (The master's perspective series)
  Collection of articles that previously appeared in the first six volumes of The master's seminary journal.
  Includes bibliographical references and indexes.
  1. Bible—Criticism, interpretation, etc.
I. Thomas, Robert L.   II. Master's seminary journal.
III. Series.
BS511.2.M345   1998   220.6—dc21   98-26787
                                                 CIP
ISBN 0-8254-3180-8

Contents

Foreword

Happy is the man who finds wisdom, and the man who gains understanding; for her proceeds are better than the profits of silver, and her gain than fine gold. She is more precious than rubies, and all the things you may desire cannot compare with her. (Prov. 3:13–15 NKJV)

One of the most astonishing achievements of design, building, and decoration in the world is the famous Taj Mahal in Agra, India. The massive white stone tomb built for the wife of its designer and builder is a sight permanently etched in my mind.

As I stood at a distance looking across the long pool of water between me and the majestic edifice, it glistened a dazzling white with an almost pearlescent sheen in the bright sunlight like a perfectly symmetrical star against the blue sky and green grass. The full view was magnificent.

But it was only when I approached it closely that I saw the true and startling beauty—the entire structure, every square inch, had been inlaid with multicolored, semiprecious stones that had been placed into its surface one stone at a time. Millions of jewels unseen from the distance were revealed by a close look.

I am struck by how that experience with the Taj Mahal illustrates the majesty of Scripture. From a distance, viewing it as a whole, one can see its awesome grandeur, symmetry, and coherence. But the true magnificence of Scripture is only yielded to the one who comes close enough to see how every precious jewel of divine truth embedded in it by God sparkles with beauty only to those who examine it closely.

In this volume, some samples of the beautiful jewels of truth in Scripture are examined carefully for your joy and blessing.

John F. MacArthur Jr.

Introduction

Throughout the Bible are passages that Christians find difficult to handle. The difficulty may stem from how hard a passage is to interpret. Scripture contains many passages for which interpreters have differing explanations of the meaning. Modeling one's Christian walk to comply with standards of behavior commanded or implied in a passage may also create difficulty. It is one thing to know what is right, but it is often a major challenge to implement right conduct in one's Christian life.

The Master's Perspective on Difficult Passages—a collection of articles that appeared in the first six volumes of *The Master's Seminary Journal*—includes treatments of Scriptures dealing with both types of difficulty. Chapters 1, 3, 5, 6, 10, and 12 focus primarily on interpretive difficulties and a resolving of problems of that nature. Chapters 2, 4, and 11 issue challenges that relate primarily to Christian conduct, with chapters 7, 8, and 9 handling both interpretive difficulties and issues of Christian behavior.

Yet segregating the two types of difficulty may be artificial, because interpretive issues are in reality inseparable from how Christians should live. And conversely, how believers conduct themselves must be in response to sound interpretation of the Bible. Sound doctrine and wholesome practice always go together. The church must beware of ever thinking that either one can successfully exist without the other.

Chapter 1 delves into the identity of the "deceiving spirit" of 1 Kings 22:22. A close examination of Psalm 113 and how it combines the doctrine of God's transcendence with that of His immanence follows in the next chapter. Then comes a full discussion of whether Isaiah 53:4–5 supports physical healing in the atonement of Christ. The fourth chapter shows—through Daniel's example from Daniel 9—the importance of conforming prayer to God's prophetic program. Chapters 5 and 6 probe some highly important issues raised in Romans 11.

Chapter 7 discusses lessons about rewards derived from the six building materials named in 1 Corinthians 3:12. Church discipline comes to the forefront in chapter 8's treatment of 1 Corinthians 5:5. New Testament teaching about homosexuality is the subject in chapter 9's analysis of an important Greek word in 1 Corinthians 6:9 and 1 Timothy 1:10. Chapter 10 deals in depth with the often overlooked contribution of 1 Corinthians 13:11 in determining the time of cessation for the gifts of prophecy, tongues, and knowledge. The next chapter emphasizes the all-important role of prayer in Ephesians, particularly Ephesians 6:10–20. Lastly, the meaning of "the sin unto death" in 1 John 5:16–17 comes under scrutiny.

The viewpoint represented in each chapter does not necessarily represent that of The Master's Seminary, its administration, or its faculty, but in each case represents a perspective that merits consideration in resolving problems raised in the selected passage.

For those unfamiliar with the Hebrew, Aramaic, and Greek languages, an English transliteration and/or translation accompanies each word or expression in the original languages.

English translations used in this volume are those of the authors of individual chapters unless otherwise indicated.

I want to express my thanks to Mr. Dennis Swanson for his help in compiling the indexes for this volume.

Robert L. Thomas
Editor

About *The Master's Seminary Journal*

For those unfamiliar with *The Master's Seminary Journal,* a word of introduction is in order. *TMSJ* began publication in 1990 with the following statement of purpose:

> With this issue, *The Master's Seminary Journal* launches its career as a medium for the publication of scholarly articles dealing with the biblical text, Christian theology, and pastoral concerns. As you have noted, or will note, it also contains reviews of current and significant books, and occasionally of articles, relating to these issues. With these emphases in mind, technical articles dealing with such issues as the philosophy of religion, linguistics, or archaeology will not be included unless they clearly, directly, and significantly contribute to the understanding or application of God's written revelation— the Holy Bible. The editors desire that all articles be understandable, not only by seminary professors and other professional scholars, but also by pastors, and, indeed, by any serious students of Scripture.
>
> While most of the articles will be contributed by the faculty members of The Master's Seminary, the editors will solicit articles and reviews from recognized evangelical scholars, will evaluate voluntary contributions for possible inclusion, and will occasionally include outstanding historical selections from the public domain.
>
> It is our fervent prayer that our Lord Jesus Christ will be honored and exalted, either directly or indirectly, on every page of this publication, and that every article and review will contribute to the understanding or application of the Holy Scriptures as we await His return. (Excerpted from "Editorial," *TMSJ* 1/1 [1990]: 1–2)

The *Journal* has continued without interruption since that time, endeavoring to fulfil the purpose established at its beginning. Those interested in a subscription to *TMSJ* may contact Professor James F. Stitzinger, *The Master's Seminary Journal,* 13248 Roscoe Blvd., Sun Valley, CA 91352, or by e-mail at the address jstitzinger@mastersem.edu.

To the following pages of *The Master's Perspective on Difficult Passages,* volume 1 (1990) of *TMSJ* has contributed three chapters (chaps. 2, 7, and 12), volume 3 (1992) has provided four chapters (chaps. 4, 6, 8, and 9), volume 4 (1993) has been the source of two chapters (chaps. 1 and 10), and volume 6 (1995) has furnished three chapters (chaps. 3, 5, and 11).

Contributors

Irvin A. Busenitz
Vice President for Academic Administration
Professor of Bible and Old Testament
The Master's Seminary

James B. DeYoung
Professor of New Testament
Western Conservative Baptist Seminary
Portland, Oregon

Simon J. Kistemaker
Professor of New Testament Emeritus
Reformed Theological Seminary
Jackson, Mississippi

John F. MacArthur Jr.
President
Professor of Pastoral Ministries
The Master's Seminary

Richard L. Mayhue
Senior Vice President and Dean
Professor of Pastoral Ministries and Systematic Theology
The Master's Seminary

James E. Rosscup
Professor of Bible Exposition
The Master's Seminary

Robert L. Thomas
Professor of New Testament
The Master's Seminary

Michael G. Vanlaningham
Senior Pastor
Fox Lake Baptist Church
Ingleside, Illinois

George J. Zemek
Pastor-Teacher
Grace Bible Church of Brandon
Brandon, Florida
and Faculty Associate in Theology
The Master's Seminary

Abbreviations

This volume employs abbreviations sparingly, but has retained the following few:

BAGD —W. Bauer, W. F. Arndt, F. W. Gingrich, and F. W. Danker, *Greek-English Lexicon of the New Testament*

BDB —F. Brown, S. R. Driver, and C. A. Briggs, *Hebrew and English Lexicon of the Old Testament*

BDF —F. Blass, A. Debrunner, and R. W. Funk, *A Greek Grammar of the New Testament*

ICC —International Critical Commentary

MT —Massoretic Text

NICNT—New International Commentary on the New Testament

Str-B —[H. Strack and] P. Billerbeck, *Kommentar zum Neuen Testament*

TDNT —G. Kittel and G. Friedrich, eds., *Theological Dictionary of the New Testament*

TDOT —G. J. Botterweck and H. Ringgren, eds., *Theological Dictionary of the Old Testament*

TLG —*Thesaurus Linguae Graecae*

TWOT —R. Laird Harris, ed., *Theological Wordbook of the Old Testament*

1 Kings 22:19–23

False Prophets and the Deceiving Spirit

Richard L. Mayhue

First Kings 22:19–23 occasions the herculean challenge of identifying "the spirit" in a way that best accounts for the reality of false prophecy in 1 Kings 22:6. From six suggested possibilities, a personified spirit of prophecy, a demon, and Satan are initially deemed the most reasonable identifications and thus merit further inquiry. Considering the philological, hermeneutical, and theological factors of the three interpretations, Satan best fits "the spirit" in 1 Kings 22:21. Demonic activity, initiated and superintended by Satan, is the most probable and immediate dynamic responsible for the false prophecy in 1 Kings 22:6 and explained by 1 Kings 22:19–23. Finally, God did not ordain this event; however, He did permit it.

* * * * *

R. A. Torrey realistically recognized that one of the most puzzling passages in the Bible is 1 Kings 22 and its parallel account in 2 Chronicles 18.[1] Nearly everyone acknowledges that no conclusive agreement regarding the meaning of "the spirit" in 1 Kings 22:21 has surfaced. The interpretation of this passage is tantalizing for students of Scripture.

Even scholars of the same tradition differ over solutions to this enigma of how a holy God apparently collaborates with deceiving spirits. The central question is how to harmonize "the spirit" in 1 Kings 22:21 with the false prophecy of 1 Kings 22:6. How can the immediate text, the holiness of God, and the inerrancy of Scripture yield a satisfactory identification of "the spirit"?

The dilemma is how a holy and true God can associate Himself with the apparent instigation of lies among false prophets? A proposed solution to this ultimate conundrum will address three significant questions:

1. Does 1 Kings 22:1–40 represent sane factual history, or is it fictionalized drama with a spiritual message?
2. Is Micaiah's vision in 22:19–23 one of reality or merely symbolic?
3. What reality or dynamic force best accounts for the false prophecy of 22:6—human, angelic, or divine?

Several secondary inquiries also provoke curiosity, even though they are not the primary objective of this study. Who is Micaiah—possibly the prophet of 1 Kings 20:35ff.? Why did Ahab call for Micaiah and not Elijah in 22:8? What caused Jehoshaphat to question Ahab's prophets at 22:7? How did Ahab recognize Micaiah's initially barbed answer in 22:15?

First Kings 22 and 2 Chronicles 18, arguably, rank as the foremost example of prophetic conflict between kings and prophets, between God and false prophets, and between true and false prophets. Other memorable encounters from the OT include Balaam (Numbers 22–24), Elijah's contest with the four hundred prophets of Baal (1 Kings 18:16–40), and Jeremiah's confrontation of Hananiah (Jeremiah 28). In the NT, Jesus (Matt. 7:15; 24:11, 24), Peter (2 Peter 2), and John (1 John 4:1–6) warned about prophetic conflict. Paul contended with Elymas (Acts 13:6–12) and Revelation records the last foray with "the false prophet" (16:13; 19:20; 20:10). However, no passage in Scripture warns as distinctly as 1 Kings 22 that (1) kings have more to fear from true prophets than true prophets from kings and (2) false prophets have more to fear from God than from kings.[2]

BIOGRAPHICAL LINEUP

Since the focal point of this investigation is to identify "the spirit" in 1 Kings 22:21, a biographical and historical sketch is foundational. Ahab, Jehoshaphat, and Micaiah are the chief personages encountered in 1 Kings 22, where Ahab faces the decision of whether to engage Ben-Hadad, king of Syria, in a military confrontation.

Ahab

The eighth king of Israel during the Divided Kingdom phase of Jewish history, Ahab was the son of Omri. His reign began in the thirty-eighth year of Asa, king of Judah, and continued for twenty-two years (1 Kings 16:29). Thiele fixed Ahab's rule from 874/73 to 853 B.C.[3]

Ahab's wife Jezebel worshiped the Tyrian god Melqart and introduced, through Ahab, the cult of Baal-Melqart to Israel.[4] She vividly demonstrated her intolerance for anything related to the LORD by her attempted annihilation of the prophets of God (1 Kings 18:13).

Because of Ahab's "religious" activities, which abundantly and absurdly violated the Mosaic standards, he had an ominous reputation. He was the ruler who did more to provoke the Lord, God of Israel, than all the kings of Israel before him (1 Kings 16:30–33).

Premature death is often the fate of those who forsake the Lord, so Ahab died from an arrow-wound (1 Kings 22:34–37) and Jezebel fell before Jehu (2 Kings 9:30–37). In fact, their whole pagan family perished, again at the hands of Jehu (cf. 2 Kings 9:8 with 2 Kings 10:1–28).

Obviously neither of the royal couple was a man or woman of God. Their religion was pagan and their activities ruthless (1 Kings 18:4; 19:2; 21:1–16). Athaliah, a daughter of Jezebel, even attempted to kill Joash, who was the only legal heir to the messianic promise through David (2 Kings 11:1–3).

Jehoshaphat

The reign of Jehoshaphat obviously contrasts with that of Ahab. The son of Asa, he reigned as the fourth king of Judah twenty-five years (1 Kings 15:24; 2 Chron. 20:31).

This righteous ruler sought the God of his fathers, followed God's commandments, and did not act as evil Israel did (2 Chron. 17:4). He removed high places and the Asherah (2 Chron. 17:6; 19:3), and did right in the sight of the Lord (2 Chron. 20:32). The writer of Chronicles characterizes Jehoshaphat as a man who sought the Lord with all of his heart (2 Chron. 22:9).

Yet Jehoshaphat's reign was not blameless. Due to military pressures from Ben-Hadad of Syria and Shalmaneser III of Assyria, Jehoshaphat allied himself to Ahab by the marriage of his son Jehoram to Athaliah, daughter of Ahab and Jezebel (2 Chron. 18:1; 21:6). This marital bond paved the way for joint military operations (1 Kings 22 and 2 Chronicles 18), which resulted in a rebuke from the Lord by Jehu, the seer (2 Chron. 19:2).

Jehoshaphat, a God-fearing ruler, allowed governmental pressures to supersede his relationship with the Creator. The Jewish nation did the same in demanding a king like all the other nations (cp. 1 Sam. 8:19–20 with 1 Sam. 12:12). In each case, God permitted sinful activities; but, as with Joseph (Gen. 50:20), He used them to fulfil His ultimate divine plan (Isa. 46:10).

Micaiah

The Bible does not speak about Micaiah, son of Imlah, except in 1 Kings 22 and 2 Chronicles 18. Apparently Micaiah was not the only true prophet of God in Israel (cf. 1 Kings 17:1; 18:4), but he probably was the only one immediately available. The Scriptures are silent and provide no basis for conjecture on why Ahab summoned Micaiah and not Elijah. It seems that Micaiah returned to the custody of Amon and Joash from whom he had been released to appear before the royal court (1 Kings 22:26; cf. "quickly" in 1 Kings 22:9).

Ahab's reaction (1 Kings 22:8) suggests that Micaiah could be the prophet who declared Ahab's death for not killing Ben-Hadad as God commanded (1 Kings 20:35–43).[5]

From the narrative of 1 Kings 22 and from the fulfilment of Micaiah's dream (cp. Deut. 18:22 and 1 Kings 22:28 with 1 Kings 22:17 and 1 Kings 22:37), it is conclusive that Micaiah was truly a prophet of the Lord. None other than Ahab himself attests this (1 Kings 22:8, 16) along with Zedekiah, son of Chenaanah (1 Kings 22:24).

In the face of severe pressure (1 Kings 22:13, 16), Micaiah was faithful to God. In spite of overwhelming unpopularity, he delivered perfectly the divine message. Zedekiah rewarded him with a humiliating facial blow (1 Kings 22:24) and a return to prison, where the *soup de jour* was water and the entree was bread (1 Kings 22:27). Whether Micaiah obtained a release when Ahab's lifeless body came back to Samaria (1 Kings 22:37) is unknown. However, it is a certainty that God did not leave Himself without a true witness in Israel!

HISTORICAL CONTEXT

The military lineup in the ancient Near East during the tenth and ninth centuries B.C. included Shishak of Egypt (945–924 B.C.), Ashurnasirpal II (883–859 B.C.) and Shalmaneser III (859–824 B.C.) of Assyria, Ben-Hadad of Syria (890–841 B.C.), and the numerous kings of Israel and Judah.[6] About 879 B.C., Asa, king of Judah, called upon Ben-Hadad I of Syria to attack Baasha and the kingdom of Israel, who were threatening Jerusalem (1 Kings 15:16–22). In 855 B.C., Ben-Hadad I struck Israel with a coalition of thirty-two kings (1 Kings 20:1). As he was getting himself drunk, the Lord delivered him into the hands of Ahab (1 Kings 20:13–21).

Again in 854 B.C. Ben-Hadad I attacked Ahab at Amphek and was soundly defeated (1 Kings 20:26–30), as the Lord prevailed for Ahab (1 Kings 20:28). The Lord indicated His displeasure at Ahab for not killing Ben-Hadad I (1 Kings 20:31–34) through a prophet of God (1 Kings 20:35–43).

In the meantime, however, Shalmaneser III of Assyria was threatening both Syria and Palestine from the east. Ahab and Ben-Hadad I formed a military alliance with neighboring kings to meet Shalmaneser and stop his southern thrust. The combatants met at Qarqar (modern Khirbet Qarqur) on the Orontes River in a decisive battle unmentioned in the Bible but recorded on the Monolith Inscription of Shalmaneser.[7] Though Shalmaneser was probably the victor, the encounter prevented further southern penetration.

After thwarting the Assyrian threat, Ahab and Ben-Hadad I renewed their mutual hostilities because of Ahab's desire to retake Ramoth-Gilead (1 Kings 22:1–3). It was this military prospect that occasioned Jehoshaphat's quest for the Lord's approval. Although the Lord caused Ahab's previous victories, the king demonstrated no interest in the things of God (1 Kings 22:3–5). The Lord delivered Israel from defeat by Ben-Hadad I not because of Ahab, but in spite of him.

This is the immediate situation of the interpretive problem of this essay. A godless pagan Ahab sought to involve the God-fearing Jehoshaphat in a military operation to regain previously lost territory. Without seeking the Lord's leading or help, he plunged forward, little realizing that God had delivered him twice before, but would seal his doom in this third engagement with Syrian forces.

INTERPRETIVE HISTORY

Aetiological View

Of thirteen theologically liberal scholars consulted, over half suggest this rationalistic view. They are not all fully agreed in their explanations, but are united in denying the literality of Scripture and the supernaturalness of God.

Heaton described "the spirit" as the Hebrew way of accounting for evil. He writes,

> The sequel is worth pausing over, because it indicated how the existence of false prophecy was accounted for. Obviously it posed a problem. Had God lost control? Couldn't he stop it? . . . The Hebrews . . . preferred even to attribute calamity to God—and so with astounding daring they also explained evil things like false prophecy as instruments used by God for his own purposes. . . . This naive explanation of evil may not satisfy us, but at least it enabled the Hebrew to maintain his faith in God's supreme sovereignty, despite what we should call "intellectual difficulties."[8]

Burney[9] and Eissfeldt[10] identify "the spirit" as an "imaginary" and "legendary" character, respectively. Eissfeldt observes,

For the vision accounts of Balaam and Micaiah ben Imlah are likely also to have been imitations by the narrators from what they could observe in the prophets of their own time. Thus we cannot go further than saying that we have only biographical narratives, some of them of a legendary character. . . .[11]

A third variation of the aetiological position is explained by Eichrodt[12] as the development of the Hebrew concept of רוּחַ (rûaḥ, "spirit"). Von Rad considers "the spirit" to be the "spirit of Yahweh," which is a well-defined concept in the progressive development of the OT prophetical office.[13] They both see it as a developing concept with possible Canaanite and Ugaritic backgrounds.

The common element in each proponent is the interpreter's rationalistic explanation of a vision given to the prophet Micaiah, supposedly from God. Their positions are not well supported by biblical data.

Self-deluded View

F. W. Farrar describes the subject passage as a "daringly anthropomorphic apologue." He writes, "The prophets were self-deceived, but this would be expressed by saying that Jehovah deceived them."[14] Typical of many older expositors, Farrar treats this enigmatic passage with little more than personal opinion expressed in somewhat elaborate and nebulous language.

More recently, this view has attracted wider support. Advocates include Dillard,[15] Kaiser,[16] and Vannoy.[17] Kaiser succinctly notes, "These prophets spoke 'out of their open minds.'"[18] In this writer's analysis, the "self-deluded" approach does not do adequate justice to the immediate text or to similar texts such as Job 1–2, Zechariah 3, 2 Thessalonians 2, and Revelation 12, because it does not allow for the reality of a heavenly encounter between God and "the spirit."

Demonic View

A popular choice among conservatives, the demonic identification also has early patristic support from Augustine (354–430 A.D.).[19] Recent advocates of this position are mostly conservatives.[20]

Though each of these scholars may have convincing arguments for his position, he usually offers sparse support. The following features have been used to identify "the spirit" as demonic:

1. The identification of מַלְאֲכֵי רָעִים (mal'ăkê rāʿîm, "messengers of evil") in Psalm 78:49 as demons.[21]

2. The identification of רוּחַ רָעָה (*rûaḥ rāʻāh,* "evil spirit") in Judges 9:23; 1 Samuel 16:14–16; 18:10; 19:9 as demonic.[22]
3. The numerous NT references to demons as spirits. Examples include Mark 1:23; Acts 8:7; 1 Timothy 4:1; Revelation 16:13–14.
4. The article with "spirit" in 1 Kings 22:21 is used in its generic sense.[23]
5. The activity of "the spirit" in 1 Kings 22:19–23 is representative of demonic activity.[24]

Against this view, however, there are some serious objections:

1. Nowhere in Scripture do demons appear before the throne of God.
2. The generic explanation of the article with "spirit" is only one of several grammatical possibilities.
3. Since demons are not omnipresent, one demon could not affect four hundred prophets simultaneously (1 Kings 22:6, 22–23).

It appears that the majority of confusion and misunderstanding in this passage has resulted from a failure to identify the cause and effect relationship between 1 Kings 22:1–7 and 22:19–23. Whoever or whatever "the spirit" in 22:21 is, it must also account for the reality of the prophets of Ahab prophesying falsely (cp. 1 Kings 22:6 with 22:34–36). The demonic view can adequately explain the false prophecy, but is weak as an identification of "the spirit."

Personified View

A majority of interpreters have adopted this, a position presented by all traditions of interpreters except Patristic.[25] Edersheim represents this view, which has been variously explained:

> It must not be understood as declaring what really took place in heaven, but as a vision in which the prophet saw before him, as in a parable, the explanation and the higher Divine meaning of the scene that had just been enacted before the two kings. . . . It was a real external vision, God directed, which the prophet describes; not a vision of what really occurred, the seduction of Ahab by his false prophets as the result of Divine judgment, was thus presented in a parable, as it were, from the heavenly point of view.[26]

As to specific identification of "the spirit," Keil comments,

> The spirit (הָרוּחַ [hārûaḥ, "the spirit"]) which inspired these prophets as a lying spirit is neither Satan, nor any evil spirit whatever, but, as the definite article and the whole of the context shows, the personified spirit of prophecy. . . .[27] [transliteration and translation added]

Unfortunately, this view creates more problems than it solves. It provides a possible interpretation, but it does not explain the cause of the false prophecy in 1 Kings 22:6. Moreover, it leaves the interpreter with the even larger problem of explaining what or who the personified spirit of prophecy is. Keil would respond,

> But the false prophets as well as the true were governed by a supernatural spiritual principle, and, according to divine appointment, were under this influence of the evil spirit in the service of falsehood, just as the true prophets were moved by the Holy Spirit in the service of the Lord.[28]

However, if the Holy Spirit is God's dynamic force for true prophecy, then what reality accounts for the numerous accounts of false prophecy in the OT? The view does not explain this satisfactorily.

One possible explanation has been suggested by Whitcomb: "In the vision, the spirit who volunteered to entice Ahab's prophets may have been a personification of the spirit of false prophecy as in Zechariah 13:2."[29] But if this be true, what reality is the spirit personifying and how does this relate to the false prophecy in 1 Kings 22:6? Who or what is the false spirit of prophecy? Both 1 Kings 22:21 and Zechariah 13:2 demand that the energizing force behind the false prophecy be identified by something more than a biblical term; it must identify the actual cause! Commentators either briefly pass over 1 Kings 22:21 with a quick identification or labor unconvincingly to find a token touch of causal meaning in the passage.[30]

Supporting arguments for this view include:

1. Grammatically, רוּחַ שֶׁקֶר (rûaḥ šeqer, "spirit of deception") is in the construct state and must be translated "spirit of deceit" rather than "deceiving spirit."
2. רוּחַ (rûaḥ, "spirit") is used in a similar sense elsewhere in Scripture.

Exodus 28:3	spirit of wisdom
Numbers 5:14	spirit of jealousy
Deuteronomy 34:9	spirit of wisdom
Judges 9:23	spirit of evil
Isaiah 11:2	spirit of wisdom and understanding
	spirit of counsel and strength
	spirit of knowledge and fear of the Lord
Isaiah 19:14	spirit of distortion
Isaiah 28:6	spirit of justice
Isaiah 29:10	spirit of deep sleep
Jeremiah 51:1	spirit of a destroyer
Hosea 4:12; 5:4	spirit of harlotry
Zechariah 12:10	spirit of grace
Zechariah 13:2	spirit of uncleanness

Heinisch explains, "The hagiographer simply wished to emphasize the fact that every event, whatever the circumstances, has been willed by God and must be traced back to God as its final cause."[31]

By far the most serious objection to this view is its implications for interpreting similar passages. If this is a parabolic personification, how then are Job 1:6–12; 2:1–6; Isaiah 6:1–13; Zechariah 3:1–10 to be understood? The normal conservative interpretation of each is that they were actual encounters in heaven. As a matter of fact, this was John's explanation of Isaiah 6 (cf. John 12:36–41.) He declares that Isaiah actually saw the glory of Christ on the throne.

Satanic View

Although this view does not have the strongest numerical support, it is the majority choice of the early scholars who wrote concerning this passage.[32] In support of this position, the following proofs have been suggested:

1. The parallel situations of Job 1:6–12; 2:1–7; Zechariah 3:1–10; Revelation 12:10, where Satan appeared before God in heaven, suggest "the spirit" in 1 Kings 22:21 be identified as Satan. Merril Unger notes, "This is an extremely attractive thesis since Satan is King and head over the demonic powers."[33]
2. The use of the article with "spirit" to indicate a particular, well-known spirit suggests Satan.[34]
3. The title of "the father of lies" given to Satan by Christ in John 8:44 characterizes "the spirit" of 1 Kings 22:21.

4. Paul's description of Satan as a disguised angel of light in 2 Corinthians 11:14 describes "the spirit" of 1 Kings 22:21.
5. Satan's activity in Genesis 3 of deceiving Eve and in 1 Chronicles 21:1 of deceiving David suggest an identification of Satan. Also compare the influence of Satan upon Ananias to lie to the Holy Spirit in Acts 5:3.
6. The deceiving activity of Satan in Revelation parallels that of "the spirit" in 1 Kings 22:21. Cf. Revelation 12:9; 20:3, 8, 10.
7. Ephesians 6:12 suggests that Satan is a spirit being. This is supported by Satan's entry into Judas. Cf. Luke 22:3 and John 13:27.
8. Second Thessalonians 2:11–12 presents a clearly different but similar situation and uses almost identical language to describe God sending a deluding influence upon the world.

The most formidable argument against this view is that Satan is not omnipresent and could not possibly have entered the mouth of all four hundred prophets (1 Kings 22:6, 22–23). Additionally, it has been suggested that שֶׁקֶר רוּחַ (rûaḥ šeqer) (1 Kings 22:22–23) is in the construct state and should be translated "spirit of deceit" rather than "deceiving spirit."

Angelic View

This view is an extreme possibility although it was not advocated by any scholar consulted. Though not supporting this idea, F. C. Cook suggests it as a possibility.[35] Because no indication is in the immediate text or anywhere else in the Bible that good angels are involved in deceiving activities, this view cannot receive serious consideration.

Noncommittal View

Several commentators, both liberal and conservative, conveniently chose to avoid dealing with the identity in question.[36]

PHILOLOGICAL CONSIDERATIONS

Text

The OT Massoretic Text has no textual variations within or between 1 Kings 22:21 and 2 Chronicles 18:20. A comparison of 1 Kings 22:21 with 2 Chronicles 18:20 in the LXX reveals a significant variation, however. The 1 Kings passage presents *"spirit"* as an anarthrous noun while in 2 Chronicles the noun is articulated. This is also at variance with the Massoretic Text.

The Aramaic Targum of Jonathon renders both verses רוּחָא (rûḥ', "the spirit"). This original spelling indeed agrees with the MT because of its use of the postpositive article א (').[37] The Latin Vulgate is noteworthy because the definite article is absent from both passages. Since Latin has no word for either the definite or indefinite article,[38] the Vulgate witness is inconclusive.

In view of the MT and Aramaic Targum evidence for the article, which is supported by the LXX reading in 2 Chronicles, the conclusion is that the article in 1 Kings 22:21 is the correct rendering. Kittel considered the LXX reading of 1 Kings insignificant and did not include this variation in the critical apparatus of *Biblia Hebraica*.[39]

Unfortunately, no Dead Sea Scroll manuscript has 1 Kings 22:21. However, there are fragments from 1 Kings that include 1 Kings 22:28–31. Examples of the Former Prophets have been located in several Qumrân caves. Milik observes, "They seem to be derived from the same Hebrew tradition as is represented in the LXX!"[40] Brownlee[41] and Baillet[42] concur with this analysis.

Several fragments of 1 Kings are included in *Les 'Petites Grottes' De Qumrân*. They are 1 Regum 3:12–14 (fragment 1), 1 Regum 12:28–31 (fragments 2, 3, and 4), and 1 Regum 22:28–31 (fragment 5).[43] These fragments are dated in the last half of the second century B.C. as verified by the antiquated orthography. In these five fragments, sixty-seven consonantal characters, all of which are in agreement with the Massoretic Text, occur. This in no way verifies that the MT is totally substantiated or validated by the DSS, but it does serve as an empirical demonstration of the MT's reliability after one thousand years of transmission through hand-lettered copies.

If LXX readings are more often reliable in the Dead Sea Scroll fragments of the Former Prophets than anywhere else in the OT, how does this affect the above conclusion that the article in 1 Kings 22:21 is correct in light of its absence in the LXX? In view of the strong supporting evidence for the Massoretic reading, it appears that the LXX rendering could possibly be marred by a scribal error of omission although there is no absolute explanation for this mistake from the evidence at hand. Therefore, the remainder of this investigation assumes the validity of the articulated reading.

Syntax
The Article (הָרוּחַ [hārûaḥ, "the spirit"])
Because of the inerrancy and infallibility of Scripture, it can be ascertained that the articulated noun *hārûaḥ* was used by the Holy Spirit for a specific reason. In Hebrew grammar the article is always omitted when a person or thing is represented as undetermined or unknown.[44] Therefore,

it is conversely true that the article is used almost exclusively when the person or thing is determinable.

Of the numerous uses of the article in Hebrew, three possibilities are applicable to this problem:

1. The article is used to limit ideas of species to definite individuals or things.[45]
2. The article may be employed in a generic sense to indicate the totality of the individuals in the genus so that the union of a singular noun with the article includes every individual under the species.[46] This same effect can be equally well accomplished by the plural.
3. A peculiarity in Hebrew is the use of the article to designate a single unknown that is to be later determined or identified.[47]

Because "the spirit" is not later identified, alternative 3 can be dismissed from consideration. Either option 1 or 2 is valid. The first alternative seems to be the natural use in its simplest sense and is preferred in light of further supporting evidence. The generic use (option 2) is legitimate grammatically, but it is the more difficult use and is not necessary to identify "the spirit."

Construct State or Attributive Adjective? (רוּחַ שֶׁקֶר [*rûaḥ šeqer,* "deceiving spirit"])

The expression *šeqer* occurs in verses 22 and 23. Those who argue for the personified view, understanding "the spirit" to be the spirit of prophecy, interpret this form as the construct state, which would best be translated "spirit of deceit." The satanic and demonic positions demand that *šeqer* function as an attributive adjective and have the meaning "deceiving spirit."

The form *rûaḥ* is used as both absolute and construct, which makes this determination difficult since the spelling is correct for either.[48] Obviously positive identification of the form is impossible, but the possibility that "the spirit" does not have to have a personified meaning is evident. It is absolutely essential to the demonic or satanic view that the attributive understanding (i.e., construct state) is legitimate. Those who use the construct state to support a personified position must recognize that the construct offers another attractive alternative.

Singular or Collective Use? (*rûaḥ šeqer*)

Almost any word may be used in the singular as a collective, especially words that name classes of persons or things.[49] The force of this observation is somewhat diminished in this particular instance by the normal plural form of "spirit," which is רוּחוֹת *(rûḫôt)*. In context, however, verses 22 and 23 speak of the effect upon the four hundred prophets of Ahab for which "the spirit" of verse 21 was to be responsible. Since one spirit (regardless of the identification) cannot be omnipresent in four hundred men simultaneously, a collective understanding of *rûaḥ šeqer* is necessary.

Syntactically, it may be understood then that "the spirit" of verse 21 was responsible for a multiple deceiving effect upon the prophets. As theological considerations will show, the only alternative that can be naturally explained is that "the spirit" is none other than Satan.

Semantics
Spirit *(rûaḥ)*

The Ugaritic *rwḥ,* meaning "wind, spirit, or breath,"[50] has four basic meanings:[51]

1. breath/wind
2. a principle that gives life to the body
3. seat of emotions, intellectual functions, and attitude of will
4. supernatural influences acting upon men

As expected, alternative 4 is the use in 1 Kings 22:21–23.

Those who espouse the Personified View have identified "the spirit" with "the spirit of prophecy" as if this spirit of prophecy was a well-known concept. On the contrary, the phrase "spirit of prophecy" appears only once in the Bible. In Revelation 19:10 the testimony of Jesus is equated with "the spirit of prophecy." This use associated with Christ could in no sense account for "the spirit" in 1 Kings 22:21, much less for the false prophecy in 22:6.

The concept of a "spirit of prophecy" is surely derived from the familiar OT phrase, "the Spirit of the LORD came upon him and he prophesied. . . ." This is strengthened by 2 Peter 1:21, which directly testifies that the Holy Spirit is God's agent for the revelation of true prophecy. However, this does not account for a "spirit of false prophecy."

Rûaḥ in the OT and πνεῦμα *(pneuma,* "spirit") in the NT are used in reference to demons. Such OT passages as 1 Samuel 16:23; 18:10; 19:9 possibly use "evil spirit" in reference to demonic activity. Far more conclusive is the NT use, especially in the Gospels. Examples include Mark 1:23; Acts 8:7; 1 Timothy 4:1; Revelation 16:13–14.

Neither Testament calls Satan a spirit, but this does not make the identification impossible. Because Satan entered into Judas (cf. Luke 22:3;

John 13:27), he must be a spirit being. Further, Paul's description of a Christian's battle against the forces of evil equates Satan (Eph. 6:11) with a force not of flesh and blood but with "spiritual" (πνευματικός [pneumatikos]) forces of evil (Eph. 6:12). Semantically, a good case can be made for either a satanic or demonic identification of rûaḥ in 1 Kings 22, but a "spirit of prophecy" responsible for false prophecy finds no support.

Entice (פָּתָה [pātāh]) and Deceive (šeqer)

Pātāh, which can be translated "deceive, entice, persuade, seduce, or prevail upon," has the basic idea of overcoming or prevailing.[52] This victorious result is obtainable either legitimately or dishonestly. In Jeremiah 20:7–9 and Ezekiel 14:9, this activity is credited to God. In Exodus 22:16, it has the sense of a man seducing a virgin sexually, and in Deuteronmy 11:16, it involves deception that results in turning away from truth. Only context can determine the legitimacy of the action whereby one prevails over another.

Šeqer involves deception by words through falsehoods and lies.[53] It speaks in Jeremiah 14:14; 23:25–26; 29:21 of prophets prophesying falsely, in Psalm 101:7 of a lie, and in Proverbs 17:4 of a liar.

The interchange of these two terms in 1 Kings 22:23 is interesting in that it highlights the difference between two almost synonymous words. In 22:20 God asks for a volunteer to entice (pātāh), and in 22:21 "the spirit" volunteers to entice or, better yet, prevail. When God asks "the spirit" in 22:22 what activity would be used, "the spirit" replies he would be a deceiving spirit (rûaḥ šeqer). In 22:22–23 God approved of the deceiving activity (šeqer) that resulted in overcoming (pātāh) Ahab in the sense that God allowed it to occur, not that He planned or approved of the dishonest means to a legitimate end.

Jeremiah 20:7–9 and Ezekiel 14:9 prove that God prevails and overcomes. The direct statement in Titus 1:2 and the fact that God is never associated with the word šeqer in the OT confirms that He never lies. However, overcoming by falsehoods is an activity characteristic of Satan and his demonic agents.

HERMENEUTICAL CONSIDERATIONS[54]

Figurative Language in Prophecy
Symbolic Speech

More than one interpreter has erred by failing to understand the purpose of symbols used prophetically. A basic maxim that provides guidance and stability is, "Prophecy arises out of a historical situation."[55]

This leads logically to a normal interpretation of prophecy, recognizing the legitimate use of speech figures. Symbols in prophetic passages represent the reality of a literal person or object about which the author writes. Mickelsen suggests three characteristics for symbols:[56]

1. The symbol is itself a literal object.
2. The symbol is used to convey some lesson or truth.
3. The connection between the literal object and the truth it teaches becomes clearer in light of the intention of the one who used the symbol.

Once a figure has definitely been pinpointed, it is then the interpreter's responsibility to seek diligently the literal idea the author intended. For example, four beasts in Daniel 7:3–7 are used symbolically, but the interpreter finds help at 7:17 where Daniel explains that these four beasts are four literal kingdoms. John describes Jesus in Revelation 1:12–16 with symbols and then furnishes the literal meaning of several of these symbols in verse 20.

What symbols did Micaiah see in his vision of 1 Kings 22:19–23, and what are their interpretations? First, it must be recognized that this vision is symbolic in terms of self-interpreting anthropomorphisms. First, the expressions "the LORD sitting on His throne" and "all the host of heaven standing by Him" are anthropomorphically communicating the setting for Micaiah's vision. Instead of requiring a separate interpretation such as in Daniel or Revelation, these phrases are self-explanatory. Second, although the surroundings have an anthropomorphic description, the main personages are not also necessarily symbolic.

In the demonic view, "the spirit" is symbolic of demonic agents, and their appearance before the Lord symbolically represents God's permissive will with respect to demonic activity. "The spirit" then symbolically pictures that real dynamic or energizing power that caused the prophets to prophesy falsely in 1 Kings 22:6. Inherent in this understanding also is the generic use of the article as discussed above. This explanation, however, ignores Satan's reign over demons and creates a bigger problem—why is Satan bypassed in this process?

While this possible interpretation is legitimate, it does require a unique happening never repeated before or after in Scripture. It is more natural to recognize the anthropomorphic background of the vision, but to interpret "the LORD" and "the spirit" literally. With this approach, "the spirit" seems certain to correspond with Satan's other literal appearances before God in Job 1; 2; Zechariah 3:1; Revelation 12:10.

Parables

Those interpreters who advocate the Personified View identify "the spirit" as the personified spirit of false prophecy in a parabolic vision that approximates the setting of 1 Kings 22:3–6. This connection between heaven and earth must be made to introduce the parable into the context. Does the vision in 1 Kings 22:19–23 qualify as parabolic, though?

According to all definitions of parables, 1 Kings 22:19–23 can legitimately be termed a parable. It is like other OT parables, e.g., 2 Samuel 12:1–4. Yet this is the only feature that qualifies the Personified View as a legitimate possibility hermeneutically.

The next issue is whether the parabolic explanation of "the spirit" accounts for the reality of false prophecy in 1 Kings 22:6. Those holding the Personified View would answer that it is "the spirit of false prophecy." But the question arises, "Who or what is the spirit of false prophecy?" It is at this point that the parabolic interpretation and its attendant identification falters.

The most defensible position is that 1 Kings 22:19–22 has not been placed alongside 1 Kings 22:6 for comparison as the parabolic understanding demands, but rather is a causal explanation for the actual false prophecy in 22:6. The more natural explanation is to understand Micaiah's vision to include a real encounter between God and Satan. Satan then performed the deception through his demonic assistants according to God's permissive will. J. Barton Payne concurs:

> I would hesitate to involve the hermeneutic of symbolic interpretation without contextual substantiation, though it is true, the statement about the "spirit" occurs in a vision (yet most of us would argue for literalism even in such a case: cf. hell in the parable of the rich man and Lazarus, or the millennium in the visions of Revelation). A connection in time and place with Job would favor satanic understanding. . . .[57]

Biblical Visions

A vision involves a supernatural presentation of certain events before the mind of the prophet that can be represented symbolically (Dan. 4:10–17) or actually (Ezek. 8:5–18). Furthermore, because some objects in a vision can be symbolic, it is not necessary that all the objects be symbolic (Rev. 4:2–5:14). A good rule of thumb is not to interpret symbolically when the object can be real, especially when there are no theological objections to doing so (Ezekiel 40–48; Isa. 65:25).

Visions can be predictive, such as that given to Micaiah in 1 Kings

22:17 and 1 Kings 22:19–23, or didactic, as when Micaiah communicated his vision to Ahab and Jehoshaphat after the fact. The subject passage affords a very rare situation because both the predictive and didactic aspects, along with the fulfilment, are present within the same context. The vision had originally been given to Micaiah by God as predictive; it was fulfiled in 1 Kings 22:6; and it was related in its didactic sense in 22:19–23.

Why was the vision given to Micaiah? Obviously, the primary purpose was didactic, for the vision was not revealed by Micaiah until after the prophecy was fulfiled. What then does the vision teach? Two elements seem prominent. First, the four hundred prophets of Ahab had indeed prophesied falsely. Second, "the spirit" was the source from which the false prophecy had originated.

"The spirit," however identified, must account for the prophecy in 1 Kings 22:6, which Jehoshaphat correctly evaluated as false. Interpreting "the spirit" as a personification of the spirit of prophecy does not provide a real answer as to the cause of false prophecy. The Holy Spirit is the source of God-breathed prophecy, but who or what is responsible for false prophecy?

A response might be that the prophets were just lying and really did not know the answer to Ahab's question. However, it would not be to the prophets' benefit to prophesy falsely, knowing that there was good reason to believe that the prophecy might fail. It was this same basic situation that the Chaldeans faced when Nebuchadnezzer challenged them to tell him his dream (Dan. 2:1–11). Even in the face of a death sentence (Dan. 2:12–13), they refused to speak falsely.

What caused Ahab's prophets to prophesy falsely? It certainly was not the Holy Spirit of God. Therefore, another source must be identified, one that would make the prophets believe their prophecy was indeed true. Biblically, that leaves two choices: Satan or his demonic assistants. This explanation fully satisfies the inquiry into the real source of false prophecy.

Additional support for a primarily literal as opposed to symbolic understanding of Micaiah's vision is added by three biblical visions whose settings approximate 1 Kings 22:19. The prophet Isaiah, through a vision, viewed the Lord with His heavenly court. In Isaiah 6, the description recalls Micaiah's account of the celestial encounter in 1 Kings 22:19. The context of Isaiah 6 suggests an essentially literal understanding as does John's God-inspired, NT commentary. John 12:40 quotes from Isaiah 6:10 and interprets that Isaiah actually saw the glory of the Lord Jesus Christ (739 B.C.).

Joshua the high priest, the angel of the Lord, and Satan were all participants in the vision recorded in Zechariah 3. Not only the setting but also the appearance of Satan before the Lord is instructive as a parallel to 1 Kings 22:19–23. Finally, the setting in Revelation 4:2 approximates that of Micaiah's vision also, as do Ezekiel 1:26–28; Daniel 7:9–10; Acts 7:55–56. These passages by themselves are not sufficient to demand a literal interpretation of "the spirit" as Satan. However, taken together, they are other positive indicators that compel serious consideration for a satanic identification of "the spirit."

THEOLOGICAL CONSIDERATIONS

Satan
Satan in the OT

Job 1–2 depicts Satan's appearing before God at the assembly of the sons of God. During this encounter, God and Satan discussed the future of an earthly inhabitant, i.e., Job. Understanding that the scene is anthropomorphically described, one is hard pressed to understand it as anything but a literal interpretation. Job 1:13–22; 2:7 record the real events resulting from this heavenly conference.

The similarities between these Job passages and 1 Kings 22 are striking in character and setting. Delitzsch, commenting on Job 1, opposes Keil's understanding of 1 Kings 22. He observes, "Finally, it agrees with 1 Kings xxii.19–22, Zech. iii., on the one hand and Apoc. xii. on the other that Satan here appears still among the good spirits. . . ."[58] Zöckler similarly states, "In 1 Kings xxii.19, where a scene greatly resembling the present is discovered, the tempter bears no name, but his individuality is distinct, for he is characterized as *the spirit*."[59]

In Zechariah 3:1 Satan personally appeared before the Lord in the presence of others. This seems to reflect the norm for Satan's appearances in the OT.

That Satan stood up against Israel and moved David to number Israel is the report of 1 Chronicles 21:1. Interestingly, the parallel passage in 2 Samuel 24:1 suggests that it was the Lord who caused David to conduct the census. John Davis explains,

> The Chronicles account and the Samuel account merely reflect two aspects of the same incident. Satan was the immediate cause of David's action, but, theologically speaking, God was the ultimate cause in that He did not prevent the incident from occurring.[60]

The 2 Samuel 24 and 1 Chronicles 21 passages not only provide an almost identical parallel for identifying "the spirit" as Satan, but also mirror the causal factors in 1 Kings 22:22–23. In verse 22 "the spirit" is the prevailer, and in 22:23 Micaiah attributes the false-prophecy phenomenon to the Lord.[61] By His permissive will, God allowed Satan to deceive the four hundred prophets of Ahab. Illustrative of Satan's deceiving activities is his encounter with Eve in the Garden of Eden. The serpent in Genesis 3:1 is certainly Satan (compare 1 Tim. 2:14; Rev. 12:9; 20:2). When man began to inhabit this earth, Satan was the chief deceiver. His character in Genesis 3 vividly recalls "the spirit" in 1 Kings 22.

These appearances of Satan in the OT and their close resemblance to 1 Kings 22 in action and character are strong reasons to identify "the spirit" as Satan. The personified spirit of prophecy has no biblical support in the realm of deceit and false prophecy, and thus is unconvincing. The possibility of "the spirit" representing demons collectively is recognized, but demons are never known biblically to have appeared before God. Old Testament theology strongly supports the satanic identification.

Satan in the NT

Satan is not directly referred to as "a spirit" in either Testament unless "the spirit" of 1 Kings 22 is Satan. This does not mean, however, that Satan is not a spirit. The Bible has indirect indications that Satan is a spirit. In 2 Corinthians 11:14, Satan is called an angel of light. Angels, of course, are spirits (Heb. 1:14; cf. Ps. 104:4). Satan must be spirit by nature, for he entered into Judas (Luke 22:3; John 13:27). Further, Paul discusses how to combat Satan in Ephesians 6:10–20. The opponent is identified in verse 11 and the nature of Satan is discussed in 6:12. The struggle is not against flesh and blood but against "spiritual" (πνευματικός [pneumatikos]) forces of wickedness. The nature of Satan as spirit in being harmonizes with a satanic identification of "the spirit" in 1 Kings 22.

The apostle John characterizes Satan as a being in whom there is no truth, who is a liar, and in fact, is the Father of Lies (John 8:44). It was "the spirit" in 1 Kings 22:22 who suggested deceit as the means to prevail over Ahab. Satan is the most likely identification.

The strongest objection to the satanic identification is that Satan is not omnipresent and could not have indwelt all four hundred prophets simultaneously; so he could not be "the spirit." It is correct that Satan is not omnipresent, but this does not negate his identification as "the spirit." Satan can be in only one place at any given time because he is not the omnipresent God.[62] However, the effect upon many prophets can be explained by Satan's relationship with demons. Matthew 12:24 identifies Satan as the ruler of demons. Matthew 25:41 and Revelation 12:9 speak of Satan and his angels. Demons are fallen angels.[63] It is this precise relationship—that of Satan's ruling over demons—that explains Satan's worldwide ministry of evil and explains how one spirit who is not omnipresent could affect many prophets simultaneously.[64] One of the many functions of demons is to disseminate false information.[65] James 3:14–15 suggests that being against the truth is from a demonic source. It is perfectly natural that demons assisted Satan in light of his ruling relationship over them.

Acts 10:38 illustrates this inseparable relationship between Satan and demons. Peter, speaking to Cornelius, relates how Christ went about doing good and healing all whom Satan had oppressed. Numerous NT cases of people whom Christ healed involved demon possession.[66] Here, Peter apparently speaks of Satan (the ultimate cause) who ruled and directed the demons (the immediate cause).

The height of attempted satanic deception is in Matthew 4:1–11. Satan attempted to deceive God in human flesh. The Lord Jesus Christ thwarted this subtle effort only because He is God. The deceiving activities of Satan in Revelation are frequent and worldwide in scope (Rev. 12:9; 20:3, 8, 10). If Satan attempted to deceive Christ, he must have found it easy to deceive Ahab's four hundred.

Satan is called the Father of Lies in John 8:44. Ananias and Sapphira knew personally of this satanic influence as Peter detected (Acts 5:1–11).

Revelation 12:10 states that Satan accuses the brethren in the presence of God day and night. The fact that Satan accuses is not significant for identifying "the spirit," but the place of the accusations is. Satan stands before the presence of God, a characteristic that fits 1 Kings 22:19–23.

Paul indicates Satan's relationship with false prophets in 2 Corinthians 11:13–15 where he notes that they disguise themselves as false apostles just as Satan disguises himself as an angel of light. False prophets are actually servants of Satan, so it is not surprising to see a direct relationship in 1 Kings 22 between false prophets and Satan.

Second Thessalonians 2:9–12 in its similarity to 2 Samuel 24 and 1 Chronicles 21 parallels 1 Kings 22 in emphasis. Satan is at work through the lawless one (2:9–10), causing God to "send upon them" a deluding influence so that they may believe what is false (2:11).[67] The close parallel between these three passages is perhaps the most convincing argument for the satanic identification of "the spirit" in 1 Kings 22:21.

CONCLUSION

This essay has examined 1 Kings 22:21 to identify "the spirit" that caused the false prophecy in 1 Kings 22:6. The disciplines of philology, hermeneutics, and theology have been used as evaluative tools. Six possible views—the aetiological, self-deluded, angelic, personified spirit of prophecy, demonic, and satanic positions—received initial attention. The aetiological view was inadequate because of rationalistic presuppositions concerning the Scriptures and God. Replacement of biblical reasoning by subjective opinion was the basis for ruling out the self-deluded view. The angelic view failed because of the absence of biblical indications that good angels practice deceiving activities. This left the personified, demonic, and satanic identifications as reasonable possibilities.

First came an investigation of philological matters. Textually the articulated reading of "spirit" was substantiated and found syntactically to support any one of the three reasonable alternatives. Next, רוּחַ שֶׁקֶר (rûaḥ šeqer) proved to be either "the spirit of deception" or "deceiving spirit," allowing for the correctness of any of the three views. Semantically, the use of רוּחַ (rûaḥ) supported only the demonic or satanic view as did the usage of פָּתָה (pātāh) and שֶׁקֶר (šeqer).

Second, a hermeneutical investigation of the symbolic speech of the passage demonstrated that it was possible to understand Micaiah's vision literally as supporting the satanic view, symbolically supporting the demonic view, or parabolically as supporting the personified spirit of prophecy view. However, in light of the literal understanding of Satan's appearances before God in Job 1 and 2, Zechariah 3, and Revelation 12, the satanic view emerged as the most natural and the most likely.

The study of biblical visions reduced the possible causes of false prophecy in 1 Kings 22:6 by one. The demonic and satanic positions remained possible although the satanic understanding was favored because of similar literal interpretations of heavenly visions in Isaiah 6, Ezekiel 1, Daniel 7, Zechariah 3, Acts 7, and Revelation 4. Hermeneutically, the satanic view was most probable in both Testaments, but was not conclusive.

Third, the theological implications of OT and NT revelation concerning Satan, which include his activities and character, best describe "the spirit." Finally, the answer to the objection to a satanic identification—i.e., that Satan is omnipresent and could not affect all four hundred prophets simultaneously—demonstrated Satan's role as ruler over demons. This relationship and the known activities of Satan theologically provided the most consistent explanation for identifying "the spirit" as Satan and demons as Satan's instrument in the mouths of Ahab's false prophets.

These philological, hermeneutical, and theological factors lead to the conclusion that "the spirit" in 1 Kings 22:21 was in fact Satan and that demonic activity, initiated and superintended by Satan, provided the dynamic force responsible for the false prophecy in 1 Kings 22:6.

ENDNOTES

[1] R. A. Torrey, *Difficulties in the Bible* (Chicago: Moody, n.d.), 73. See Ray Dillard, "The Chronicler's Jehoshaphat," *TrinJ* NS (1986): 20, for a discussion of why the Chronicles' account is unique to Chronicles and also differs from 1 Kings 22.

[2] Patrick Miller Jr., "The Prophetic Critique of Kings," *Ex Auditu* II (1986): 82.

[3] Edwin R. Thiele, *The Mysterious Numbers of the Hebrew Kings,* rev. ed. (Grand Rapids: Eerdmans, 1965), 66.

[4] William F. Albright, *From the Stone Age to Christianity,* 2d ed. (Baltimore: Johns Hopkins Press, 1957), 234–35.

[5] C. F. Keil, *The Books of the Kings,* trans. James Martin, vol. 3 of *Biblical Commentary on the Old Testament* (reprint, Grand Rapids: Eerdmans, n.d.), 274.

[6] See John C. Whitcomb Jr., *Chart of Old Testament Kings and Prophets* (Chicago: Moody, 1968).

[7] James B. Pritchard, *The Ancient Near East: An Anthology of Texts and Pictures* (Princeton: Princeton University Press, 1958), 188–92.

[8] Eric William Heaton, *His Servants the Prophets* (London: SCM, 1949), 25. Matheney (M. Pierce Matheney and Roy L. Honeycutt Jr., "1–2 Kings," in *The Broadman Bible Commentary,* ed. C. J. Allen [Nashville: Broadman, 1970], 223), Oesterly (W. O. E. Oesterley and T. H. Robinson, *Hebrew Religion: Its Origin and Development* [1944; reprint, London: Society for Promoting Christian Knowledge, n.d.], 222), Seigman (Edward F. Siegman, *The False Prophets of the Old Testament* [Washington: The Catholic University of America, 1939], 3–4), and Wellhausen (Julius Wellhausen, *History of Israel,* trans. J. S. Black and A. Menzies [Edinburgh: Adam and Charles Black, 1885], 403) also take this basic position.

[9] C. F. Burney, "Notes on the Hebrew Text of the Books of Kings," in *The Library of Biblical Studies,* ed. Harry M. Orlinsky (New York: KTAV, 1970), 255.

[10] Otto Eissfeldt, *The Old Testament: An Introduction,* trans. P. R. Ackroyd (New York: Harper and Row, 1965), 148.

[11] Ibid.

[12] Walther Eichrodt, *Theology of the Old Testament,* 2 vols., trans. J. A. Baker (Philadelphia: Westminster, 1967), 2:52.

[13] Gerhard Von Rad, *Old Testament Theology,* trans. D. M. G. Stalker (New York: Harper and Row, 1962), 2:56–57.

[14] F. W. Farrar, "The First Book of Kings," in *The Expositor's Bible,* ed. W. R. Nicoll (New York: A. C. Armstrong and Son, 1903), 492–93. Also see Adam Clarke, *The Holy Bible* (New York: Eaton and Mains, n.d.), 476; W. A. L. Elmslie, "The Book of Chronicles," in *The Cambridge Bible for Schools and Colleges,* 2d ed., ed. A. F. Kirkpatrick (Cambridge: University Press, 1916), 243–44.

[15] Raymond B. Dillard, "2 Chronicles," in *Word Biblical Commentary,* ed. David A. Hubbard and Glenn W. A. Barker (Waco: Word, 1987), 15:142.

[16] Walter C. Kaiser Jr., *Toward Old Testament Ethics* (Grand Rapids: Zondervan, 1983), 256. Also idem, *Hard Sayings of the Old Testament* (Downers Grove: InterVarsity, 1988), 120–21.

[17] J. Robert Vannoy, *The NIV Study Bible* (Grand Rapids: Zondervan, 1985), 520.

[18] Kaiser, *Hard Sayings,* 120.

[19] Augustine, "Expositions on the Book of Psalms," in *Nicene and Post-Nicene Fathers,* vol. 8, ed. A. Cleveland Cose and P. Schaff (New York: The Christian Literature Company, 1888), 376.

[20] These include Chafer (L. S. Chafer, *Systematic Theology* [Dallas: Dallas Seminary Press, 1948], 4:294), Dickason (C. Fred Dickason, *Angels, Elect and Evil* [Chicago: Moody, 1975], 180, who seems to identify "the

spirit" with demons, but does not rule out Satan), Feinberg (Charles Lee
Feinberg, personal correspondence dated October 11, 1973, a view never
formally published apparently), Gates (John T. Gates, "1 Kings," in *The
Wycliffe Bible Commentary,* ed. C. F. Pfeiffer and E. F. Harrison [Chicago:
Moody, 1962], 339), Hoyt (Herman Hoyt, "Biblical Eschatology" [un-
published class notes; Winona Lake: Grace Theological Seminary, 1966],
158), Jacob (Edmond Jacob, *Contemporary Old Testament Theologians,*
ed. R. B. Laurin [Valley Forge: Judson, 1970], 154), Kleinknecht (Hermann
Kleinknecht, "πνεῦμα, πνευματικός," *TDNT,* ed. Gerhard Friedrich, trans.
Geoffery W. Bromily [Grand Rapids: Eerdmans, 1968], 4:363), McClain
(Alva J. McClain, John C. Whitcomb Jr., and Charles R. Smith, "Christian
Theology—God and the World" (unpublished class notes; Winona Lake:
Grace Theological Seminary, n.d.], 119–20), Merrill (Eugene H. Merrill,
"1 and 2 Chronicles," in *The Bible Knowledge Commentary,* ed. John F.
Walvoord and Roy B. Zuck [Wheaton: Victor, 1985], 633), Scott (Tho-
mas Scott, *The Holy Bible* [Boston: Samuel T. Armstrong, and Crocker,
and Brewster, 1831], 2:288), Strong (Augustus H. Strong, *Systematic Theology* [1970; reprint, Old Tappan: Revell, n.d.], 457), and Wood (Leon J.
Wood, personal correspondence dated October 3, 1973, a view never formally published apparently, but commented upon briefly in *The Holy Spirit
in the Old Testament* [Grand Rapids: Zondervan, 1976], 131).

[21] Augustine, *Expositions on the Book of Psalms,* 376.

[22] Note the article is lacking in each instance.

[23] John Gray, *I and II Kings,* 2d ed. (Philadelphia: Westminster, 1970),
452. Leon Wood reasons differently: "The article is only to designate a
definite spirit . . . rather than merely spirits in general . . ." (personal
correspondence).

[24] A. J. McClain, et al., "Christian Theology—God and the World,"
119–20; Augustus H. Strong, *Systematic Theology,* 457.

[25] Included are Alden (Robert L. Alden, personal correspondence dated
September 28, 1973), Barry (Alfred Barry, "1 Kings," in *Ellicott's Commentary on the Whole Bible,* ed. C. J. Ellicott [reprint, Grand Rapids:
Zondervan, n.d.], 2:95), Brown (R. E. Brown, et al., *The Jerome Biblical Commentary* [Englewood Cliffs: Prentice-Hall, 1968], 197), Burrows (W. O. Burrows, *The First Book of Kings* [London: Rivingtons,
1899], 95), DeVries (Simon J. DeVries, *Prophet against Prophet* [Grand
Rapids: Eerdmans, 1978], 45; also idem, "1 Kings," in *Word Biblical*

Commentary [Waco, Tex.: Word, 1985], 268 and "The Three Comparisons in 1 Kings XXII 4B and Its Parallel and 2 Kings III 7B," *Vetus Testamentum* 39, no. 3 [1985]: 283–306), Cook (F. C. Cook, ed., "1 Samuel–Esther," in *The Bible Commentary* [1970; reprint, Grand Rapids: Baker, n.d.], 222), Edersheim (Alfred Edersheim, *The History of Israel and Judah* [New York: James Pott and Company, n.d.], 69), Eichrodt (Walther Eichrodt, *Theology of the Old Testament,* 2:52; Eichrodt terms this the demonic aspect of the developing doctrine of the spirit), J. C. Gray (James C. Gray, *The Biblical Encyclopedia and Museum* [Hartford: S. S. Scranton, 1900], 3:102), J. Gray (John Gray, *I and II Kings,* 452), Hammond (J. Hammond, "1 Kings," in the *Pulpit Commentary,* ed. H. D. M. Spence and J. S. Excell [New York: Funk and Wagnalls, n.d.], 535), Honor (Leo L. Honor, *Book of Kings 1* [New York: Union of American Hebrew Congregations, 1955], 319), Keil (C. F. Keil, *The Books of the Kings,* 276), Lumby (J. R. Lumby, "The First Book of the Kings," in *Cambridge Bible for Schools and Colleges,* ed. J. J. S. Perowne [Cambridge: University Press, 1894], 233), Montgomery (J. A. Montgomery and H. S. Gehman, "A Critical and Exegetical Commentary on the Book of Kings," in *ICC,* ed. C. A. Briggs, et al. [Edinburgh: T & T Clark, 1930], 339), Nichol (F. D. Nichol, *The Seventh-Day Adventist Bible Commentary* [Washington: Review and Herald, 1954], 840), Patterson and Austel (R. D. Patterson and Hermann J. Austel, "1 & 2 Kings," in *The Expositor's Bible Commentary,* ed. Frank E. Gaebelein [Grand Rapids: Zondervan, 1988], 4:165), Rawlinson (George Rawlinson, "Kings—Books I and II," in *The Holy Bible,* ed. F. C. Cook [New York: Scribner, Armstrong and Co., 1875], 619), Torrey (R. A. Torrey, *Difficulties in the Bible,* 73–75), Whitcomb (J. C. Whitcomb Jr., *Solomon to the Exile* [Winona Lake: BMH, 1971], 46), and Young (E. J. Young, *My Servants the Prophets* [Grand Rapids: Eerdmans, 1952], 136–42).

[26] Alfred Edersheim, *The History of Israel and Judah,* 69.

[27] C. F. Keil, *The Books of the Kings,* 276.

[28] Ibid., 277.

[29] J. C. Whitcomb Jr., *Solomon to the Exile,* 46.

[30] E.g., E. J. Young, *My Servants the Prophets,* 136–42.

[31] Paul Heinisch, *Theology of the Old Testament,* trans. William Heidt (Collegeville, Minn.: The Liturgical Press, 1955), 122.

[32] Advocates of identifying "the spirit" as Satan are Cassian (John Cassian, "The Conferences of John Cassian," in *Nicene and Post-Nicene Fathers,* 2d series, ed. P. Schaff and Henry Ware, trans. E. C. S. Gibson [1955; reprint, Grand Rapids: Eerdmans, n.d.], 11:304), Chrysostom (John Chrysostom, "Epistles of Paul to the Corinthians," in *Nicene Fathers,* First Series, ed. P. Schaff, trans. T. W. Chambers [New York: The Christian Literature Company, 1888], 12:169), Davidson (A. B. Davidson, *The Theology of the Old Testament,* ed. S. D. F. Salmond [Edinburgh: T & T Clark, 1904), 302–3), Gill (John Gill, *An Exposition—The Old Testament* [London: W. H. Collinridge, 1853], 393), Heinisch (Paul Heinisch, *Theology of the Old Testament,* 138), Kittel and Noth (R. Kittel and M. Noth, *Liber Regum* [Stuttgart: Wurttembergische Bibelanstalt, 1966], 554; see critical note on 1 Kings 22:21); John MacArthur, *God, Satan, and Angels* [Panorama City, Calif.: Word of Grace, 1987], 75), Oehler (G. F. Oehler, *Theology of the Old Testament,* trans. G. F. Oehler [New York: Funk and Wagnalls, 1883], 449), Origen (Origen, *"Origen De Principiis,"* in *The Ante-Nicene Fathers,* ed. A. Roberts and J. Donaldson, trans. F. Crombie [Grand Rapids: Eerdmans, 1951], 4:329), Payne (J. Barton Payne, *Theology of the Older Testament* [Grand Rapids: Zondervan, 1962], 294; personal correspondence dated October 2, 1973 agrees as does "1 & 2 Chronicles," in *The Expositor's Bible Commentary,* ed. Frank E. Gaebelein [Grand Rapids: Zondervan, 1988], 4:499), Wordsworth (Charles Wordsworth, *The Holy Bible* [London: Rivington's, 1868], 84).

[33] Merrill F. Unger, personal correspondence dated September 25, 1973.

[34] J. Barton Payne, *Theology,* 294.

[35] F. C. Cook, *1 Samuel–Esther,* 222.

[36] These included Benson (Joseph Benson, *The Holy Bible* [New York: T. Carlton and J. Porter, n.d.], 114), Dentan (R. D. Dentan, "The First and Second Books of the Kings," in *The Laymen's Bible Commentary,* ed. B. H. Kelly [Richmond: John Knox, 1964], 68–70), Josephus (Flavius Josephus, *Antiquities of the Jews,* VIII:15, trans. W. Whiston [Philadelphia: John E. Potter, n.d.], 224–25), Myers (Jacob M. Myers, "II Chronicles," in *The Anchor Bible,* ed. Wm. F. Albright and David N. Freedman [Garden City: Doubleday, 1965], 104–5), and Poole (Matthew Poole, *Annotations upon the Holy Bible* [New York: Robert Carter and Brothers, 1853], 713).

[37] Franz Rosenthal, *A Grammar of Biblical Aramaic* (Weisbaden: Otto Harrassowitz, 1961), 23.

[38] N. J. DeWitt, J. F. Gummere, and A. Horn, *College Latin* (Chicago: Scott, Foresman, 1954), 12.

[39] R. Kittel and M. Noth, *Liber Regum,* 554.

[40] J. T. Milik, *Ten Years Discovery in the Wilderness of Judaea,* trans. J. Strugnell (Naperville: Alex R. Allenson, 1959), 25.

[41] W. H. Brownlee, *The Meaning of the Qumrân Scrolls for the Bible* (New York: Oxford, 1964), 12.

[42] M. Baillet, J. T. Milik, and R. deVaux, *Les 'Petites Grottes' De Qumrân* (Oxford: Clarendon, 1962), 107.

[43] Ibid., 107–8.

[44] E. Kautzsch, *Gesenius' Hebrew Grammar,* 2d ed., ed. A. E. Cowley (Oxford: Clarendon, 1910), 377.

[45] Ibid., 376, and A. B. Davidson, *Hebrew Syntax,* 3d ed. (Edinburgh: T & T Clark, 1901), 25.

[46] E. Kautzsch, *Gesenius' Hebrew Grammar,* 377. Also see Bruce K. Waltke and M. O'Connor, *An Introduction to Biblical Hebrew Syntax* (Winona Lake: Eisenbrauns, 1990), 114.

[47] E. Kautzsch, *Gesenius' Hebrew Grammar,* 378.

[48] F. Brown, S. R. Driver, and C. A. Briggs, *A Hebrew and English Lexicon of the Old Testament* (1972; reprint, Oxford: Clarendon, n.d.), 924.

[49] A. B. Davidson, *Hebrew Syntax,* 19.

[50] Cyrus H. Gordon, *Ugaritic Handbook* (Rome: Pontificium Institutum Biblicum, 1947), 323, and Stanislaw Segert, *A Basic Grammar of the Ugaritic Language* (Berkeley: University of California, 1984), 201.

[51] David Hill, *Greek Words and Hebrew Meanings* (Cambridge: University Press, 1967), 206–15; Hermann Kleinknecht, "πνεῦμα, πνευματικός,"

Theological Dictionary of the New Testament, ed. Gerhard Friedrich, trans. Geoffery W. Bromily (Grand Rapids: Eerdmans, 1968), 4:359–67; Paul Younger, "A New Start Towards A Doctrine of the Spirit," in *Canadian Journal of Theology* 13, no. 2 (1967): 123–33.

[52] F. Brown, et al., *A Hebrew and English Lexicon,* 834; Ludwig Koehler and Walter Baumgartner, *Lexicon in Veteris Testamenti Libros* (Leiden: E. J. Brill, 1958), 786; also see R. Laird Harris, et. al., *Theological Wordbook of the Old Testament* (Chicago: Moody, 1980), 2:742–43.

[53] Brown, et al., *Lexicon,* 1010, 1055.

[54] Two recent volumes can be consulted for key aspects of the hermeneutical process. See Elliot E. Johnson, "Hermeneutical Considerations of the Goal of Interpretation," in *Expository Hermeneutics: An Introduction* (Grand Rapids: Zondervan, 1990), 31–53. Also William W. Klein, Craig L. Blomberg, and Robert L. Hubbard Jr., *Introduction to Biblical Interpretation* (Dallas: Word, 1993), 87–116, discuss presuppositions and preunderstanding.

[55] A. J. McClain, *The Greatness of the Kingdom* (Chicago: Moody, 1959), 135.

[56] A. B. Mickelsen, *Interpreting the Bible* (Grand Rapids: Eerdmans, 1963), 265–66.

[57] J. Barton Payne, personal correspondence dated October 2, 1973.

[58] F. Delitzsch, "Job," in *Commentary on the Old Testament,* trans. Francis Boltin (reprint, Grand Rapids: Eerdmans, n.d.), 4:53.

[59] Otto Zöckler, "The Book of Job," in *Lange's Commentary on the Holy Scriptures,* trans. L. J. Evans (1971; reprint, Grand Rapids: Zondervan, n.d.), 4:294.

[60] J. J. Davis, *The Birth of a Kingdom* (Winona Lake: BMH, 1970), 164; also see Richard Mayhue, *Unmasking Satan* (Wheaton: Victor, 1988), 138–39.

[61] James L. Crenshaw, *Prophetic Conflict* (Berlin: Walter de Gruyter, 1971), 83, notes, "The divine responsibility for false prophecy is nowhere expressed more unequivocally than in the story of Micaiah ben

Imlah (I Kings 22:1–40)." See also J. J. M. Roberts, "Does God Lie? Divine Deceit as a Theological Problem in Israelite Prophetic Literature," in *Congress Volume: Jerusalem 1986*, ed. J. A. Emerton (Leiden: E. J. Brill, 1988), 211–20. Although this subject deserves at least an article-length discussion, let it suffice for now to say that, while God is ultimately the first cause of all, He is not the morally responsible, immediate agent of sin such as false prophecy (Job 2:10; Isa. 45:7; Lam. 3:38). Thus, it is asserted that the events of 1 Kings 22 were not caused by God's decreed will, but rather allowed by His permissive will, for which there is then human and angelic accountability to God in judgment.

[62] Compare Job 1:7 and 1 Peter 5:8. Also see Revelation 20:2–3 where Satan is confined to the abyss for one-thousand years.

[63] C. R. Smith, "The New Testament Doctrine of Demons," *Grace Journal* 10, no. 2 (spring 1969): 32–35. Dr. Smith has written a well-documented case for demons being identified as fallen angels. Also see Psalm 78:49 where demons are referred to as a band of destroying ("evil," NASB margin) angels.

[64] M. F. Unger, personal correspondence dated September 25, 1973. Dr. Unger writes that הָרוּחַ ("the spirit") is "probably a reference to הַשָּׂטָן ["Satan"] since the רוּחַ ("spirit") has the article. This is an extremely attractive thesis since Satan is King and Head over the demonic powers."

[65] M. F. Unger, *Biblical Demonology,* 199.

[66] See Matthew 4:24; 9:32; 12:22; 15:21–28.

[67] Robert L. Thomas, "1, 2 Thessalonians," in *The Expositor's Bible Commentary,* ed. Frank E. Gaebelein (Grand Rapids: Zondervan, 1978), 11:327–28.

CHAPTER TWO

Psalm 113

Grandeur and Grace: God's Transcendence and Immanence

George J. Zemek

Psalm 113 is a rich treasury for all. Literarily, it is a masterpiece of semantical, syntactical, and structural development. The Spirit of God inspired this psalmist to combine beauty with bounty, resulting in a highly functional piece of art that amplifies the psalm's theological substance and applicational summons. Liturgically, this hymn of praise has played a significant role in both Passover week and Passion week. Applicationally, it has served as a well of refreshment for needy people throughout its history. Theologically, the psalm's message of God's transcendence and immanence provides substance to the promise of refreshment. Today Psalm 113 continues to invite the people of God to come and drink deeply.

* * * * *

A TRANSLATION

1 Praise the LORD!
  O servants of the LORD, praise *Him!*
  Praise the name of the LORD!
2 Let the name of the LORD be blessed
  both now and forever!
3 From east to west,
  let the name of the LORD be praised!
4 The LORD *is* high above all nations;
  His glory *rises* above the heavens.
5 Who is like the LORD our God,
  who is enthroned on high,
6 who condescends to care for *things*
  in the heavens and upon the earth?

7 *He* lifts up *the* downtrodden from *the* dust;
   He raises *the* destitute from the dump
8 to make *them* dwell with nobles,
   with the nobles of His people.
9 *He* makes the woman barren in household to dwell
   as a joyful mother of sons.
   Praise the LORD!

INTRODUCTION

One reason for the spiritual poverty of some Christians is their ignorance of or failure to reflect on who God is. In so doing, they have robbed themselves of a vital source of help and encouragement. No better solution to their problem is available than a careful study of Psalm 113.

"Presence-theology" discussions and debates about whether or not in the OT the Lord is ever genuinely conceived of as dwelling on earth have generally been counterproductive in the edification of the church.[1] Finite and fallible deliberations, energized by overly simplistic assumptions, have both impugned key texts and skewed their balanced theology. Conclusions that see contradiction rather than complementary truths have resulted, especially in reference to God's transcendence and immanence. Consequently, this investigation will undertake a long-overdue examination of the psalm's data without recourse to critical agenda.

Psalm 113 provides a natural theological entrance into two corollary truths about God, His transcendence (i.e., lying beyond the limits of ordinary experience) and His immanence (i.e., operating within a domain of reality or realm of discourse). As in other texts, God's attributes of greatness and goodness, His characteristics of grandeur and grace, harmoniously blend in a theological duet. The psalm is an excellent avenue to a deeper appreciation of God's attributes.

LITERARY ENHANCEMENTS

Before proceeding with an exposition of the psalm, a look at how its two great themes are enhanced by a variety of stylistic features is beneficial.

Semantical

Wordplays on the roots רום (*rwm*, "to be high, exalted") and ישׁב (*yšb*, "to dwell") magnify this psalm's astounding development.[2] God's *rank*, appropriately summarized by the qal forms רָם (*rām*, "he is exalted") and לָשֶׁבֶת (*lāšebet*, "to dwell") in verses 4a and 5b, does not inhibit God's ability to *rescue* those in distress, as well depicted in the corresponding hiphil forms יָרִים (yārîm, "to raise, lift up"), לְהוֹשִׁיבִי (lĕhôšîbî, "to make [them] dwell"), and מוֹשִׁיבִי (môšîbî, "to make [her] dwell, abide") (i.e., vv. 7b, 8a, 9a³). This exalted One mercifully and characteristically exalts lowly and exasperated people. He who is transcendent enables them to transcend their stifling circumstances.

Syntactical
Syntactical subtleties also accentuate the psalm's theological motifs. For example, the introductory crescendo of *hallels* (i.e., "praises") (v. 1) establishes the *priority* of praise to Yahweh. Then in the next two verses an inverse parallelism of four lines conveys the *propriety* of praise.⁴ The pual participle מְבֹרָךְ (mĕbôrāk, "blessed") from בָּרַךְ (brk, "to bless")⁵ in verse 2a is paralleled by its counterpart מְהֻלָּל (mĕhullāl, "to be praised") in verse 3b. Correspondingly, the עַד ('ad, "unto, until") . . . מִן (min, "from") prepositional combination of verse 2b is immediately followed by its counterpart in verse 3a.

Verse 4, containing explicit assertions of God's transcendence, is highlighted by progressions and parallels. The abbreviated יָהּ (yh, "the LORD") of verse 1a, the יהוה (yhwh, "the LORD") of verse 1b, and the circumlocution שֵׁם יהוה (šēm yhwh, "the name of the LORD") of verses 1c, 2a, and 3b anticipate the exalted one, yhwh, who is the subject of verse 4a. The tetragrammaton (i.e., yhwh) is followed by another significant circumlocution in verse 4b, כְּבוֹדוֹ (kĕbôdô, "His glory").⁶

Especially important in verse 4 are the corresponding phrases with עַל ('al, "above"), a preposition eminently suited to convey the concept of transcendence.⁷ An upward and outward movement from "over/above all people/nations" (v. 4a) to "over/above the heavens" (v. 4b) emphasizes the concept, possibly creating the impression that God is far removed from the cares of His creatures and creation. Nevertheless, the widening concentric circles of transcendence subsequently reverse, and the reality of the Lord's immanence emerges (vv. 6–9). This "reversal" is dramatically portrayed through a downward and inward movement (v. 6): He makes low⁸ to care for matters not only "in the heavens" but also "upon the earth."⁹ This reality is vividly documented by selected examples of intervention (vv. 7–9).

The rhetorical question¹⁰ of verse 5 is pivotal. Patterns of the basic "who-is-like" formula recur throughout the OT (e.g., Exod. 15:11; Deut. 3:24; Ps. 35:10; Isa. 40:12ff.; 46:5; etc.) as a part of theological affirmations and in personal names.¹¹ Both usages serve as reminders of the Lord's uniqueness.¹² There is no one like Yahweh!

In the middle of verse 5 comes a shift of emphasis from being to doing. Yet the articular causative participles of verses 5b and 6a still function substantively in apposition with the יְהוָה אֱלֹהֵ֫ינוּ (yhwh 'ĕlôhênû, "the LORD our God") (v. 5a).[13] Furthermore, the tight apposition of . . . הַמַּגְבִּיהִי (hammagbîhî, "to make high, exalt") (v. 5b) with . . . הַמַּשְׁפִּילִי. (hammašpîlî, "to make low, condescend")[14] (v. 6a) is extraordinary. The Lord who literally "makes high to dwell" (i.e., a poignant summary of His transcendence) is the very one who "makes low to see," that is, *to care for* the needs of His subjects (i.e., an arresting introduction to His immanence). By this stark apposition, transcendence and immanence join hands in complementary manifestation of the incomparable one (i.e., v. 5a).

Structural
   Depending upon emphases on form and/or content, the psalm may be divided differently into major sections.[15] A basic analysis of the psalm's form leads to the following twofold division: "a hymnic introduction" (i.e., vv. 1–3) and "the reasons why God is worthy of praise and homage" (i.e., vv. 4–9).[16] Most structural analysts, however, prefer a threefold division.[17] A few of these end divisions after verses 1 and 3 (i.e., vv. 1, 2–3, 4–9),[18] while the majority prefer the following strophes: verses 1–3, 4–6, 7–9.[19]
   Kidner's "high above . . ." (i.e., vv. 1–4)/"far down . . ." (i.e., vv. 5–9) separation represents a twofold division based largely on thematic considerations.[20] This breakdown naturally emphasizes the psalm's overarching pedagogy: there is "nothing too great for Him, no-one too small."[21] A shift to the interrogative motif at verse 5 lends some weight to this twofold division (i.e., coming between vv. 4 and 5).[22] The following propositional outline attempts to integrate the psalm's various literary phenomena with its two thematic divisions:

Two choruses of thanksgiving flow from primary theological incentives.
1A.   (vv. 1–4) The first chorus of thanksgiving flows from
      the incentive of God's transcendence.
   1B.   (vv. 1–3) The worshipful response to God's transcendence
      1C.   (v. 1) The exhortation:
         1D.   Its reverberation: the threefold *hallel*
         2D.   Its responsibility: the servants/worshipers
               of the Lord
         3D.   Its Recipient: the Lord
      2C.   (vv. 2–3) The extent:
         1D.   (v. 2) considered temporally
         2D.   (v. 3) considered geographically

2B. (v. 4) The worshipful recognition of God's transcendence
   1C. (v. 4a) He transcends all that is earthly
   2C. (v. 4b) He transcends all that is heavenly
2A. (vv. 5–9) The second chorus of thanksgiving flows from the incentive of God's immanence.
   1B. (vv. 5–6) The interrogatives develop His immanence
      1C. (v. 5) The interrogatives of v. 5 reveal that God's immanence is uncompromising (i.e., it does not come at the expense of His transcendence)[23]
      2C. (v. 6) The interrogative of v. 6 reveals that God's immanence is unassuming[24]
   2B. (vv. 7–9) The illustrations dramatize His immanence
      1C. (vv. 7–8) The general illustration of God's concern for the downtrodden
      2C. (v. 9) The special illustration of God's consolation for the childless

BACKGROUND

Another helpful preliminary to the psalm's exposition is an awareness of its background. Leslie conjectured that Psalm 113 "is a liturgical choir hymn which was sung antiphonally by two Levitical choirs."[25] The specific details of its early usage are unknown, although "the setting was clearly cultic."[26]

That it came to be recognized as "a classical Hebrew hymn"[27] is confirmed by its inclusion in the "Hallel" (i.e., Psalms 113–118), which "is recited on all major biblical festivals, with the exception of Rosh Ha-Shanah and the Day of Atonement."[28] This grouping "is also recited during the Passover *seder* service (Tosef., Suk. 3:2), when it is known as *Hallel Mizri* ('Egyptian *Hallel*') because of the exodus from Egypt which the *seder* commemorates."[29] The latter use probably relates to "The Last Supper":[30] "It is interesting to recall that probably just as Jesus and the disciples sang a hymn after they had eaten the Passover meal (Matt. 26:30)—almost certainly Psalms 115–118—so most likely before the meal they had sung Psalms 113–114."[31] Craigie's summary helps to complete the historical survey of Psalm 113 in worship:

> With the passage of centuries, the psalm became more closely associated with the celebration of Passover. Indeed, in the modern *Passover Haggadah,* Psalm 113 is still recited in the context of the blessing of the cup of wine, prior to the participation in the Passover meal as such. And in Christianity, Psalm

113 was traditionally designated as one of the Proper Psalms for evening worship on Easter Day, thus linking the Christian use of the psalm to its more ancient Jewish antecedents. In both Judaism and Christianity, Psalm 113 was a special psalm, employed in the worship of God at those times in the liturgical calendar when praise *par excellence* should be addressed to the Almighty.[32]

Verses 7–9 of the psalm have been seen as "a connecting link between the Song of Hannah and the Magnificat of the Virgin."[33] In fact, Craigie calls 1 Samuel 2:1–10 the prehistory of Psalm 113:7–9 and Luke 1:46–55 its posthistory.[34]

EXPOSITION

The psalm opens and closes with הַלְלוּ יָהּ (*halĕlûyāh,* "praise the LORD"),[35] a fitting boundary, since

Psalm 113 bids all men to let the praise of God resound all the world over and motivates the appeal with the declaration that this incomparable God, transcending the heavens in glory, is the Sovereign of the world who controls the affairs of men below from his throne on high.[36]

Outside this psalm, the reverberating invitations to praise in verse 1 most closely parallel Psalm 135:1.[37]

Selected from an arsenal of worship synonyms,[38] הלל (*hll,* "praise") is especially suited to elicit jubilant praise[39] from the community.[40] The vocative construction עַבְדֵי יהוה (*'abĕdê yhwh,* "servants of the LORD")[41] is a designation for the "worshiping community,"[42] "the loyal among Israel."[43] It is also noteworthy that the root עבד (*'bd,* "to serve, worship") denotes both service and worship,[44] emphasizing "the privileges of the worshipers as well as their duties and responsibilities."[45]

"The name of the LORD" (שֵׁם יהוה *[šēm yhwh]*) is the object of the third echoing imperative from *hll.* Remembering that *šēm* "in the OT often included existence, character, and reputation,"[46] "the *name of* the LORD" "signifies the whole self-disclosure of God."[47] Passages such as Exodus 33:19–23 and 34:5–7 indicate that *šēm,* when applied to God, encompasses the totality of His attributes and actions.

The origin of the tetragrammaton *yhwh* is in question. "While no consensus exists, the name is generally thought to be a verbal form derived from the root *hwy,* later *hyh,* 'to be at hand, exist (phenomenally), come to pass.'"[48] Significantly, "the consensus of modern scholarship supports the biblical text [cf. Exod. 3:14] in associating the name of Yahweh with the root *hyh*. . . ."[49]

The jussive exhortation יְהִי (*yĕhî*) standing at the head of verses 2–3 (i.e., "*May/Let* the name of the LORD *be* . . .") centers on the *priority* of praise, and the subordinate *pual* participles in these two verses with their compound prepositional phrases combine to introduce the *propriety* of universal praise. Indeed, "no less response in space or time is worthy of him."[50]

Blessing formulas are common throughout ancient Near Eastern literature. The OT is saturated with them (for an identical parallel to Ps. 113:2a, see Job 1:21).[51] Based on the previous *hallels* and a subsequent parallelism with מְהֻלָּל (*mĕhullāl*, "being praised") in verse 3b, יהוה מְבֹרָךְ יְהִי שֵׁם (*yĕhî šēm yhwh mĕbōrāk*, "let the name of the LORD be blessed") stands as "an expression synonymous with 'Praise the LORD.'"[52] Such praise is to be unrestricted in its duration (i.e., מֵעַתָּה וְעַד־עוֹלָם *[mē'attāh wĕ'ad-'ôlām]*).[53] Literally, it should continue "from now and forever,"[54] i.e., "forever, without ceasing."[55]

In the middle of the inverted parallelism of verses 3–4, a spatial focus replaces the emphasis on time: מִמִּזְרַח־שֶׁמֶשׁ עַד־מְבוֹאוֹ (*mimmizrah–šemeš 'ad–mĕbô'ô*, "from the sun's place of rising to its entrance,"[56] "throughout the world from east to west."[57]) (v. 4a). Concerning מְהֻלָּל (*mĕhullāl*, "being praised") (v. 3b),[58] "the part. pual describes God as 'worthy of praise.'"[59] The following assertions of His transcendence and immanence support the praiseworthiness of His name always and everywhere.

One of the major spheres of usage of רוּם (*rûm*, "to be high, exalted") (cf. *rām* at the head of v. 4) is "height as symbolic of positive notions such as glory and exaltation."[60] Besides verse 4a, several passages corroborate God's exaltation, e.g., Psalms 46:11; 99:2; 138:6;[61] Isaiah 6:1; 57:15[62]; etc.[63] Furthermore, the prepositional phrase עַל־כָּל־גּוֹיִם (*'al–kol–gôyim*, "above all nations") provides greater resolution to this portrait of God's transcendence.[64] When attention is fixed upon the exalted Lord, all the *gôyim* pale into insignificance (cf., e.g., Ps. 46:11; Isa. 40:17).

The Lord's *kābôd* ("glory," v. 4b), like His *šēm* ("name"), refers to "God's self-disclosure,"[65] often standing for "Yahweh himself."[66] It is that very "glory," representing all He is and does, that surpasses the highest heavens.

These affirmations of transcendence (v. 4) are a powerful incentive for the invited praise (vv. 1–3). Although the order is switched, similar choruses in Psalms 57:6, 12 and 108:6 also observe the priority and propriety of praise: "Be exalted above the heavens, O God; and Your glory above all the earth!"

The implied response to the rhetorical questions in verse 5 is "No one!" Not one compares with "the LORD, our God."[67] It seems that אֱלֹהֵינוּ ('ĕlôhênû, "our God") has covenantal overtones[68] and anticipates the gracious interventions of verses 7–9.[69] Yet it must be remembered that this personal God "makes high to dwell" (v. 4a).[70] Expressed in the participle הַמַּגְבִּיהִי (hammagbîhî, "who sits on high," v. 5b), the verb גָּבַהּ (gābah, "to be high, make high"[71]), a synonym of rûm and an antonym of שָׁפֵל (šāpal, "below"),[72] "is often used to describe the greatness, height, or high position of a person. . . ."[73] Gābah combines idiomatically with the complementary infinitive lāšebet (from יָשַׁב [yšb, "to dwell"]) in a vivid statement of the Lord's exalted enthronement: "who is enthroned on high."[74]

Even though verse 6a is conceptually antithetical to verse 5b, it is also syntactically appositional.[75] Delitzsch captures the apparent irony of a transcendent/immanent God:

> He is the incomparable One who has set up His throne in the height, but at the same time directs His gaze deep downwards . . . in the heavens and upon the earth, i.e., nothing in all the realm of the creatures that are beneath Him escapes His sight, and nothing is so low that it remains unnoticed by Him; on the contrary, it is just that which is lowly, as the following strophe presents to us in a series of portraits so to speak, that is the special object of His regard.[76]

Consequently, while the hammagbîhî of verse 5b trumpets exaltation, the hammašpîlî of verse 6a whispers condescension.[77]

The complementary infinitive לִרְאוֹת (lirĕ'ôt, "to see"), from the common רָאָה (rā'āh), carries an uncommon theological significance. In contexts such as this and Genesis 22:8, 14; 29:32; 1 Samuel 1:11;[78] 2 Samuel 16:12; Psalm 106:44, rā'āh means to look at with interest, kindness, and helpfulness.[79] Used here to confirm the Lord's intervention, it is acceptably rendered, "Who condescends to care for"[80] (things) "in the heavens and upon the earth." His gracious condescension more than compensates for life's hard conditions (e.g., vv. 7–9).

The anarthrous causative participles of verses 7–9 (i.e., מְקִימִי [mĕqîmî, "raising up"], יָרִים [yārîm, "lifting up"], מוֹשִׁיבִי [môšîbî, "causing to dwell"]) illuminate His merciful immanence via forceful illustrations. In verses 7–8 a general but extremely significant illustration of God's active concern for the downtrodden arouses the reader's amazement first. Then another unexpected example follows: God's consolation for the childless (v. 9). In reference to both illustrations, Allen recalls that "the third strophe [i.e., vv. 7–9] uses 1 Samuel 1–2 to illustrate this grace in terms of the providential reversal Yahweh brings about, raising the socially underprivileged to positions of respect."[81] Kidner appropriately digresses regarding the theological ramifications of this psalm's great climax:

> Consciously . . . those verses look back to the song of Hannah, which they quote almost exactly (cf. 7, 8a with 1 Sa. 2:8). Hence the sudden reference to the childless woman who becomes a mother (9), for this was Hannah's theme. With such a background the psalm not only makes its immediate point, that the Most High cares for the most humiliated, but brings to mind the train of events that can follow from such an intervention. Hannah's joy became all Israel's; Sarah's became the world's. And the song of Hannah was to be outshone one day by the *Magnificat*. The spectacular events of our verses 7 and 8 are not greater than this domestic one; the most important of them have sprung from just such an origin.[82]

The דָּל (*dāl*, "poor") and the אֶבְיוֹן (*'ebyôn*, "needy"),[83] normally social outcasts, are the focal point of God's bold intervention in verses 7–8.[84] Although "the *dāl* was not numbered among dependents who have no property,"[85] He still represented "those who lack."[86] The plight of the *'ebyôn* in the OT generally seems to be more aggravated: "The destitution of the *'ebyôn* is to be inferred from the whole tenor of the appropriate psalms: it manifests itself in affliction, illness, loneliness, and nearness to death."[87] Therefore, He represents those who are materially, socially, and spiritually in need.[88] God really cares for such people![89]

In the parallelisms of verse 7, the *dāl* was associated with the עָפָר (*'āpār*), "dust," "an emblem of lowly estate,"[90] and the *'ebyôn* with the אַשְׁפֹּת (*'ašpōt*), an "ash-heap, refuse-heap, dung-hill,"[91] certainly "an emblem of deepest poverty and desertion."[92] Anderson briefly describes the imagery of such an ancient garbage dump as this when he comments,

> It was the rubbish heap outside the village or town, which had become the pitiful shelter of the poor, the outcasts, and the diseased (cf. Lam. 4:5; also Job 2:8). There they begged, ransacked the refuse dump to find some scraps of food, and slept.[93]

But the Lord mercifully extricates the needy from (cf. the two occurrences of מִן [*min*, "from"]) such dire circumstances. He "lifts up, raises"[94] them from their predicament. The lifted up and exalted One (vv. 4–5) "can make men high in rank (i.e., 'exalt' them . . .)."[95] Verse 8 confirms that by its progression from extrication to exaltation. The Lord's intention is "to cause [them] to dwell,"[96] "to make [them] sit" (i.e., *lĕhôšîbî*)[97] in fellowship with[98] נְדִיבִים (*nĕdîbîm*, "nobles, princes"), those of "exalted material and social position."[99] Verse 8 is therefore "a figure for elevation to the highest rank and dignity,"[100] and compared with the plight of verse 7, it "is meant to bring out by way of contrast the magnitude of divine power and grace."[101]

Barrenness (v. 9) in the cultural context of the OT was a pitiful status.[102] "The lot of a childless wife must have been hard (cf. 1 Sam. 1:6), for barrenness was often regarded as a disgrace and a curse from God (cf. Gen. 16:2; 20:18; 1 Sam. 1:5; Lk. 1:25 . . .)."[103] It is no wonder that, from a woman's perspective, a barren womb was among the insatiable things in Proverbs 30:15–17 (cf. Rachel's agonizing cry in Gen. 30:1). From a man's perspective, it occasioned ultimate frustration as indicated by Abraham's response in Genesis 15:2 and Jacob's in Genesis 30:2.

Although the syntactical options of verse 9 are diverse,[104] the overarching impact of its illustration is incontestable. The gracious Lord "makes the woman barren in the household to dwell[105] *as* a joyful mother of sons," i.e., "he grants her security."[106] Consequently, He not only prospers the poor (v. 8), but He also blesses the barren (v. 9). The appropriate הַלְלוּ יָהּ (*halĕlûyāh*, "praise the LORD") closes the psalm.

What a majestic God Psalm 113 reveals! Yet His grandeur does not nullify His grace, and conversely, His grace does not undermine His grandeur:

> The bridge which man himself cannot throw across to reach the remote, transcendent God nevertheless exists; it is built by God himself so that in spite of all the disparity between God and man a communion exists between them which enables man to believe that the God who is far off is also the God of the here and now. What remains a mystery to the mind of man is revealed to the eyes of faith: that the exalted God not only looks down upon men but inclines graciously to them.[107]

CONCLUSION

Since God is supreme in the universe for all time and yet has still shown concern for His creatures, how should His children respond?

Certainly a reverent gratitude is in order, as is a God-consciousness that pervades every activity and attitude. In times of need, reminders of a transcendent God's involvement in human life can be important sources of strength. These and other lessons derive from Psalm 113, a gem among gems. Disclosures about God that arise from the exquisite beauty of the language should be adorning the bride of Christ. Furthermore, preachers and teachers of God's word should shine their expositional floodlights on this Scripture more regularly. God's infinite greatness and inexplicable grace need more attention. The richly blessed should voice spontaneous thanksgiving and praise to Him who reigns in heaven and yet responds to human needs.

ENDNOTES

[1] See John Gray, *I and II Kings: A Commentary* (Philadelphia: Westminster, 1970), 215; Moshe Weinfeld, *Deuteronomy and the Deuteronomic School* (Oxford: Clarendon, 1972), 37, 194–95, 325–26; Walter Zimmerli, *Old Testament Theology in Outline* (Atlanta: John Knox, 1978), 70–81; Eugene H. Maly, "'The Highest Heavens Cannot Contain You': Immanence and Transcendence in the Deuteronomist," *Standing Before God,* ed. A. Finkel and L. Frizzell (New York: KTAV, 1981), 29; G. von Rad, "οὐρανός," *TDNT,* 5:504–7; cf. the critical hypotheses that undergird most of the related discussions pertaining to "place-theology" and "name-theology." For brief critiques and interaction, note W. C. Kaiser, "יָשַׁב," *TWOT,* 1:411–12; idem, "שֵׁם," *TWOT,* 2:934–35.

[2] Cf. Leslie C. Allen, "Psalms 101–150," in *Word Biblical Commentary* (Waco, Tex.: Word, 1983), 100.

[3] Most interpreters construe מוֹשִׁיבִי as a hiphil participle from יָשַׁב ("dwell"); contra David Freedman, "Psalm 113 and the Song of Hannah," in *Pottery, Poetry, and Prophecy* (Winona Lake, Ind.: Eisenbrauns, 1980), 249, who suggests it derives from שׁוּב ("turn"; i.e., "who transforms . . .").

[4] A bridge to this chiasm is provided by the אֶת־שֵׁם יהוה ("name of the LORD") at the end of verse 1, since occurrences of אֶת־שֵׁם יהוה ("name of the LORD") serve as book ends for verses 2–3.

[5] ברך ("bless") is part of a repertoire of OT praise synonyms; cf. הלל ("praise"), ידה ("give thanks"), רנן ("give a ringing cry"), שׁיר ("sing"), גדל ("magnify"), רום ("exalt"), זמר ("make music"), etc.

[6] The כְּבוֹדוֹ of verse 4b may be construed as standing at the head of a parallel noun clause or as also governed by the רָם (rām, "high") of verse 4a. Concerning the latter option, Buttenweiser translates, "His glory transcends . . . ," arguing that "ram is a case of zeugma and is to be construed as a predicate also with kebodo" (Moses Buttenweiser, The Psalms Chronologically Treated with a New Translation [New York: KTAV, 1969], 348).

[7] Cf. BDB, 752, 755; Ronald J. Williams, Hebrew Syntax: An Outline (Toronto: University of Toronto, 1967), 51; and G. L. Carr, "עָלָה," TWOT, 2:669–70.

[8] Cf. E. Kautzsch and A. E. Cowley, eds., Gesenius' Hebrew Grammar [GKC] (Oxford: Clarendon Press, 1970), 350 (par. 114n).

[9] Besides the impacting reversal of order (i.e., v. 4: earthly, heavenly; v. 6: heavenly, earthly), the shift from the preposition עַל ("above") in verse 4 to occurrences of בְּ ("in") in verse 6 contributes to the change in mood (i.e., from separation to involvement).

[10] Obviously, when proper attention is paid to the immediate context, "there is . . . much more than rhetoric in the question of verse 5, 'Who is like the LORD our God?'" (Derek Kidner, Psalms 73–150 [Leicester, England: InterVarsity, 1975], 402).

[11] Survey BDB, pp. 567–68, for the proper names built upon this theological formula.

[12] Cf., e.g., C. J. Labuschagne, The Incomparability of Yahweh in the Old Testament (Leiden: Brill, 1966), 22, 99, 102.

[13] Through a less formal syntactical relationship, even the anarthrous participles of verses 7–9 continue as vital links in a strong theological chain.

[14] For various views on the so-called hireq compaginis, see discussions in GKC 253–54 (par. 90m, n); Mitchell Dahood, "Psalms III: 101–150," in The Anchor Bible (Garden City, N.Y.: Doubleday, 1970), 130; F. Delitzsch, "Psalms," in Commentary on the Old Testament in Ten Volumes, ed. C. F. Keil and F. Delitzsch (Grand Rapids: Eerdmans, n.d.), 3:203–4; Avi Hurvitz, "Originals and Imitations in Biblical Poetry: A Comparative Examination of 1 Samuel 2:1–10 and Psalm 113:5–9," in

Biblical and Related Studies Presented to Samuel Iwry, ed. A. Kort and S. Morschauser (Winona Lake: Eisenbrauns, 1985), 119–22; A. A. Anderson, "The Book of Psalms," in *New Century Bible Commentary* (Grand Rapids: Eerdmans, 1972), 2:782; and Allen, "Psalms 101–150," 99 n. 6a. Cf. also the forms in verses 7a, 8a (probably), and 9a.

[15] For an excellent survey of the options, see Allen, "Psalms 101–150," 99–100.

[16] Anderson, "The Book of Psalms," 2:780.

[17] Based upon an older method of grouping various combinations of parallelism, Briggs adopted a fourfold strophic division (Charles Augustus Briggs, *A Critical and Exegetical Commentary on the Book of Psalms*, ICC [Edinburgh: T & T Clark, 1907], 2:387).

[18] See Allen, "Psalms 101–150," 99.

[19] Cf. the strophic and poetic analyses of K. K. Sacon, "A Methodological Remark on Exegesis and Preaching of Psalm 113," *Nihon no Shingaku* 25 (1986): 26–42 (see *Old Testament Abstracts* 10, no. 1 [February 1987]: 65); Peter C. Craigie, "Psalm 113," *Interpretation* 39, no. 1 (January 1985): 70–74. Craigie astutely develops the strophes in reverse order because "we will only be able to respond honestly to the opening summons to praise when we have perceived God's merciful dealings with human beings (vv. 7–9) and his majesty in heaven and earth (vv. 4–6)" (ibid., 71).

[20] Kidner, *Psalms 73–150,* 401.

[21] I.e., Kidner's title for Psalm 113 (ibid.).

[22] Cf. Allen, "Psalms 101–150," 100.

[23] This particular reminder of an uncompromised transcendence at the outset of a consideration of our Lord's immanence* is supported by scriptural parallels. The most obvious example is Isaiah 57:15:

> 1A.   He has a transcendent manifestation of glory above
>   (Isaiah in introducing the Lord focuses upon His
>   transcendence)
>   1B. He is separate in position: "Thus says the high and
>   lifted-up One"

2B. His is separate in existence: "*who* perpetually exists"
3B. He is separate in character: "*whose* name is holy"
2A. He has an immanent manifestation of grace below (the Lord in speaking focuses upon His own immanence)
*1B. *He is near but without compromise*: "I dwell in a high and holy place"
2B. He is near with grace: "and with the crushed and lowly in spirit"
3B. He is near with purpose: "in order to revive . . ."

[24] The ultimate proof of this came in the Incarnation.

[25] Elmer A. Leslie, *The Psalms* (New York: Abingdon, 1949), 192.

[26] Allen, "Psalms 101–150," 99.

[27] Craigie, "Psalm 113," 70.

[28] "Hallel," in *Encyclopedia Judaica,* 7:1198–99.

[29] Ibid. On the so-called Egyptian Hallel, cf. Sigmund Mowinckel, *The Psalms in Israel's Worship,* trans. D. R. Ap-Thomas (Nashville: Abingdon, 1962), 1:3.

[30] On the Passover setting of "The Last Supper," see J. Behm, "κλάω," *TDNT,* 3:732–34, and J. Jeremias, "πάσχα," *TDNT,* 5:896–904.

[31] Leslie, *The Psalms,* 192–93.

[32] Craigie, "Psalm 113," 70.

[33] J. J. Stewart Perowne, *The Book of Psalms* (Grand Rapids: Zondervan, 1966), 1:322. The 1 Samuel 2 parallels are not an automatic indication of a postexilic date for Psalm 113; cf. John T. Willis, "The Song of Hannah and Psalm 113," *Catholic Biblical Quarterly* 35, no. 2 (April 1973): 154.

[34] Craigie, "Psalm 113," 71.

[35] See Sacon in *Old Testament Abstracts* 10, no. 1 (February 1987): 65. There is no solid evidence for suggesting that both occurrences are later

liturgical additions (e.g., Buttenweiser, *The Psalms,* 348). Additionally, the placement of the final הַלְלוּ יָהּ before Psalm 114 (LXX 113) in the LXX is incorrect. Consequently, two of the twenty-four occurrences of the formula הַלְלוּ יָהּ bracket this great hymn.

[36] Buttenweiser, *The Psalms,* 348.

[37] If the *hallel* pattern of Psalm 113:1 is designated as a, b, c, then the corresponding *hallel* exhortations of Psalm 135:1 reflect an a, c, b order.

[38] For some of the most important ones, note H. Ringgren, "הלל *hll* I and II," *TDOT,* 3:406; and L. J. Coppes, "הָלַל II," *TWOT,* 1:217.

[39] *TDOT,* 3:404; Coppes adds, from an overall assessment of הלל *(hallel),* that "belief and joy are inextricably intertwined" (*TWOT,* 1:217).

[40] Ringgren notes that the summons to praise with הלל *(hallel)* is almost always in the plural being associated with the community, while הודה ("thanksgiving") is generally singular being associated with the individual (*TDOT,* 3:408). Cf. Coppes' discussion of the propriety of such a corporate response (*TWOT,* 1:217).

[41] LXX tradition takes ("the LORD") as the object of הַלְלוּ ("hallelujah"), thereby construing the עַבְדֵי ("servants") as an independent vocative (i.e., as if it were עֲבָדִים ["servants"]). As Allen notes in the reference to this tradition, "Probably at some stage abbreviation . . . has been *assumed*" [emphasis added] ("Psalms 101–150," 99).

[42] W. Zimmerli and J. Jeremias, "παῖς θεοῦ," *Theological Dictionary of the New Testament [TDNT],* 5:475 n. 122.

[43] A. Cohen, *The Psalms,* Soncino books of the Bible (London: Soncino, 1945), 378; in the light of verse 3, Cohen widens the scope of inclusion, commenting "the call is made to all, Israelites and Gentiles, who acknowledge God" (ibid.). On the other hand, some would restrict יהוה עַבְדֵי ("servants of the LORD") to the Levitical circle. Both Allen and Anderson entertain this option; however, they commendably opt for the more comprehensive interpretation (see "Psalms 101–150," 99, and "The Book of Psalms," 2:780, respectively).

[44] E.g., its occurrences in 2 Kings 10:18–24 and Jesus' association of the twin concepts in Matthew 4:10 (referring to Deuteronomy 6:13).

[45] Anderson, "The Book of Psalms," 2:780; for a basic survey, see W. C. Kaiser, "עָבַד‎," *TWOT,* 2:639–41.

[46] W. C. Kaiser, "שֵׁם‎," *TWOT,* 2:934. Kaiser documents his conclusion with 1 Samuel 25:25, among other passages.

[47] Ibid.; cf. Delitzsch, "Psalms," 3:204–05. Anderson corroborates, noting that אֶת־שֵׁם יהוה‎ ("name of the LORD") "comprises primarily the whole self-revelation of Yahweh to his people; the phrase may be a circumlocution for 'Yahweh'" ("The Book of Psalms," 2:780). Kidner's reference to "the Revealed" is also telling (*Psalms 73–150,* 401).

[48] D. N. Freedman, M. P. O'Connor, and H. Riggren, "יהוה‎," *TDOT,* 5:500.

[49] Ibid., 5:513. Cf. Payne's conclusions in "הָוָה‎ II," J. B. Payne, *TWOT,* 1:210–12; contra some of R. L. Harris' editorial comments within Payne's article.

[50] Allen, "Psalms 101–150," 101.

[51] For a survey, see J. Scharbert, "בְרֵךְ‎," *TDOT,* 2:284–88; for a condensed presentation, see J. N. Oswalt, "בָּרַךְ‎," *TWOT,* 1:132–33.

[52] Anderson, "The Book of Psalms," 2:780.

[53] For occurrences of this identical compound, cf. Psalms 115:18; 121:8; 125:2; 131:3; Isaiah 9:6; 59:21; Micah 4:7; and for similar compounds, cf. Psalms 41:14; 90:2; 103:17; 106:48; Jeremiah 7:7; 1 Chronicles 16:36; 29:10.

[54] BDB, 763.

[55] Anderson, "The Book of Psalms," 2:780.

[56] Cf. BDB, 99–100, 280–81. See also this compound prepositional phras in Psalm 50:1; Malachi 1:11.

[57] A. F. Kirkpatrick, "The Book of Psalms," in *Cambridge Bible for Schools and Colleges* (Cambridge: University Press, 1906), 678.

[58] Cf. the occurrences of the pual participle from הלל‎ ("praise") in Psalms 18:4; 48:2; 96:4; 145:3.

[59] J. Herrmann and H. Greeven, "εὔχομαι," *TDNT*, 2:786; for some discussion see *TDOT*, 3:409.

[60] A. Bowling, "רום," *TWOT*, 2:837.

[61] Note the interesting juxtaposition of the roots רום ("be high") and שׁפל ("be low") in Psalm 138:6; cf. Psalm 113:4a with 113:6aff.

[62] Note the parallelism between רָם ("be high") and the root נשׁא ("lift") in both of these verses from Isaiah.

[63] For some pertinent observations, see Robert Baker Girdlestone, *Synonyms of the Old Testament* (Grand Rapids: Eerdmans, 1973), 35.

[64] Cf. רָם ("be high") with עַל־כָּל הָעַמִּים ("above all the peoples") in Psalm 99:2.

[65] J. N. Oswalt, "כָּבֵד," *TWOT*, 1:427.

[66] Anderson, "The Book of Psalms," 2:781.

[67] For a concise summary of the conjectural emendations and transpositions that have been suggested in verses 5–6 of the MT, see Allen, "Psalms 101–150," 99 n. 6a. His first observation (i.e., no transpositions) is preferable, his last is permissible, and the others are unacceptable.

[68] Cf. Anderson, "The Book of Psalms," 2:781, who draws attention to Jeremiah 24:7; 30:22; 31:1.

[69] Consequently, amidst a recapitulation of God's transcendence (v. 5), the stage is set for a concentration upon His immanence (vv. 6–9).

[70] On the hiphil expressing action in a definite direction see, once again, *Gesenius' Hebrew Grammar*, 350 (para. 114n).

[71] R. Hentschke, "גָּבַהּ," *TDOT*, 2:356–60.

[72] Ibid., 2:357–58; note the textual documentation cited for both assertions.

[73] Ibid., 2:358; concerning the theological significance of גָּבַהּ ("be high"), Hamilton appropriately notes that "God's position is said to be 'on high'

(Ps. 113:5; Job 22:12) and his ways are 'higher' than those of mankind (Isa. 55:9)" (V. P. Hamilton, "גָּבַהּ," *TWOT,* 1:146).

[74] Cf. Anderson, "The Book of Psalms," 2:781.

[75] See the discussion above under syntactical enhancements.

[76] Delitzsch, "Psalms," 3:205.

[77] In reference to שָׁפֵל, Austel notes that "though the idea 'be low' in the physical sense underlies the verb and its derivatives, its most important use is in the figurative sense of 'abasement,' 'humbling,' 'humility'" (H. J. Austel, "שָׁפֵל," *TWOT,* 2:950). An examination of the roots רום ("be high") and שפל in Psalm 138:6a would be appropriate here.

[78] In light of these particular texts, note the appropriateness of the illustration in Psalm 113:9.

[79] BDB, 907–8.

[80] Cf. Anderson, "The Book of Psalms," 2:781.

[81] Allen, "Psalms 101–150," 101.

[82] Kidner, *Psalms 73–150,* 402. There are no compelling reasons to construe these illustrations corporately as a reference to Zion according to targumic tradition (e.g., Cohen, *Psalms,* 378; and Buttenweiser, *The Psalms,* 248).

[83] For other combinations of דַּל and אֶבְיוֹן in various contextual settings, see 1 Samuel 2:8; Isaiah 14:30; 25:4; Amos 4:1; 8:6; Psalms 72:13; 82:4; Proverbs 14:31; Job 5:15–16; etc. Commenting upon this particular combination in our psalm, Botterweck concludes that "according to the context, the *dal* and the *'ebyôn* belong to the same group as the feeble, hungry, poor, and godly" (P. J. Botterweck, "אֶבְיוֹן," *TDOT,* 1:40).

[84] For a good review of the humiliation of such people along with God's interest in them, see W. Grundmann, "ταπεινός," *TDNT,* 8:9–10.

[85] H. J. Fabry, "דַּל," *TDOT,* 3:219.

[86] L. J. Coppes, "דָּלַל," *TWOT,* 1:190. Coppes concludes that "we might consider *dal* as referring to one of the lower classes in Israel" (ibid.).

[87] *TDOT,* 1:36; Botterweck's whole survey is illuminating (ibid., 36–37).

[88] Cf. L. J. Coppes, "אֶבְיוֹן," *TWOT,* 1:4–5.

[89] Cf. "The *dallim* Under the Protection of Yahweh, the King, and His Fellow Men (Psalms)" *TDOT,* 3:226–30; also notice Allen's New Testament applications ("Psalms 101–150," 101–2).

[90] Delitzsch, "Psalms," 3:205.

[91] BDB, 1046.

[92] Delitzsch, "Psalms," 3:205.

[93] Anderson, "The Book of Psalms," 2:781–82.

[94] Cf. BDB, 878–79, 927; the hiphils from קוּם ("arise") and רוּם ("be high") are near synonyms as shown by their parallelism here. Interestingly, since מְקִימִי ("raising up") is synonymously related to יָרִים ("He lifts"), it not only relates semantically to God's description as רָם ("be high") in verse 4 (cf. the previous discussion under semantical enhancements), but also conceptually to the root גבה ("be high") in verse 5 (cf. R. Hentschke, "גָּבַהּ," *TDOT,* 2:357–58, for a general discussion of these synonyms). In reference to קוּם ("arise") with God as subject, Coppes observes that "the word may denote his creative, saving, and judging action" (L. J. Coppes, "קוּם," *TWOT,* 2:792); cf. A. Oepke, "ἐγείρω," *TDNT,* 2:334.

[95] A. Bowling, "רוּם," *TWOT,* 2:838.

[96] BDB, 443.

[97] Most emend the final י of the MT to ו based largely on LXX and Syriac tradition (e.g., *Gesenius' Hebrew Grammar,* 254 [par. 90n]), but there are other options: Dahood takes it as a "third-person suffix-y" ("Psalms III: 101–150," 130); Delitzsch says, "ver. 8 shows how our Ps. cxiii in particular delights in this ancient *i,* where it is even affixed to the infinitive as an ornament" ("Psalms," 3:204); and Buttenwieser argues, "Though Gr. reads *lĕhōshîbō,* the reading of the Hebrew is equally correct: according

to this reading the objects of vs. 7 are to be construed also with *lĕhōshîbō,* being a case of brachylogy" (*The Psalms,* 249).

[98] The two occurrences of עִם ("with") in verse 8 balance the two occurrences of מִן in verse 7. עִם in such contexts emphasizes "fellowship and companionship" (BDB, 767).

[99] L. J. Coppes, "נָדַב," *TWOT,* 2:555. His brief summary of the major synonyms of by נָדִיב ("nobles") is quite informative (ibid.).

[100] Kirkpatrick, *The Book of Psalms,* 679.

[101] *TDOT,* 3:228.

[102] Cf. other occurrences of the adj. עָקָר ("barren") in Genesis 11:30; 25:21; 29:31; Judges 13:2–3; 1 Samuel 2:5; and Job 24:21.

[103] Anderson, "The Book of Psalms," 2:782.

[104] E.g., BDB, 443; Buttenweiser, *The Psalms,* 349; Delitzsch, "Psalms," 3:206; etc.

[105] Again, note the causative verbal from יָשַׁב ("dwell"; i.e., מוֹשִׁיבִי ["makes to dwell"], v. 9; cf. לְהוֹשִׁיבִי ["to make to dwell"], v. 8).

[106] Anderson, "The Book of Psalms," 2:782.

[107] Artur Weiser, *The Psalms: A Commentary* (Philadelphia: Westminster, 1962), 707.

CHAPTER THREE

Isaiah 53:4–5

For What Did Christ Atone?

Richard L. Mayhue

Isaiah 53:4–5 raises the question, "For what did Christ atone?" or more specifically, "Is physical healing in the atonement?" Outside Isaiah 53, Scriptures touching on Christ's atonement in Leviticus and Hebrews deal only with sin, not sickness. The context and language of Isaiah 53:3–12 address sin alone. A broad range of Scriptures teach that Christ died to deal with humankind's sin dilemma. Matthew 8:16–17 uses an illustration of physical healing to demonstrate a spiritual truth about the Christian's resurrection hope of being sinless and thus in perfect health. First Peter 2:24, studied in both broad context (vv. 18–25) and narrow (vv. 24–25), reasons that Christ atoned for sin, not sickness. Therefore, the conclusion is that physical healing is not in the atonement, but rather comes through the atonement after resurrection, because only then does the atonement eliminate the moral cause of physical infirmities, which is sin in one's personal experience.

* * * * *

As I browsed through some commentaries at my favorite Christian bookstore in Columbus, Ohio, a dear lady whom I had recently visited in the hospital and prayed for entered and walked toward me. Greeting her, I remarked how well she looked. She responded, "By His stripes I have been healed. Praise God there is healing in Christ's atonement."

The bookstore was no place that day for a theology lesson. I did not want to dampen her joy, nor did I want to rob her confidence that God had somehow been involved in her physical restoration (Deut. 32:39). However, her understanding of Isaiah 53:5 and 1 Peter 2:24 did not relate biblically to what she had experienced.

I wondered where she had learned those proof texts. Perhaps she had read or listened to a faith healer's explanation of Isaiah 53.[1] A friend or neighbor may have told her. Possibly she heard this on Christian TV or radio. For certain, many explanations of Isaiah 53:4–5 at the popular level raise more questions than they answer and frequently prove to be less than precise biblical treatments of the subject at hand.

By a careful look at Isaiah 53 and related passages, the following discussion purposes to entertain biblically such questions as, "Is there healing in the atonement?" "If there is, what kind, how much, and when do I get it?" Perhaps it would be more accurate to inquire, "Was Christ punished for our diseases?"[2] Or "In what way is physical healing related to the atonement?" or even "For what did Christ atone?"[3] Did Christ bear our diseases in His body the same way He bore our sins? Can we have freedom from sickness in this life as we have forgiveness of sins?

The search for biblical answers begins by looking not at healing, but rather at the atonement.

The Atonement[4]

Mention of the atonement sacrifice (כָּפֻר [*kippūr,* "pacify, atone"]) first appears in Scripture as a part of the Mosaic sacrificial system[5] (cf. Exod. 29:33, 36–37; 30:10, 15–16). On this one day of the year, Israel's high priest entered the Holy of Holies, approached the ark of the covenant, and sprinkled blood to atone for the sins of Israel.

Aaron, the brother of Moses, was the very first high priest to enter the Holy Place with a bull for an offering (Lev. 16:3). Was it for a sin or a sick offering? Unquestionably, it was a sin offering (v. 11). Aaron offered a bull for a sin offering—first for himself and his household (vv. 5–6). "And he shall make atonement for the holy place, because of the impurities of the sons of Israel, and because of their transgressions, in regard to all their sins . . ." (v. 16, cf. v. 34). "Then Aaron shall lay both of his hands on the head of the live goat, and confess over it all the iniquities of the sons of Israel, and all their transgressions in regard to all their sins . . ." (v. 21).

Moses instituted the Day of Atonement by the authority of God about 1450–1400 B.C. Hundreds of years later (about 700–680 B.C.), Isaiah wrote prophetically concerning a coming servant who would be "the ultimate atonement." The Atonement ritual that Moses established and the atonement prophecy that Isaiah penned, Jesus Christ would later fulfil in reality when He died for sins—not sicknesses.

The book of Hebrews (the "Leviticus" of the NT) demonstrates the unity of Scripture. When the final atonement that propitiated God's wrath occurred, Christ served as both the high priest and the sacrifice.

> But when Christ appeared as a high priest of the good things to come, He entered through the greater and more perfect tabernacle, not made with hands, that is to say, not of this creation;

and not through the blood of goats and calves, but through His own blood, He entered the holy place once for all, having obtained eternal redemption. (Hebrews 9:11–12 NASB)

Jesus Christ as God incarnate became the Lamb slain for the sins of the world (John 1:29, 36; 1 John 2:2). Hebrews 10 addresses the atonement's fulfilment in Jesus Christ. For example, "Then He said, 'Behold, I have come to do Thy will.' He takes away the first in order to establish the second. By this will we have been sanctified through the offering of the body of Jesus Christ once for all" (Heb. 10:9–10).

In the old economy, year after year the high priest had to make atonement first for himself and his family and then for the nation. But with the new covenant, Christ had to sacrifice only once for everyone else, not for Himself. Isaiah 53 anticipated Christ's one time sacrifice: "But He, having offered one sacrifice for sins for all time, sat down at the right hand of God. . . . For by one offering He has perfected for all time those who are sanctified" (Heb. 10:12, 14).

Both Leviticus and Hebrews demonstrate that in God's mind the atonement dealt immediately with sin, not sickness. It had everything to do with humankind's sin problem and the redemption needed to remove sin and its penalty, so that true believers might stand eternally justified before a holy God. Christ's atonement paid the due penalty for sin when God poured out His wrath upon Jesus Christ while upon the cross.

Textual Comments on Isaiah 53

Isaiah 53 serves indispensably as the heart of anyone's healing theology.[6] One's biblical expectations for eventually restored health rest on this biblical bedrock. The "Magna Charta" of God's healing promise focuses on Christ's sacrificial death at Calvary. Clearly the emphasis of Isaiah 53 centers on spiritual salvation.[7] Since sin is the moral cause of physical infirmities, it is not surprising (1) that sin and sickness are related and (2) that dealing with sin (the cause) eventually addresses sickness (the effect).

Isaiah 53 raises the question then, "What, if anything, does the prophet promise about physical restoration?"[8] Or put another way, "Is Isaiah 53:4–5 limited to dealing only with sin and salvation?"

Surely our griefs He[9] Himself bore, and our sorrows He carried; yet we ourselves esteemed Him stricken, smitten of God, and afflicted. But He was pierced through for our transgressions, He was crushed through for our iniquities; the chastening for our well-being fell upon Him, and by His scourging we are healed. All of us like sheep have gone astray, each of us has turned to his own way; but the Lord has caused the iniquity of us all to fall on Him. (Isaiah 53:4–6 NASB)

The Hebrew words[10] translated "griefs" (חֲלִי [ḥŏlî,[11] "sick, weak"]) and "sorrows" (מַכְאוֹב [mak'ôb, "pain"])[12] in Isaiah 53:3–4, 10 can legitimately refer to either physical infirmities, mental pain, or spiritual problems. Those who limit this language only to physical problems should more accurately say that the words "may" refer to physical problems, but not necessarily.[13] Note also that none of the primary translations—NASB, NIV, and NKJV—reflect the physical idea, but rather all translate with the spiritual in view.

Words should always be understood in a context and with a meaning intended by the author. Normally, the surrounding context indicates what the author meant by the words he used. A careful analysis of context frequently clarifies whatever definitional ambiguities may exist.

Contextually, Isaiah 53 uses three different Hebrew words for sin—translated "sin," "iniquity," and "transgression"—at least nine times to identify decidedly the passage's intent. For example, in 53:5 Christ was "pierced through for our transgressions" and "crushed for our iniquities," so that in 53:6, "the Lord has caused the iniquity of us all to fall on Him." Further, He will "bear their iniquities" (v. 11), and "He Himself bore the sins of many" (v. 12). The obvious focus of Isaiah 53 is on sin, not on its immediate effects upon the body.[14]

Isaiah 53:4 reads that he "bore" (נָשָׂא, nāśā) our griefs and "carried" (סָבַל, sābal) our sorrows. Isaiah used these same verbs in verses 11 and 12. As one compares verse 3 with verse 4 and then verse 4 with verse 11 and verse 12, one can see that the emphasis relates to salvation. The more frequent use of redemption (vv. 3, 11–12) interprets the use in 53:4. Christ took upon Himself sin, not sickness. It is also no small consideration that the LXX rendered the first part of 53:4 as an interpretive translation, "He bore our sins."

Note additionally that "He would render Himself as a guilt offering" (53:10), that "He will bear their iniquities" (53:11), and that "He Himself bore the sin of many" (53:12). Hebrews 9:28 also comes to this grand conclusion: "So Christ also, having been offered once to bear the sins of many. . . ." Both Hebrews and Isaiah 53 focus on spiritual redemption.

The "scourging" or "wounds" (53:5) received by Christ, translated חַבּוּרָה (ḥăbûrâ, "stripe, blow"), can speak of actual physical wounds (Gen. 4:23;

Exod. 21:25) or the spiritual afflictions of sin (Ps. 38:5; Isa. 1:6). Although Christ was physically afflicted by man before and while upon the cross, it is most consistent with the remainder of Isaiah 53 to see this in the latter sense of Christ being afflicted by the Father for the sins He bore (53:10–12).

Further, note that Isaiah used, רָפָא (rāpā', "heal, make healthful") six times in his prophetic book (6:10; 19:22; 30:26; 53:5; 57:18; 57:19). While rāpā' can either be literal with regard to physical healing (Gen. 20:17) or figurative in the OT, in each of Isaiah's five uses, other than 53:5, he employs it figuratively of healing from sin. In light of (1) this otherwise exclusive figurative use by Isaiah, (2) the previous discussion concerning metonymy of effect, and (3) the figurative use of "wounds," it is reasonable to conclude that Isaiah intended the use of rāpā' in 53:5 to be figurative also.

Even though there might seem to be a veiled inference to the physical benefit that sin's removal can produce upon the body, the language of Isaiah 53 demands an understanding in terms of Christ's redemption of sinners. Isaiah intended to convey the thought that Christ atoned for sin.

Theological Comments Relating to Isaiah 53

Consider from other Scriptures some clarifying theological observations relating to sin and salvation.

First, the present body is corruptible; that is, it will degenerate until death (1 Cor. 15:50–58; 2 Cor. 5:1–4). The physical element in this life will ultimately separate from the spiritual (James 2:26). But the good news for believers is that one day they will put on the incorruptible—a form that will remain eternally constant, pure, and without sin. "And not only this, but also we ourselves, having the first fruits of the Spirit, even we ourselves groan within ourselves, waiting eagerly for our adoption as sons, the redemption of our body" (Rom. 8:23).

Believers have only the firstfruits of the Spirit now and will not begin to see what God will do in them until they leave this world and enter into His presence. Now they groan within themselves, eagerly awaiting their adoption as sons and the redemption of their bodies. The future will be fantastic by comparison. They will experience afflictions no more because the moral source of sickness—sin—will be no more.

Second, Christ died for sins. The gospel immediately becomes good news about the sin problem, but not necessarily so with physical problems. Read about this in such biblical texts as Matthew 1:21; John 1:29; Romans 1:16; 1 Corinthians 15:1–3; Ephesians 1:7; Colossians 1:14; Hebrews 9:1–28; 1 John 3:5.

Disease is not sin, but a consequence of sin. Disease carries no penalty which must be atoned for as sin does. Disease does not interfere with a man's fellowship with God like sin does. A sick man can still enjoy fellowship with God in spite of suffering from disease, and his experience of sickness may even deepen that fellowship. Once we recognize that sin and disease belong to different categories we can readily see that the atonement will affect them in different ways. In the case of sin we can know forgiveness in this present life, but there is nothing corresponding to this experience of forgiveness in the case of disease. The only thing which could correspond to forgiveness would be an immunity to disease which would be as permanent as our forgiveness. Those who were healed by Jesus in the gospels were not given such an immunity for this would have meant that they would never have died. Even Lazarus who was raised from the dead eventually died again. What was true for them is also true for us today. When we receive forgiveness on putting our faith in Jesus Christ and His atonement on our behalf, we are not made perfect by having sin and its effects removed from us. Sin will only be finally removed at the resurrection. What applies to sin, also applies to its effects such as disease for these too will only be removed at the resurrection.[15]

Next, Christ was made sin and not sickness. Paul writes about the ministry of reconciliation: "He made Him who knew no sin to be sin on our behalf, that we might become the righteousness of God in Him" (2 Cor. 5:21). Christ was never made sickness.

Fourth, Christ forgave sins, not sicknesses. John notes, "I am writing to you, little children, because your sins are forgiven you for His name's sake" (1 John 2:12).

Fifth, Christ gave Himself for sins and not for sicknesses: "Grace to you and peace from God our Father, and the Lord Jesus Christ, who gave Himself for our sins, that he might deliver us out of this present evil age, according to the will of our God and Father . . ." (Gal. 1:3–4).

Next, the Bible teaches that if people are truly saved, they cannot lose their salvation (John 10:28–29; Rom. 8:28–39; Phil. 1:6; Jude 24). Now, carrying this thought out to its logical conclusion, assuming (for argument's sake) that physical healing is as much in the atonement for today as is redemption, yields an interesting conclusion. A truly saved person cannot lose salvation (John 5:24), and God has given salvation through no human merit—through no price that human beings have paid.

Since these two biblical facts are true, then if physical healing did share in the atonement as does spiritual healing, people ought not to lose their physical health and thus would never die.

But is that what really happens or what the Scriptures teach? No! The Scripture teaches that all must die (Heb. 9:27)! The deaths of such godly examples as Abraham, Isaac, Daniel, Paul, and Timothy show that God's greatest saints were sick and eventually died. Therefore, it is biblical to conclude that though a related physical aspect may be in the atonement, it will not apply until after death and the redemption of Christians' bodies by resurrection (Rom. 8:23).[16]

Seventh, genuine believers have assurance of their salvation but have no guarantee concerning the quality of physical life or health.

> Come now, you who say, "Today or tomorrow, we shall go to such and such a city, and spend a year there and engage in business and make a profit." Yet you do not know what your life will be like tomorrow. You are just a vapor that appears for a little while and then vanishes away. (James 4:13–14 NASB)

Believers have no certainty that any will be here tomorrow. But every biblical assurance is that placing faith in Jesus Christ will enable one to remain His son and daughter forever (Eph. 1:5).

Next, if healing is in the atonement and if it applies physically today, those who ask by faith for physical healing and do not receive it have no logical right to assurance of their salvation. However, Scripture teaches that if someone is saved, then that person has every right to believe in his or her eternal salvation (Rom. 8:28–39; Phil. 1:6). So, if physical healing were in the atonement and if someone asks to be healed and is not, not only does that person lose assurance of the physical restoration, but also assurance of spiritual redemption. Fortunately, one can reach these unbiblical conclusions only by first taking a wrong approach to what the atonement is really all about—the forgiveness of sins.

Ninth, assuming that physical healing in the atonement were to apply today, logic dictates that eternal life must also apply today with the acquisition of immortal bodies. But death is the great nemesis and stumbling block to this proposed truth. All are going to die (Heb. 9:27). Death will not totally disappear in earthly human experience until the eternal state commences (1 Cor. 15:25–26). Therefore, whatever physical benefits, if any, are found in the atonement, they will not begin until the resurrection. The Bible does not teach anywhere that sickness needs atonement, but it does teach everywhere that sinners require Christ's atonement for forgiveness of their sin.

If Christ paid the penalty for sin and if sin is the moral cause of sickness and is still continuing, what then ought to be the current experience in the physical realm? Total or impaired health? Just as believers have impaired *spiritual* health, so they will continue to have impaired *physical* health until sin is no more. Total health will not happen until death or until the Lord comes!

In reality, Christ paid the penalty for sin, but He did not remove sin from the life of the believer. Christ died for the moral *cause* of sickness, i.e., sin. But He did not remove sickness from the life experience of believers because He did not eliminate besetting sin.

Finally, if the conclusions reached in Isaiah 53 and elsewhere are true, then the NT should verify them. The Scriptures are marvelously unified and will not contradict themselves. As expected, Isaiah 53 is not without its New Testament witness.[17]

Philip encountered the Ethiopian eunuch reading Isaiah 53 (Acts 8:28, 32–33). When the eunuch asked Philip for an explanation, he preached Jesus to him (8:35). Apparently, the eunuch embraced Christ as his personal Savior and Lord because he next asked about baptism (8:36). The point to note is this—both Philip and the Ethiopian eunuch understood Isaiah 53 to be dealing with sin, not sickness. That is as anticipated from the above inductive study of Isaiah 53.

Matthew on Isaiah 53
Matthew 8:14–17 presents another challenge in referring back to Isaiah 53:4:

> And when Jesus had come to Peter's home, He saw his mother-in-law lying sick in bed with a fever. And he touched her hand, and the fever left her; and she arose, and began to wait on Him. And when evening had come, they brought to Him many who were demon-possessed; and He cast out the spirits with a word, and healed all who were ill; in order that what was spoken through Isaiah the prophet might be fulfiled, saying, "He Himself took our infirmities, and carried away our diseases."

The challenge is to understand what use of Isaiah 53:4 Matthew intended. A cursory reading of the English text does not provide that clarification. It is a very difficult passage, and without an understanding of original language, comprehending what Matthew taught is elusive.

The Greek words translated "took" (λαμβάνω, *lambanō*) and "carry" (βαστάζω, *bastazō*) in Matthew 8:17 are different from the corresponding

Greek word, "to bear," in the Greek translation (the Septuagint, also referred to by LXX) of Isaiah 53:4, i.e., φέρω (pherō, "bear, carry"). They are never used in the NT with the sense of atonement or propitiation. The words in Matthew 8 (lambanō and bastazō) mean "to take away from" or "to remove." Matthew's dramatic word change indicates that he is *not* saying that Christ "bore" sickness, but rather He "removed" sickness. In contrast, the Hebrew words used in Isaiah 53:4 (nāśā and sābal) mean "to bear sacrificially" as does pherō in the LXX. Thus, the idea in Isaiah is that "He took our sins upon Him." A good reason then accounts for the word change.

Matthew is saying that Christ "took away" (lambanō) their sicknesses. Christ did not "bear" (pherō) in a substitutionary sense the sickness of Peter's mother-in-law. He did not say, "Fever, move from her into Me." He just touched her and it was gone. He bore in His body neither the afflictions of those who were ill nor the spirits of those who were possessed (8:16). Later, He would "bear" sin on Calvary, but at this point in Matthew 8 He had only "taken away" their sicknesses.[18]

Matthew uses θεραπεύω (therapeuō, "heal, restore") in 8:16, whereas Isaiah (53:5) and Peter (2:24) use רָפָא (rāpāʾ, "heal") and ἰάομαι (iaomai, "heal, cure") respectively. *Therapeuō* always refers to real physical infirmities in the New Testament; on the other hand, rāpāʾ and its LXX/NT counterpart iaomai regularly indicate either actual physical healing (Matt. 8:8; 15:28; Mark 5:29; Luke 5:17) or spiritual healing (cf. Isa. 6:10; Matt. 13:15; John 12:40; Acts 28:27). Contexts in Isaiah and 1 Peter point clearly to a figurative use of iaomai in the realm of salvation. However, Matthew's purposeful change to *therapeuō* signals his obvious intent to focus on the physical alone. From Christ's perspective, those healings provided messianic credentials. From the perspective of the present time, they pointed to the resurrection hope that when sin disappears, human bodies will be free of physical infirmities.

Advocates of contemporary physical healing in the atonement overlook the fact that what Christ did at Calvary actually occurred several years after His healing ministry at Capernaum.[19] This means that there could be no effectual relationship between Christ's healings in Capernaum and His later atonement on the cross at Calvary. Rather, Matthew employed a normal illustration from the OT when commenting on Christ's healings. He found a point of continuity, a point of identity between Isaiah 53 and Christ's healing ministry in Capernaum. Matthew used Isaiah analogically.

Matthew 2:14–15 illustrates this principle when quoting Hosea 11:1: "And he arose and took the Child and His mother by night, and departed for Egypt; and was there until the death of Herod; that what was spoken by the Lord through the prophet might be fulfilled, saying, 'Out of Egypt did I call My son.'"

Matthew writes in the context of the Lord's childhood and Herod's desire to put Him to death. Hosea, on the other hand, was writing about the historical exodus of Israel out of Egypt's bondage. So what relation is there between Israel and Christ? By analogy it is true that (1) they both were in Egypt, (2) they both are referred to as God's Son, and (3) God brought them both out from Egypt. These then are the points of analogy that explain why Matthew used the prophecy of Hosea 11:1.

Consider this perspective: Matthew 8 is to Isaiah 53 (in terms of its analogy) as Matthew 17 (the transfiguration of Christ) is to Revelation 19 (the second coming of Christ). Matthew 17 is a preview, just as Matthew 8 is a foretaste of (1) resurrection life, (2) the coming millennial kingdom in which there will be healing, and (3) the ultimate eternal kingdom, which will be free of sin and therefore of sickness too.[20]

D. A. Carson has reasoned,

> Indeed, as I have argued elsewhere, Matthew 8:16–17 explicitly connects Jesus' miracles of healing and exorcism with the atonement that had not yet taken place. They serve as foretastes of and are predicated on the cross work that is their foundation and justification.[21]

The conclusion is there is no more basis for believing that because Christ cared for physical affliction at Calvary there is now no sickness in the believer's life experience, than there is to suggest that because Christ bore our sins at Calvary sin has now been fully eliminated from the believer's life. As long as sin exists, the moral basis for sickness and physical debilitation will continue.

Believers have the present potential for incurable physical distress and the promise of eventual physical death. What Christ did at either Capernaum or Calvary eliminated neither sickness nor dying from the life of the Christian.[22] Matthew 8 is best understood as a preview of Christ's future messianic ministry which authenticated his claim to be the Son of God and an illustration of the resurrection hope of true believers that when sin is gone, sickness will be also. At Capernaum, He merely removed sickness; He did not become the believer's substitutionary sickness bearer.

Peter on Isaiah 53

Before some final conclusions, a consideration of Peter's use of Isaiah 53 is in order.

For you have been called for this purpose, since Christ also suffered for you, leaving you an example for you to follow in His steps, who committed no sin, nor was any deceit found in His mouth; and while being reviled, He did not revile in return; while suffering, He uttered no threats, but kept entrusting Himself to Him who judges righteously; and He Himself bore our sins in His body on the cross, that we might die to sin and live to righteousness; for by His wounds you were healed. (1 Peter 2:21–24 NASB)

Did Christ die for our sins or for our sicknesses? A wider reading from 2:18 to 2:25 shows that Peter is preparing his audience to endure more suffering, not to be relieved of it. Physical healing is not in Peter's thinking here. He teaches just the opposite. The context demands an understanding that Christ died for sins.

Now, consider the following, more narrow contextual analysis of 1 Peter 2:24–25:

1. The fact of salvation (2:24a)
   ". . . He Himself bore our sins in His body on the cross, . . ."
2. The purposes of salvation (2:24b)
   ". . . that we might die to sin and live to righteousness;"
3. The means of salvation (2:24c)
   ". . . for by His wounds you were healed."
4. The need for salvation (2:25a)
   "For you were continually straying like sheep, . . ."
5. The result of salvation (2:25b)
   ". . . but now you have returned to the Shepherd and guardian of your souls."

Given the fact that elements 1, 2, 4, and 5 deal with sin, it would be surprising to find element 3, "for by His wounds you were healed," to deal with the physical. Since nothing in the context supports this kind of anomaly and since the previous discussion of Isaiah 53:5 (which Peter quotes here) pointed to Isaiah's use of metonymy in substituting effect for cause, the conclusion is that Peter intended to address Christ's atonement for sin alone.

Peter used ἀναφέρω (*anapherō*, "bring up, offer, bear") in 2:24 to indicate the sin-bearing role of Christ (cf. Heb. 7:27; 9:28; 13:15; 2 Peter 2:5).[23] This corresponds directly with Isaiah's use of *nāśā, sābal,* and the LXX use of *pherō* in the sense of atonement sacrifice. This consistent use of sacrificial language stands in stark contrast to Matthew's use of *lambanō* and *bastazō,* meaning to "take away" in a spatial sense of disease being removed. What does μώλωπι (*mōlōpi,* "wound" or "by His stripes") mean (2:24)? Translated "stripes" in the KJV and "wounds" in the NASB and NIV, *mōlōpi* is best translated from חַבּוּרָה (*ḥăbûrâ,* "stripe, blow") in Isaiah 53:5 as "wounds from physical abuse." Peter quoted Isaiah exactly, using a physical illustration (sickness) to portray a spiritual cause (sin), i.e., Peter used the speech figure "metonymy of effect" as did Isaiah.

In context, it is questionable whether Peter refers to the scourging and crucifixion that Christ received at the hands of the soldiers. The beatings and afflictions that Jesus suffered before He was nailed to the cross were nothing in comparison with the agony He suffered when God the Father afflicted God the Son with His wrath for the sins of the world (cf. Ps. 22:14–17). Christ did not propitiate God's wrath with His suffering at the hands of men, but rather by that which was inflicted by His Heavenly Father (Isa. 53:10).

Peter refers to healing in 2:24 with *iaomai,* which corresponds to the LXX translation of the Hebrew text of Isaiah 53:5. Four other times (of 26 NT uses) *iaomai* is used in a spiritual sense.[24] Given the context of 1 Peter 2:18–25 and given the otherwise exclusive spiritual use of *iaomai* by NT writers when quoting Isaiah, it is most reasonable to conclude that this was Peter's intention when he quoted Isaiah 53:5 in 1 Peter 2:24. Oepke notes, "In 1 Pt. 2:24, Is. 53:5 is referred to the atoning work of Christ. In such passages ἰᾶσθαι denotes the restoration of divine fellowship through the forgiveness of sins, and all the saving benefits which accompany it."[25]

The context and language in 1 Peter 2:24–25 consistently deal with spiritual healing and Christ's payment for sin, not for sickness.[26]

CONCLUSION

Isaiah 53 refers to the atonement and its redemptive features, not to its therapeutic effect in a physical sense. Five lines of evidence support this conclusion:

1. The idea of atonement in both Leviticus and Hebrews applies to salvation.
2. The context of Isaiah 53 focuses on Christ's atonement as provision for sin.
3. The theological context of Christ's death and salvation centers on sin.
4. Matthew used Isaiah 53:4–5 illustratively to indicate that

what Christ did at Capernaum (8:14–17) with physical healing pictured the resurrection consequence of salvation, i.e., the end of sickness when sin has been eliminated.

5. Peter, the Ethiopian eunuch, and Philip understood Isaiah 53 in reference to sin.[27]

Isaiah 53 deals with man's spiritual being, not his physical. Its emphasis is on sin, not sickness. It focuses on the moral cause of sickness, which is sin, and not on the immediate removal of one of sin's results—sickness.

Matthew 8 is a limited and localized preview of Christ's millennial rule and a believer's resurrection experience when sickness will be no more because sin will have been eliminated. Christ did not personally bear sickness at Capernaum in a substitutionary way, but instead He removed it, even though illness would later return and those whom He had healed would eventually die.

Matthew referred to Isaiah 53 for illustrative and anticipatory purposes, but by no means intended to teach that Christ ultimately fulfiled the prophecy of Isaiah 53 two years before He went to Calvary.

First Peter 2:24 rehearses the redemptive implications of Isaiah 53. Christ's atoning death provided the basis for spiritual health and eternal life. Christ bore our iniquities to satisfy God's righteous demand against sin. Physical health and healing are in view only in the sense that once the cause of sickness (i.e., sin) disappears, then sickness (i.e., the effect of sin) will also be no more.

Recall the question raised at the beginning. "Is there healing in the atonement?" This writer's answer is, "No." However, there is healing "through" the atonement or "as a result" of the atonement, but it is never promised to believers for the present time.[28] With the ultimate removal of sin, believers will receive physical healing in full; but only in the future, when our bodies have been redeemed by the power of God (Rom. 8:23; Rev. 21:4). Christ atoned for sin, not sickness.

No, healing for our mortal bodies is not in the atonement. This conclusion is supported at once by the fact that forgiveness of sins and cleansing from guilt are offered through the cross freely and certainly and at the present moment to all who sincerely "believe" whereas healing for all our infirmities and sicknesses is not offered freely and certainly at present to all who believe. Not one of those who have believed for forgiveness and cleansing has ever been denied, but thousands and thousands who have believed for physical healing have been denied. That cannot be gainsaid—for a very pertinent reason. Permitted sin in the present is never a part of God's plan or purpose for us, but permitted sickness often is, as we learn both from Scripture and from Christian testimony (more on this later). Both Scripture and experience, then, say no; bodily healing is not in the atonement.[29]

By (1) looking at the original languages used, (2) understanding the context in which the above passages are found, (3) appreciating the complementing passages in Leviticus and Hebrews, and (4) realizing what the atonement actually involved, the conclusion is that the atonement dealt with sin and the need to satisfy the righteous wrath of a just and holy God. Not until sin is removed from our personal existence will Christians have any hope of guaranteed physical well-being.[30] J. I. Packer carefully captures the intent of Isaiah 53 with this insightful summary:

> We must observe that perfect physical health is promised, not for this life, but for heaven, as part of the resurrection glory that awaits us in the day when Christ "will change our lowly body to be like His glorious body, by the power which enables Him even to subject all things to Himself." Full bodily well-being is set forth as a future blessing of salvation rather than a present one. What God has promised, and when He will give it, are separate questions.[31]

ENDNOTES

[1] For brief historical summaries of the faith healing movement in the United States and Canada see Richard Mayhue, *The Healing Promise* (Eugene, Ore.: Harvest House, 1994), 27–39, and John Wilkinson, "Physical Healing and the Atonement," *Evangelical Quarterly* 63, no. 2 (April 1991): 149–55. For more in-depth treatments consult J. Sidlow Baxter, *Divine Healing of the Body* (Grand Rapids: Zondervan, 1979), 29–105; Frank C. Darling, *Biblical Healing* (Boulder, Colo.: Vista, 1989); *Christian Healing in the Middle Ages and Beyond* (Boulder, Colo.: Vista, 1990); *The Restoration of Christian Healing* (Boulder, Colo.: Vista, 1992); David E. Harrell Jr., *All Things Are Possible: The Healing and Charismatic Revivals in Modern America* (Bloomington, Ind.: Indiana University, 1975); Michael G. Moriarity, *The New Charismatics* (Grand Rapids: Zondervan, 1992), 20–86; Benjamin B. Warfield, *Counterfeit Miracles* (reprint, Edinburgh, Scotland: Banner of Truth, 1972), 33–69.

[2] Alva J. McClain, *Was Christ Punished for Our Diseases?* (Winona Lake, Ind.: BMH, n.d.).

[3] W. Kelly Bokovay, "The Relationship of Physical Healing to the Atonement," *Didaskalia* 3, no. 2 (April 1991): 26, 35.

[4] The other significant question raised by Isaiah 53:4–5, "For whom did Christ atone?" is treated in such standard works as R. L. Dabney, *Systematic Theology,* 2d ed. (reprint, Edinburgh: Banner of Truth, 1985), 513–35; R. B. Kuiper, *For Whom Did Christ Die?* (Grand Rapids: Eerdmans, 1959); John Murray, *Collected Writings of John Murray* (Edinburgh: Banner of Truth, 1976), 1:59–85; and George Smeaton, *The Doctrine of the Atonement According to the Apostles* (reprint, Peabody, Mass.: Hendrickson, 1988).

[5] Read John V. Dahms, "Dying With Christ," *Journal of the Evangelical Theological Society* 36, no. 1 (March 1993): 15–23, which carefully relates the OT atonement to Christ's substitutionary death.

[6] I have been greatly surprised by the deficiency of attention given to Isaiah 53 by some of the most recent, highly visible volumes advocating a contemporary healing ministry. For instance, Jack Deere, *Surprised by the Power of the Spirit* (Grand Rapids: Zondervan, 1993), 169, devotes only one paragraph in a 299 page book on healing. John Wimber and Kevin Springer, *Power Healing* (San Francisco: Harper & Row, 1987) take less than four pages (152–56) out of 269 pages, but spend most of that space discussing what men have said rather than what the Scriptures teach. Benny Hinn, *Lord, I Need a Miracle* (Nashville: Nelson, 1993) provides less than two pages (55–56). Even Jeffrey Niehaus in *The Kingdom and the Power* (Ventura, Calif.: Regal, 1993) devotes less than three pages (48–50). For an excellent exegetical discussion of Isaiah 53 see Edward J. Young, *The Book of Isaiah* (Grand Rapids: Eerdmans, 1972), 3:340–54.

[7] The New Testament consistently presents Christ as the Christian's substitutionary sin-bearer in His atonement. See Matthew 20:28; John 1:29; Romans 4:25; 5:6–8; 8:3; 1 Corinthians 15:3; 2 Corinthians 5:21; Galatians 1:4; 3:13; 4:4–5; Hebrews 9:28; 1 Peter 3:18; 1 John 2:2; 4:10.

[8] This is a legitimate question in light of other passages in Isaiah that point to a time of physical healing, e.g., 29:18; 33:24; 35:5–6; 65:20.

[9] This writer has assumed the messianic identification of Jehovah's servant in Isaiah 52–53. See detailed discussions of this issue in David Baron, *The Servant of Jehovah* (reprint, Minneapolis: James Family, 1978), 3–47, and Kenneth D. Litwak, "The Use of Quotations from Isaiah 52:13–53:12 in the New Testament," *Journal of the Evangelical Theological Society* 26, no. 4 (December 1983): 385–94. Litwak notes, "Though quotations from Isaiah 53 are not numerous in the New Testament, allusions to the passage are deeply imbedded in the work of all the principal New Testament writers as well as the early fathers, particularly Clement and Barnabas. From this fact it is certain that the interpretation of Isaiah 53 as referring to Jesus belongs to the earliest thought of the primitive church" (387). For a classic Jewish example of rejecting messianic implications see Gerald Sigal, *The Jew and the Christian Missionary: A Jewish Response to Missionary Christianity* (New York: KTAV, 1981).

[10] The language of Isaiah 53 is decidedly that of the atonement in Leviticus 16, which points strongly to a primary, if not exclusive, focus on the atonement's relationship to sin, not sickness. Read Douglas Judisch, "Propitiation in the Language and Typology of the Old Testament," *Concordia Theological Quarterly [CTQ]* 48, no. 4 (October 1984): 221–43; "Propitiation in Old Testament Prophecy," *CTQ* 49, no. 1 (January 1985): 1–17; W. Kay, "Isaiah," in *The Bible Commentary,* ed. F. C. Cook (reprint, Grand Rapids: Baker, 1981), 5:266; F. Duane Lindsey, "The Career of the Servant in Isaiah 52:13–53:12," *Bibliotheca Sacra* 139, no. 556 (October–December 1982): 312–29 and 140, no. 557 (January–March 1983): 21–39.

[11] See Isaiah 1:5; Jeremiah 6:7; 10:19; Hosea 5:13 for examples other than actual sickness.

[12] See Psalm 32:10; Jeremiah 30:15; Lamentations 1:12, 18 for examples other than actual sickness.

[13] "The terms 'infirmities' and 'sorrows,' each of which should be identified as a metonymy of effect for cause, are used generally for all suffering which is viewed as the result of sin. This does not mean that Christ became sick or infirm in a substitutionary sense, nor that divine healing is guaranteed through the atonement (except in the ultimate sense of a resurrection body)" (Lindsey, "The Career," 23). See E. W. Bullinger, *Figures of Speech in the Bible* (reprint, Grand Rapids: Baker, 1968), 538, 560, for a discussion of metonymy in general and metonymy of

effect in particular. Certainly, if metonymy is not the speech figure intended in 53:4–5, then metaphor easily explains the use of "healing" (רָפָא) in 53:5 (cf. J. Ramsey Michaels, "1 Peter," in vol. 49 of *Word Biblical Commentary,* ed. David A. Hubbard and Glenn W. Barker [Dallas: Word, 1988], 149, who opts for metaphor in both Isaiah 53:5 and 1 Peter 2:24). Hebrews 12:12–13 provides a fine example.

[14] See also the parallel in 53:6 between "sheep going astray" and humans having turned to their own way and thus the Lord causing "the iniquity of us all to fall on Him." Christ was cut off out of the land of the living for the transgressions (53:8). He was numbered with the transgressors and interceded for the transgressors (53:12).

[15] Wilkinson, *Physical Healing,* 162–63.

[16] See Mayhue, *The Healing Promise,* 85–116, for a detailed analysis of healing history in the OT, Gospels, Acts, and the NT Epistles.

[17] The NT directly quotes Isaiah 53 six times. (1) Matthew 8:17—Isaiah 53:4; (2) Luke 22:37—Isaiah 53:12; (3) John 12:38—Isaiah 53:1; (4) Acts 8:32–33—Isaiah 53:7–8; (5) Romans 10:16—Isaiah 53:1; (6) 1 Peter 2:24—Isaiah 53:4.

[18] Young, *Isaiah,* 3:35, writes, "The reference in Matthew 8:17 is appropriate, for although the figure of sicknesses here used refers to sin itself, the verse also includes the thought of the removal of the consequences of sin. Disease is the inseparable companion of sin."

[19] Wilkinson, "Physical Healing," 157, provides another frequently overlooked point: "There is, however, one detail which is different from all the rest. All the injuries and their effects which are described of the servant were produced by external agents at the time of His suffering." Thus Christ did not bear sickness within as He did with sin.

[20] Donald A. Hagner, "Matthew 1–13," in vol. 33A of *Word Biblical Commentary,* ed. David A. Hubbard, et al. (Dallas: Word, 1993), 211: "Properly perceived, these healings are most important as symbols of the much greater 'healing' that is at the heart of the gospel, the healing of the cross. At the same time, they foreshadow the fulfilment of the age to come when all suffering and sickness are finally removed (cf. Rev. 21:1–4)."

[21] D. A. Carson, *Showing the Spirit* (Grand Rapids: Baker, 1987), 156–57. Baron, *The Servant*, 86, perceptively notes, "The miracles of healing not only served to certify Him as the Redeemer, and as *'signs'* of the spiritual healing which He came to bring, but were, so to say, pledges also of the ultimate full deliverance of the redeemed, not only from sin but from every evil consequence of it in body as well as in soul."

[22] Hagner, "Matthew 1–13," 211: ". . . Isa. 53:4 guarantees no one healing in the present age. What is guaranteed is that Christ's atoning death will in the eschaton provide healing. . . ." Baxter, *Divine Healing,* 136, unequivocally states, "Therefore, that the healing is in the atonement should not be preached on the basis of Matthew 8:16–17 unless it is endorsed by Scripture statements elsewhere. But it is not taught elsewhere, and it certainly cannot be safely adduced solely from Matthew 8:16–17."

[23] Wayne Grudem, *The First Epistle of Peter* (Grand Rapids: Eerdmans, 1988), 133–34.

[24] Matthew 13:15, John 12:40, and Acts 28:27 quote Isaiah 6:10 while Hebrews 12:12–13 alludes to Isaiah 35:3.

[25] Albrecht Oepke, "ἰᾶσθαι, κ.τ.λ.," *TDNT,* 3:214.

[26] It is noteworthy that Wayne Grudem, who might be thought to reason otherwise because of his Vineyard Fellowship connection, understands 1 Peter 2:24 in reference to salvation (*The First Epistle of Peter,* 132). Of this "healing" D. Edmond Hiebert concludes, "The verb 'healed' here does not denote physical healing . . ." (*1 Peter* [Chicago: Moody, 1992], 189).

[27] A sixth evidence, although not from Scripture, is the latter first-century and early second-century use of Isaiah 53:4–5 by the post-apostolic fathers. Neither 1 Clement 16 nor Barnabas 5 quotes Isaiah 53 as teaching a contemporary healing ministry or even that physical healing is in the atonement. Nor do the fathers teach such elsewhere (cf. J. B. Lightfoot, *The Apostolic Fathers* [reprint, Grand Rapids: Baker, 1976], 19–20, 140).

[28] It seems more biblically precise to say, "There *will* be physical healing *through* the atonement," rather than "There *is* physical healing *in* the atonement." I agree with Doug Moo ("Divine Healing in the Health and Wealth Gospel," *Trinity Journal* 9 [1988]: 204): "We would prefer, then,

to say that physical healing is one *effect* of the atoning death of Christ."
See also Bokovay ("Physical Healing," 35): "It is misleading for anyone
to suggest that healing is 'in' the atonement without major qualifications;
sickness is only dealt with in the sense that it is an *effect* of sin and its
eventual eradication is guaranteed because our sin has been atoned for."

[29] Baxter, *Divine Healing,* 136–37. Dr. Baxter, who believes in a contemporary healing ministry, minces no words here in utterly denying
that the atonement provides any basis for present physical healing.

[30] Wimber and Springer, *Power Healing,* 154, cite R. A. Torrey (*Divine
Healing* [reprint, Grand Rapids: Baker, 1974], 53 [actually on page 43])
writing on Isaiah 53 as meaning ". . . that based on what Jesus experienced on the cross, we as a consequence may experience one hundred
percent healing here on earth." At best, this is an overstatement of Torrey's
discussion (43–46); at worst, a misrepresentation.

[31] James I. Packer, "Poor Health May Be the Best Remedy," *Christianity
Today* 26, no. 10 (May 21, 1982): 15.

CHAPTER FOUR

Daniel 9:1–19

Prayer Relating to Prophecy

James E. Rosscup

Daniel's prayer for Israel in Daniel 9 precedes the famous prophecy of the "seventy sevens" in the same chapter. The prayer models submission to God's will both in heartfelt confession of Israelite sin and passionate intercession for deliverance from exile and the blessing of restoration. Daniel adeptly uses OT books such as Deuteronomy, Psalms, Jeremiah, and Ezekiel. Chapter 9 is one of many OT examples of how God uses human prayer to accomplish His predetermined sovereign plan.

* * * * *

The prayer of Daniel 9 ranks high among OT texts that demonstrate a unity between prayer for God to work out His will and prophecy that He will fulfil His sovereign purposes. Coming from the man most noted for prayer among OT prophets, the passage is all the more significant. As he does in Daniel 2, 6, and 10, Daniel exemplifies a servant sensitive to God's concerns and expends himself in prayer for the fulfiling of the divine program.

THE AUTHENTICITY OF DANIEL'S PRAYER

Before an examination of the text, attention must be directed to efforts that impugn the prayer as an artificial patchwork interpolated by a second century writer borrowing from others of post-exilic days.[1] There is no valid cause to fault the prayer, as though it mixes together phrases from prayers in Ezra 6:6–15; Nehemiah 9:5–38; 2 Baruch 1–3. Charles urged seven reasons against the prayer's authenticity,[2] but Leupold answered these in some detail.[3]

Jones, though erring in holding a second-century date, rebuts several arguments to show how the prayer blends appropriately with its context.[4] First he notes that it is mere arbitrary opinion to conjecture that the prayer was composed in Palestine, not Babylon. Second, he sees it as unconvincing to deny the validity of the prayer because of "unnecessary" repetitions. It is natural to repeat in prayers, sermons, or personal conversations.[5] Third, he calls it a mistake to hold that 9:20–27 pays no attention to Daniel's substance in the prayer for pardon and restoration. Jones points out that the angel *does* answer his prayer for forgiveness and deliverance (v. 24). Fourth, he sees as arbitrary the requirement that 9:1–4a call for a prayer for illumination, not pardon and restoration. No adequate proof exists to restrict the type of prayer needed to elicit a revelatory response. Besides, Daniel combines concern for illumination (v. 22, reflecting back on the prayer) and restoration (v. 24, relating back to vv. 15–19).[6]

Jones misconstrues Daniel 9 in other regards, however. First, he states that the prayer's use of the reward/retribution motif—blessings and cursings (Deuteronomy 28–29)—stems from Daniel's mistaken notion and is irrelevant to Daniel 9:24–27. Arbitrarily assuming a second-century dating, he contends that a retribution view in 9:4b–19 would be inappropriate as a comfort to Israel because they were still suffering after already being restored to their land. Jones sees the author being swayed to accept Gabriel's determinism (9:20ff.) as a better answer to Israel's need than his own theory of retribution.

Jones has missed the thrust of Daniel 9. Though Israel suffers because of its sin, in both his prayer and his prophecy Daniel bases deliverance on God's covenant grace. He confesses Israel's sin, but does not imagine that Israel merits favor. Merited favor contradicts a hope in God's gracious covenant.[7] Further, Daniel 9 nowhere suggests inconsistency between a plan God is certain to fulfil finally and His interim blessing or judgment in moral harmony with obedience or disobedience.[8] Inconsistency originates only in the mind of an interpreter and is not found in the biblical accounts seen in their integrity.

Second, Jones wrongly reasons that since God's word went forth "at the beginning of [Daniel's] supplications" (9:23), his prayer "made little difference to God."[9] He sees the prophecy (vv. 24–27) as taking no account of the subject of the prayer, but ignoring it to make the point that God had previously determined His plan. It is better, however, to recognize that God's response does not ignore the prayer, but implements it in fulfiling His will. Jones has himself noted ties between the prayer and the prophecy, but does not follow through with this. Daniel's earnest cries for city, sanctuary, and people are needs about which the prophecy offers reassurance (v. 24).[10]

To say that prayer makes little difference to God mishandles Scripture not only here, but in scores of passages. God has a sure decree of what He will do (cf. Dan. 4:35) but has already correlated with this an opportunity for surrendered people to be involved in its implementation through prayer. Prayer should be submission to and involvement in God's carrying out His will. God's plan is certain from beginning to end (Isa. 46:9–10) and need not be decided piecemeal along the way or at the dictates of men. Yet He Himself challenges man to pray (Jer. 33:3) for His own concerns, including the restoration of Israel (Jer. 33:6ff.). As events advance toward His appointed fulfilment, He appeals to mankind to be prayerfully involved in His work, and these prayers do make a difference to God. He does not choose to work, as Jones reasons, "quite apart from prayers and quite apart from previous ideas of retribution."[11] Harris differs with him: "How such a prayer of confession and petition to God could 'make little difference to God' is beyond imagination."[12] The prayer's answer in Daniel 9:24–27 is not an interpretive *change* from the truth Daniel expresses in 9:4b–19, but correlates well with it.

The notion that Daniel borrowed from Ezra, Nehemiah, and others is unnecessary, because Daniel was a man rich in the Word of God. In fact, the notion is impossible with a sixth-century dating of the book. Daniel, Ezra, and Nehemiah were all beneficiaries of the same scriptural treasure. A person saturated with such books as Exodus, Deuteronomy, Psalms, Jeremiah, and Ezekiel could spontaneously incorporate words or phrases from these sources into his prayers. God's word is spiritual food for His people (Job 23:12; Jer. 15:16). Strong reliance on earlier biblical books is natural in a prayer featuring a guilt and history of the same people. Then too, while prayers in Ezra and Nehemiah, or even Baruch, are similar to Daniel's, they also show marked differences.[13] Nehemiah, for example, praised God for His mercies, saw Him as righteous, then he confessed, and repented. Yet he voiced none of the intercession for Israel's restoration as is found in Daniel 9, because in Nehemiah's day, many had already returned. Each of the prayers relates to its own context: Daniel's in 539 B.C., Ezra's in 457 B.C. and after, and Nehemiah's around 445/444 B.C.

Because of no convincing evidence to the contrary, this study assumes a sixth-century B.C. setting and a perspective of unparalleled blessing for Israel after their Messiah's second coming.[14] The Messiah will do His work as a catastrophic "stone" (2:44) and as "one like a son of man coming on the clouds of heaven" (7:13–14).[15] He will dramatically defeat all enemies of His covenant people and restore His people to blessing.

Daniel's prayer is one of praise, confession, petition, and intercession in circumstances that are for his people the very reverse of unprecedented blessings. That God's people deserve exile from their land (9:4b–14) is clear. The prayer pleads for God to restore the people (9:15–19). The following discussion develops the aspects of the prayer and the way it fits its historical and literary context.

DANIEL'S READINESS TO PRAY (9:1–4a)

Daniel's prayer is appropriate in this context, e.g., Daniel's situation of 9:1–2, the visit by Gabriel (vv. 20–23), and the answer of Gabriel (vv. 24–27). Daniel is sensitive to his people's need, saturated with Scripture, sympathetic with his people in their need, and surrendered to God.

Sensitive to the Need
The timing of this prayer is strategic in God's plan. It is relevant both to Israel and to Babylon, her captor in exile. The first year of Darius is significant to Daniel. His peril with the lions in chapter 6 and this prayer probably came in the same year, 539/538 B.C. By faith he "shut the mouths of lions" (Heb. 11:33) because God shut those mouths in answer to his prayer (Dan. 6:22). Daniel's God sent an angel to protect him in peril as He miraculously answered him in chapter 9.

The situation is relevant also as to timing in God's prophetic plan. Darius's first year was his first year of reign over Babylon after Persia's conquest of that nation. God sovereignly accomplished this, for He "removes kings and establishes kings" (Dan. 2:21). This is a new era. Daniel, sensitive to the momentous change and its effect on his people, mentions the "first year" twice for emphasis (9:1–2). After years of neo-Babylonian lordship, Daniel's people are at a point that provoked inquiry regarding God's next move on their behalf.

Saturated with Scripture
The man who prays, meditates first on prophecy that affirms God's plan. In the initial year of Nebuchadnezzar, king of Babylon, Jeremiah had predicted Israel's subjection to Babylon for seventy years (Jer. 25:9–11). He foresaw that God would punish the king of Babylon and his nation at the end of that time (vv. 12–13). It is relevant in Daniel 9 that the demise of Babylon's king and Cyrus's designation of Darius[16] as his sub-ruler over Babylon was of extreme interest as a sign that the seventy years were near their end. It was high time to seek God's plan for His people, whose exile was expiring.

Jeremiah's later words in Jeremiah 29 were of further help to Daniel. After 597 B.C., when Babylon deported Judah's King Jehoiachin with 50,000 subjects, Jeremiah wrote to the exiles. He advised them to build houses, plant crops, marry, and pray for the welfare of Babylon to which their own welfare was related (vv. 5–7). Settling into exilic life was sensible, because God would not bring them back to their land until "seventy years have been completed in Babylon" (v. 10). God's aims for Israel are reassuring in Jeremiah 29:11 (NASB): "For I know the plans that I have for you . . . plans for welfare and not for calamity to give you a future and a hope."

Within the seventy years, near or at their end, the Lord tells the Israelites,

> Then you will call upon Me and come and pray to Me, and I will listen to you. And you will seek Me and find Me, when you shall search for Me with all your heart. And I will be found by you . . . and I will restore your fortunes and will gather you from all the nations . . . and I will bring you back to the place from which I sent you into exile. (Jeremiah 29:12–14 NASB)

In harmony with God's plan, prayer strategically fits with prophecy affirming restoration in Jeremiah 29.

Daniel, being full of knowledge (1:17; 2:17–30; 4:8–9; 5:10–16), is steeped in God's promises in chapter 9. He submits himself to God and becomes a representative of his people. As Jeremiah 29 directed, he commits himself to "call," "come," "pray," "seek," and "search" for God with all his heart. God articulates His will in Jeremiah 29:12–14, putting His own authority on prayer as a means in restoring Israel. Daniel is part of a program that God foreordained. He prays, probably kneeling,[17] calling on God to act and forward His purposes. In this he joins a band of others who prayed in agreement with God's purposes to restore Israel.[18] Another thing is clear about Daniel, his sympathy for his people.

Sympathetic with His People

The first person "we" (v. 5, etc.) shows Daniel's deep involvement with and for the sake of his people. In so doing, he fills the role of earlier leaders on behalf of Israel. Moses prayed for Israel's benefit at a crucial time when the people fashioned a golden calf (Exod. 32:11–14). Jeremiah also prayed with many tears, seeking the correction of his people (13:17; 14:17).[19] The psalmists are often moved to such prayer.[20] In such a chain of prayer warriors, Daniel longs to see God lift Israel to a bright future (vv. 15–19). He is painfully aware that God's "people" continue to erect a road block against the moral direction God wants. They are unrepentant and do not appropriate the way to blessing (v. 13).[21] For seventy years, plus many years before, they had needed repentance. Israel had "be-wailed its sad lot."[22] They regretted their sentence but failed to attain a significant repentance. Daniel rushes to the crux of concerns, acknowledging sin (vv. 4b–14). He deals thoroughly with sin before he intercedes for restoration from sin and its consequences (vv. 15–19).

Surrendered to God

"So," i.e., consequentially (וְ *[wā]*, v. 3), when Daniel prayed, he was sensitive to his time, steeped in God's plan, and sympathetic with the need for help. Those three characteristics also reflect his surrender to God. His surrender is also visible in his flint-like concentration in verse 3. He says literally, "I set my face toward the Lord. . . ." He resolutely applied his attention, fixed his focus.[23] The verb נָתַן (*nātan*, "to give, set") appears with the accusative "my face," followed by the infinitive "to seek." In surrender, Daniel stations himself to seek "the Lord," אֲדֹנָי (*'ǎdōnāy*), a word that has in view His almighty authority or Lordship.[24] This is the "Lord" Daniel often addresses in this prayer (vv. 4, 7–8, 16–17, 19). He combines it here with אֱלֹהִים (*'ĕlōhîm*, "God") the word used for God the creator in Genesis 1:1–2:4a. That Daniel approaches God in the humility of "fasting, sackcloth and ashes"[25] with a sincere heart also suggests the seriousness of surrender. Daniel is not just going through the motions. His actions express inward earnestness, in harmony with his genuine walk with God throughout the book.

The surrender of the man emerges in the form of "prayer and suppli-cations" (9:3). The former word תְּפִלָּה (*tĕpillāh*) does not in itself neces-sarily mean "intercede" as some assume.[26] Sawyer more definitively notes that the noun or its verbal form refers to prayer in general. This could sometimes narrow to distinct aspects such as praise, thanksgiving, con-fession, petition, and intercession, but not here.[27]

The latter word "supplications" (וְתַחֲנוּנִים *[wĕtaḥănûnîm]*) occurs often in this prayer (9:3, 17–18, 20, 23). It is one of several words denoting the idea found in חָנַן (*ḥānan*), "he is gracious." It is a prayer for favor.[28] Jeremiah employs it in 3:21 and 31:9 as a parallel with "weepings," the outpourings of a soul in trouble, desperate for grace. Such a term is apt when a person approaches God in "particularly urgent prayer, loud or tearful supplication. . . ."[29]

Probably remembering King Solomon, Daniel does the same thing as Solomon did in the prayer of temple dedication. "Listen," Solomon had pled before God, "to the supplications of Thy servants and Thy people Israel, when they pray toward this house . . ." (2 Chron. 6:21).[30]

DANIEL'S ACKNOWLEDGMENT OF BLAME (9:4b–14)

Daniel's prayer acknowledges Israel's blame, first giving prominence to God's glory (vv. 4b, 7a, 9a) and then confessing their guilt in comparison to that glory. Daniel "prayed" using the same umbrella word for prayer as in verse 3. Then he uses a specific word for prayer (יָדָה *[yādah]*) in confessing the sins of his people (cf. v. 20 also). Confession is an implicit acknowledgment of worthiness in God and in His standards while admitting guilt because of factors that violate His character and values.

God's Glory First (9:4b)
Daniel first saw the guilt in the light of God's glory, similar to what Jesus taught in His model prayer, which begins with God as heavenly and hallowed (Matt. 6:9; Luke 11:2). To Daniel, one title for God is אֲדֹנָי *(ʾădōnāy)* as articulated twice in verse 4. He is also "the great and awesome אֵל *(ʾēl*, 'God')." It is apropos for Daniel to conceive of God this way, not because of borrowing from post-exilics but through his meditation on Deuteronomy, which was written centuries before his day.[31] Deuteronomy 10:17 says, "For the LORD your God is the God of gods and LORD of lords, the great, the mighty, and the awesome God . . ." (cf. also Deut. 7:21; 10:21). Daniel knew such a God whom he has already described as the "Prince of princes" (8:25).[32] As *ʾădōnāy*, the mighty God, nothing was too hard for Him as proven by His deeds in Egypt, at the Red Sea, and at the Jordan. He was awe-inspiring, incredible, and not to be taken lightly, but greatly feared.

He is a God of glory also as "one who keeps" His covenant. He is so different from the Israelites who had broken their covenant. He made a covenant with Abraham and his people in Genesis 12:1–3, 7. As the covenant God He kept Jacob wherever he went (Gen. 28:15, 20) and keeps those who love Him (Ps. 145:20). His blessing and preservation of Israel is invoked (Num. 6:24). He is asked to keep Israel as a precious pupil of an eye (Ps. 17:8). He can be trusted to enliven His servant, to keep His word (Ps. 119:17, 44). By the authority of Scripture as borne out in personal experience, Daniel knew that God keeps His covenant.

God also keeps His covenant loving-kindness—His חֶסֶד *(ḥesed)*. Daniel knew this from a vast number of passages. The covenant God is a God of kindness (Pss. 59:18; 130:7). He delights in it and, because of it, assures Israel that He will stand true to His covenant even when they are in exile (Micah 7:18). He is kind in His deliverance from enemies and other troubles (Pss. 21:8; 143:8, 12). So men rejoice in His kindness and hope in it (Ps. 33:18). He is kind in keeping His covenant with David

(2 Sam. 7:15 = 1 Chron. 17:13 = 2 Sam. 22:51) and in quickening with spiritual life (Pss. 109:26; 119:41, 76, 88, 124, 149, 159). He is the God who gives what Daniel and his people need—forgiveness, hope, covenant fulfilment.

It is fitting for Daniel to accent these positives before spelling out the sin for which God's lovingkindness is a remedy.

Still, God is not an impersonal machine that automatically cranks out forgiveness. He is what He is for Israel and does what He does for Israel toward the goal of what He wants Israel to be toward Him. He is such a God toward "those who love Him and keep His commandments." Loving Him and obeying His commandments entwine with one another in Scriptures familiar to Daniel (cf. Deut. 5:10; 7:9). They would eventually combine in the teaching of Daniel's "anointed one"—the Messiah (cf. Dan. 9:25; John 14:21–23). A psalmist, long before Daniel, knew the people whom God keeps are those who love Him (Ps. 145:20a). "But all the wicked He will destroy" (Ps. 145:20b).

Daniel learned from the Word that Israel was to keep (שָׁמַר *[šāmar]*) God's covenant (Exod. 19:5) and commandments (Exod. 20:6; Deut. 4:2; 5:29). Some did, though not sinlessly, and found God's blessing in a life of intimacy (Pss. 103:18: 106:3; 119:63, 67). This also would happen later in NT times (John 14:21–23; 1 John 2:5; 3:24). The OT had other ways to articulate this obedience, besides through *šāmar*. Some people walked blamelessly in the law of God, seeking Him (Ps. 119:1–2), delighting in His law, and bearing fruit (Ps. 1:1–3). Daniel was this kind of person (Daniel 1, 6). God has His remnant (Isa. 6:13) and can restore by turning Israelites to Himself (Jer. 31:18; cf. Ps. 80:3, 7, 19 [Heb. text, 80:4, 8, 20]).[33]

The prophecy later in Daniel 9 tells how the covenant God will terminate Israel's sin. He will bring in "everlasting righteousness" (9:24).

Israel's Guilt in Light of God's Glory (9:5–14)

Using different terminology, the prayer acknowledges Israel's sin at least nineteen times. In verse 5 Daniel reels off four finite verbs for sin followed by a fifth verb—an infinitive absolute. He also has other expressions for sin or repeats some of these words for emphasis.

The enormity of sin. Heaping up terms, he candidly acknowledges serious guilt before God. Solomon's prayer, which had used three verbs to acknowledge sin (1 Kings 8:47 = 2 Chron. 6:37), resembles verse 5. But here two more words are added to Solomon's list.

Daniel includes himself with his people by using "we." Whatever the degree and nature of his sin, he confesses it along with theirs.

Israel has "sinned," חָטָא *(ḥāṭāʾ),* i.e., "missed the mark" of God's will.

Daniel uses this word often (vv. 5, 8, 11, 15). His competency in the Scriptures provides him many examples of the word. Often, these name Israel's sin (Num. 14:40; Josh. 7:11; 1 Sam. 12:10; Ps. 78:32). As Jerusalem is in wreckage, Jeremiah says, "we have sinned" (Lam. 5:16). Cases of an individual who sinned, such as a priest (Lev. 4:3), Balaam (Num. 22:34), Saul (1 Sam. 15:24, 30), David (2 Sam. 24:10), are frequent.

Not only did they "miss the mark," they also "committed iniquity" (עָרָה [ʿārāh]), another word used frequently in the prayer (Dan. 9:5, 13, 16). God promises an eventual solution to iniquity (v. 24). The term speaks of doing wrong. Its noun form is exemplified in the iniquity of the Amorites (Gen. 15:16) with Leviticus 18 specifying hideous perversions, Cain's murder of Abel (Gen. 4:13), the ten spies' belittling of God as inadequate to conquer walled villages and giants (Num. 14:34), and David's ugly escapade with Bathsheba (Ps. 51:2a).

Daniel strengthens his description of the enormity of the sin even more. "We acted wickedly," רָשַׁע (rāšaʿ, vv. 5, 15). The word sometimes contrasts with righteousness (Ps. 45:7; Eccl. 3:16). It describes the misdeed when King Jehoshaphat "acted wickedly" in tolerating an alliance with wicked King Ahaziah, causing God to destroy his ships as a sign of displeasure (2 Chron. 20:35). The word also describes resistance to God's ordinances and departing from His statues (2 Sam. 22:22f. = Ps. 18:22f.; cf. also Ps. 106:6; Neh. 9:33).

Daniel continues: "and rebelled" (cf. also v. 9). Joshua and Caleb urged Israel to act on their scouting report and not rebel (מָרַד [mārad]) against the Lord (Num. 14:9). Israel's sin of rebellion was so enormous to God that He would shut them out of Canaan. In context, the essence of that rebellion was a shrinking back in unbelief. They preferred their own notions of what was reasonable over the specific direction of God.

Daniel incorporates a fifth word: "and turned aside" (סוּר [sûr], vv. 5, 11). The idea is that they apostatized, or veered off course from the path of God. This resembles a woman who turns aside (sûr) into a shamefu impurity (Prov. 11:22). Israel turned aside (sûr) to make a molten im age—a revolt, in essence—from fidelity to God's commandments (Deut 9:12). A new generation after Joshua turned aside (sûr) quickly fron obeying the commandments (Judg. 2:17). The word occurs with anothe word, עָזַב (ʿāzab, "forsake"), in Jeremiah 17:13: "Those who turn away from the LORD the hope of Israel . . . have forsaken the fountain of living waters."

Daniel includes still more phrases to show the enormity of sin that warranted a great judgment.

The embarrassment of sin. Literally, "shame of faces" belongs to Israel (vv. 7–8). Theirs is an "open shame," a humiliation. The same expression describes King Sennacherib of Assyria (2 Chron. 32:21). He saw the overwhelming destruction of his military personnel in a single night's visitation by God's angel and retreated with shame of face to his own country. In Psalm 69:20 (Eng. text, 69:19), David prays for deliverance from shame. The context links the shame with sinking in the mire, being caught in deep waters, distress, reproach, and dishonor. Shame is the humiliation a broken heart can feel; it is a sick feeling, pain, and a wiped-out feeling producing weeping. In another case, Jeremiah 2:26 likens Israel's shame in its ruin to the ignominy of a thief when exposed—a downcast, hopeless sensation. Jeremiah himself is ashamed before a rejecting people. He feels it in the whisperings, the ridicule, and the torture of the stocks (20:18).

In the context of Daniel 9:7, the shame is the same. It is the emptiness produced when God has left some in Judah to behold a shattered existence and driven others to distant countries to taste bitterness without their land, city, temple, and other blessings.

Daniel knew from the Scriptures about God's promise of replacing shame with blessing in the messianic day (Isa. 61:7). Only God could do this, because righteousness (not shame) belongs to Him (Dan. 9:14, 16). God loves righteousness (Ps. 11:7), and His right hand is full of it (Ps. 48:10). It was because of God's own nature and not for Israel's righteousness that God has blessed the nation (Deut. 9:5). And it was because of His nature that He judged. Yet hope is in Him, in spite of judgment. From the Scriptures Daniel knew that God pledges to eventually establish Israel in righteousness (Isa. 54:14). The prophecy corresponding to the prayer in Daniel 9 will show that God guarantees everlasting righteousness in place of earlier shame (v. 24).

The result of sin. The consequence for Israel's sin was the "curse and the oath" (v. 11). Daniel refers to the judgment God had warned He would bring if the people disobeyed. By His servant Moses He had promised blessings in the case of obedience (Lev. 26:1–13; Deut. 28:1–14), but curses as a penalty for disobedience (Lev. 26:14–39; Deut. 28:15–68).

The two nouns "curse" and "oath" are linked by a conjunction, which brings some to see a hendiadys. If so, the idea is "the curse of the oath" or "the curse [pronounced] under oath."[34] It makes no sense to take the oath as a promise to bring judgment and the curse as the punishment itself, i.e., the content of the oath.

The judgment about which God warned Israel was the calamity that Daniel says "has been poured out" (תֵּתַּךְ *[nātak]*). The word can picture a downpour of rain (Exod. 9:33), but it usually pertains to pouring out God's wrath on Jerusalem.[35] It is forecast (Jer. 7:20), then carried out (Jer. 42:18). Sin's end was a "great calamity," so utter that Daniel says no city had been dealt a judgment as great as Jerusalem's (v. 12). The great (גָּדוֹל *[gādôl]*) God of verse 4 brought the great *(gādôl)* judgment of verse 12.[36] God in carrying out this devastation "caused His words to stand." The hiphil form registers a causative thrust of קוּם *(qûm,* "to stand, rise up," v. 12).[37] He promised His *wrath* against Israel would be great (Deut. 29:24, 28) and their *calamity* at His hand would be great (Jer. 30:14–15).

A man schooled in Scripture could see that as God was absolutely faithful to fulfil His judgment, He will be absolutely faithful to fulfil the promised blessing. He knew that the same word for "great," *gādôl,* attaches not only to calamity but also to God's great compassion (1 Kings 3:6; Ps. 57:10). Joining Daniel in prayer for Israel's future, Jeremiah assures that God will hear those who call upon Him and show them "great *(gādôl)* and mighty things . . ." (Jer. 33:3). In that very context he defines these as a restoration of Israel to her land (33:6–22).

Lamentations depicts Jerusalem's awesome destruction, misery, desperation even to the point of parents eating their own children, and bankruptcy of all temporal comforts.[38] Jeremiah 16:1–9 portrays rampant death, lack of burial or regular mourning (vv. 4, 7), and emptiness of peace or joy (vv. 5, 9).

True, terrible doom overtook other cities such as Sodom and Gomorrah and Admah and Zeboim, which are used as later examples.[39] But Jerusalem was in a class all its own. Its destruction was greater because it was distinctive as the city in which God had promised to dwell (v. 19; cf. Ps. 9:11).[40] The greater fullness of light given Israel, light she chose to reject (e.g., Dan. 9:5–6, 10), matches the greater degree of judgment.

DANIEL'S REQUEST FOR BLESSING (9:15–19)

Pointing to the Past Deliverance (9:15)

Daniel selects two great acts of God's power in Israel's history. One was at the beginning of the nation: the deliverance from Egypt (v. 15). The other came at the end of her past kingdom: the doom of Jerusalem (v. 12). He appeals to the past exodus as a backdrop for future restoration.[41]

Both main sections of the prayer (9:4b–14 and 9:15–19) begin with a look at God's greatness (vv. 4b, 15). Both times Daniel contrasts God's glory with Israel's guilt. In each he links God with His people, and the source of God's action in blessing His people is what He is. In the first section Daniel prays in view of God's perpetual action in keeping His covenant and lovingkindness. In the second he cites the one case in the past when God restored Israel to the promised land. This has direct relevance. Restoration is the specific need Israel has in Daniel 9.

Pleading for the Prospective Deliverance (9:16–19)
The man of prayer, alert in verses 1–2 to a turning point in God's dealings, now intercedes by asking God to restore Israel. He bases this on God's concern for them—they are His people (v. 16)—and also on His compassion for them. What drives Daniel is zeal for the Lord to act to uphold *His* interests.

The basis of His concern for them. Noting the relationship in which God took the initiative in making a covenant and has maintained His plans for Israel, the supplicant makes his plea.

What God did in judgment He did in fulfilment of His word and because of His own integrity, His own interests, and His own purposes. As he prays, Daniel is sensitive to God's anger and wrath (v. 16). He sees things from God's standpoint with a zeal for matters that He is concerned about. His perspective speaks of *God's* city, *God's* holy mountain, *God's* people, *God's* servant, *God's* sake, and *God's* sanctuary (vv. 16–17). The intercession begins and ends on the note of *God's* name (vv. 15, 19).

"Our desolations" are Israel's heartaches (v. 18), but the intercessor's chief focus is on God's heartbeat. And so Daniel prays aggressively for three accomplishments. All, he can be scripturally confident, are God's will by His own promises.[42] God's yes answer to them is certain in honor of His plan. In essence Daniel implores, "Bring back your city" (v 16), "Bring back your temple" (v 17), and "Bring back your people" (vv. 16, 19).

The basis of His compassion for them. Daniel approaches the God who hears "prayer" (Ps. 65:2)[43] on the ground of His righteousnesses (v. 16), not that of Israel (v. 18). His approach rests also on His great compassion (v. 18). Already Daniel has enumerated Israel's demerits, enough to sink her into depths of hopelessness. He now flees to the steadfast refuge. God in the past has been compassionate in working good for His people and exalting His name. Daniel believes that God, being what He is, will perform other comparable acts to glorify His name because He has not yet done for Israel all He promised.

Earlier in the book, God uses Daniel to describe His gracious designs for Israel (cf. Jer. 29:11). After four empires conquer Israel, the God of heaven will establish His kingdom on earth (Dan. 2:35, 44). It will never pass to another people (Dan. 2:44). He will bless His people in ruling as king over them and the other nations (7:15–28).

Later in the book, God pledges further assurance. God's people will be rescued at a time when resurrection and reward combine (Dan. 12:1–3).

When praying in chapter 9, Daniel already knew God's intent as expressed in chapters 2 and 7. It was natural for him to plead in light of

God's plan for the future. His request for help is plain, primary help being asked for the city and sanctuary.

1. If God does let His anger and wrath "turn away" (v. 16), this in effect will result in the restoration of the city. This is a direct reversal of the problem at the moment. It also is plain in prophecies prior to Daniel's time.[44]

2. If God resolves the "reproach" before other peoples (v. 16), it will entail a return to the land from which Daniel and others had been taken (Dan. 1:1–3). Ezekiel observed that nations brought insults not only on Israel (36:1–15) but also on her Lord—defaming His reputation and profaning His holy name (Ezek. 36:20). Restoration to the land would "vindicate the holiness" of His great name, causing the nations to know that He is the Lord (Ezek. 36:23). God established His reputation when He restored Israel from Egypt (Dan. 9:15). Now He will be glorified again by a restoration. The stakes are high, with His honor on the line. Moses had prayed, pleading God's honor (Exod. 32:11–13). Daniel does the same with great passion. Note phrases such as "Thy sake" (v. 17), "Thy name" (v. 18), "called by Thy name" (v. 19).

3. The prayer grasps for a solution for the problem of seventy years away from the land. Daniel knew the same passage that predicted the seventy-year duration of desolation of the city assured Israelite reentry into her land (Jer. 29:10–14). He also was aware of other prophecies to bring them back and comfort them, which equates with a reversal of the current desolations (Dan. 9:18). The return presumably would be just as literal as the desolations, so Daniel naturally prayed for this.

4. Daniel sees the best solution for a return as based on God's compassion, not human merits. God initiated the covenant (Gen. 12:1–3, 7). He often reaffirmed His pledge, even when His people had failed (e.g., Genesis 13, 20–21). He ratified the covenant by walking alone between the sacrifices while Abram slept (Genesis 15). By this God pledged by His very being that He would graciously bring the covenant to fulfillment.[45] Later He made a covenant with David (2 Sam. 7:16) verifying that even though His people failed and had to be disciplined, He would not break His promise (Ps. 89:30–37).[46]

5. Daniel's passion that God "listen" (שָׁמַע [*šāmaʿ*]) to his prayer (v. 17) agrees with God's avowal in Leviticus 26:40–45 to remember His covenant by not destroying Israel even when they were in exile. It also accords with what Solomon prayed would be the response of God's people in exile (2 Chron. 6:36–39) and with God's direct promise to "listen" to prayer by the exiles (Jer. 29:12, also *šāmaʿ*) and reinstate Israel in her land.

His concern also extended to the temple in the city:

  a. God's face shining on the temple (v. 17) implied a
     restoration of it, too. Such a connection is confirmed by
     Psalm 80:3, 7, 19 (Heb. text, 80:4, 8, 20).
  b. It is in the interests of the Lord Himself, i.e., for His sake
     (v. 17), that the temple be restored. God needed to
     restore it to uphold His very honor as in Ezekiel 36.

GOD'S PROVISION FOR BLESSING (9:20–27)

God uses an angel with a prophecy of His future plan to answer the
prayer of Daniel. This assures Daniel and his people that God has determined to provide a future of blessing for them.

The Angelic Messenger (9:20–23)

The accord with God (v. 20). God's provision for Israel's needs was
revealed while Daniel was praying about them.[47] He was speaking to
God,[48] in particular confessing the sin of his people Israel and present-
ing[49] supplication, i.e., his intercessions for favor in a situation of need.[50]
He was zealous for God's interests too, praying on behalf of "the holy
mountain" of his God.

The arrival of Gabriel (9:21). When Gabriel arrives, Daniel is "wearied with weariness,"[51] or, as some prefer, Gabriel comes, "being caused
to fly swiftly," a rapid transit since the beginning of the prayer (cf. v.
23).[52] The evening arrival time was at the important moment of Israel's
evening sacrifice (cf. Exodus 29). In exile and away from the temple,
they could not offer a sacrifice, but they could pray toward the temple
(Dan. 6:10). Daniel and other godly Israelites aspired that their prayer
would ascend as fragrant incense to God (Ps. 141:1–2).

The assurances of Gabriel (9:22–23). The angel explains that his
visit purposes to give Daniel "insight and understanding," for which
Daniel obviously longed (vv. 1–2). Gabriel quickly responds with the
assurances by coming while the prayer was in progress. He encourages Daniel by observing the esteem in which he is held by God, calling him "a precious treasure."[53] The intensive plural of the Hebrew
noun here and in Daniel 10:11, 19 could be rendered "you are one of
precious qualities."[54] Daniel abounds in traits pleasing to God: He is
pure (Dan. 1:8), humble (2:9), righteous (4:27), selfless (5:17), depends on God (2:17–18), and models integrity (6:4) and consistency
(6:10–11). He is persistent (10:2–3), sincere (chap. 9), earnest (9:3),
saturated with Scripture (9:4b–19), and involves himself for the sake

of others (chaps. 2, 4–5, 7–12). God's high regard assures His willingness to answer Daniel's prayer. *The admonition of Gabriel (9:23).* Gabriel exhorts Daniel to pay attention to the message and gain insight. He wants Daniel to *grasp* the truth communicated through him by God (v. 22).

The Answer Expressing God's Aim (9:24–27)

God covers the same subjects about which Daniel had prayed. He sums up in verse 24 the good status to which He will restore Israel and does so in a prophecy that corresponds to the precise concerns of the prayer: "your people," "your holy city," and the temple, "the most holy place" (v. 24).

God's blessing on Daniel's people is enumerated in six parts.[55] They involve the resolution of sin and the provision of righteousness. Through "the anointed one," i.e., the Messiah (v. 25), God will implement these. According to verse 26 the Messiah will be "cut off," presumably in death. Other parts of the book reveal more details about what the Messiah will be and do. From our twentieth-century perspective we see how these details connect with a second coming of this Messiah in that as a "stone," He will catastrophically and abruptly pulverize into fine dust the Gentile kingdoms who control Israel (2:35, 44; Luke 20:18). This naturally means conquest of a military and political nature that is as literal as empires subjecting other empires in the context of Daniel 2. It is not just spiritual control. The Messiah also is portrayed as "one like a son of man coming on the clouds of heaven" (7:13–14; cf. Mark 14:62; Rev. 1:14; 14:14), as one linked with humanity but also heavenly and doing what God does in other OT passages.[56]

God's answer to Daniel's prayer provides encouragement by speaking of restoration and rebuilding. The temple would be rebuilt as during Ezra's ministry[57] and later, in a final sense, in the messianic kingdom after the second advent (Ezekiel 40–47).[58] The city also would be rebuilt as in Nehemiah's era.[59] Time has revealed that the perspective of Daniel 9:24–27 covers many centuries and extends to the final restoration of the city when "everlasting righteousness" gains complete control.

The scope of this essay does not include detailed interpretive issues of verses 24–27. This has been done elsewhere.[60] Primary attention here is toward how prayer relates to prophecy, but the compatibility of this prophecy can be shown to harmonize in general with other prophecies in Daniel and the OT.

The perspective of Daniel. Some of Daniel's prophecies span many centuries, stretching to Israel's complete deliverance from other nations and possession of spiritual blessings (Dan. 2:44; 7:15–28; 12:1–3, 13).

The promised kingdom of Israel's blessing will fill the entire earth (2:35) and embrace peoples of all nations, with God ruling over all (7:27). The perspective also includes resurrection and final reward (12:2–3, 13), integrating with the second advent of the Messiah and beyond.

The perspective of other prophecies. Daniel's prophecies (9:24–27) correlate well with OT prophecies outside of Daniel too. They constitute a comprehensive summary of several ways in which God will answer the prayers of other prophets (cf. Jer. 29:12; 33:3). The process will result in the welfare for Israel (Jer. 29:12–14; 33:6ff.) Details from Daniel 9 integrate meaningfully with details of other OT predictions.

The first sixty-nine "sevens" (Dan. 9:25), "sevens" being composed of years,[61] are the early part of the process that will issue in Israel's good. The time period covered spans the interval until the Messiah, the Lord Jesus Christ, and His death.[62] A suggested placement of the seventieth "seven" of years has been at the first advent of Jesus Christ and shortly after,[63] but it fits better after a hiatus of time between His first and second advents.[64]

It is difficult to place the covenant in the last seven years (v. 27) at the first advent. The new covenant Jesus inaugurated (Jer. 32:40; Luke 22:20; Heb. 13:20) is eternal, and the "he" of Daniel 9:27 is more likely the "prince" of verse 26, the nearest antecedent of the pronoun. He is a prince (ruler) rising from the fourth empire, the Roman (Daniel 2, 7), that will bring desolation to Israel immediately before the second advent. Further, the panorama of Daniel 9:24–27 more probably agrees with Daniel's other prophecies (chaps. 2, 7, and 12) that reach to the second advent.

This harmonizes with other OT prophecies that speak of the installation of God's king over Israel and the world (Jer. 23:5–6; Ezek. 34:11–31; Zech. 14:1–3, 9). The NT also supports this anticipation as it looks beyond the Messiah's crucifixion to His second appearance (Mark 14:62; Rev. 1:7; 14:14; 19:11ff.).

So Daniel 9:24 sums up in a comprehensive unit the facets of reassurance by noting God's full restoration of Israel. These bring comfort to Daniel's people, while other parts of Daniel show the inclusion of Gentiles in the provisions (7:27). This coincides with much OT and NT prophecy too.[65]

Verses 25–27 spell out the broad steps by which God will make verse 24 a reality. These extend from the rebuilding of Jerusalem (v. 25), to the cross of the Messiah (v. 26), and then to the end of desolations (v. 27). The last of these was still future from Jesus' vantage point at His first advent (Matt. 23:37–39). God decrees the welfare described in Daniel 9:24 as the final solution, not an intermediate one that leaves Israel still in difficulty. God's unalterable word is a pledge of "everlasting righteousness."

CONCLUSION

Daniel's prayer for Israel concerns matters of sin that have been road-blocks to blessing. He confesses the sin, but recognizes that Israel's bless-ing—a direct reversal of its desolation—will come from the God who is faithful to His covenant and His compassions. He depends on God's righteous acts, not the nonexistent ones of Israel. He pleads for restora-tion of the people, the city, and the sanctuary. God answers with reassur-ances that He will restore all three. The answer does not correct Daniel, but correlates with his prayer formulated in light of earlier OT Scripture. Submissive to God, he prays for the fulfilment of blessings God has promised. So he makes himself available to participate in what God wants to do. God has a plan from beginning to end (Isa. 46:9–10) and affirms His good designs for Israel (Jer. 29:12–14). He allows men the privilege of laboring together with Him by yearning and praying for the same wonderful ends (Jer. 29:12).

Christians of the present generation can learn many important les-sons from the prayer in Daniel 9 as they engage themselves in the vital ministry of prayer.

ENDNOTES

[1] E.g., Werner Kessler, *Zwischen Gott und Weltmacht: Der Prophet Daniel* (3d ed.; Stuttgart: Botschaft Altentestament, 1961), 130–31. James Montgomery suggested a second-century author, but felt that he could have used such a prayer as fits this context, *A Critical and Exegetical Commentary on the Book of Daniel,* ICC (Edinburgh: T & T Clark, 1927), 362.

[2] R. H. Charles, *A Critical and Exegetical Commentary on the Book of Daniel* (Oxford: The Clarendon House, 1929), 226–27.

[3] H. C. Leupold, *Exposition of Daniel* (Columbus: Wartburg, 1949), 395–99.

[4] Bruce W. Jones, "The Prayer in Daniel IX," *Vetus Testamentum* 18 (1968): 488–93.

[5] Repetition is a characteristic of Hebrew and other Semitic poetry and narrative. In prayer heartfelt reiteration similar to these can be expected. Repetition can be a mark of humanness and spontaneity before God. This is one way people voice all-important concerns. In an onrushing

burden of prayer, concentration is on perils and fears, not polish and finesse, though these are not necessarily excluded.

6 Even Jones reasons that linguistic ties connect the prayer with God's response. Daniel prays for Israel to have "insight" (v. 13) (cf. שָׂכַל *[śākal]*, BDB, 968; John E. Goldingay, *Daniel,* vol. 30 of *Word Biblical Commentary,* ed. David A. Hubbard, et al. [Waco, Tex.: Word, 1989], 249; the word means "to consider, have insight, pay attention" in an understanding way based on wise reflection [cf. Deut. 32:29; Pss. 41:2; 64:10; 106:7; 119:99; Dan. 1:4, 17; 9:25]), which Gabriel in turn supplies. In verse 13, "turning" and "have insight into" are used together. Then in verse 25 new verbs represent these two concepts (Jones, "The Prayer" 489–91), though not with the same precise connotation. This is a step toward Israel's eventual deliverance.

7 Rogers shows that God's covenant with Abram was gracious and unconditional (Cleon L. Rogers Jr., "The Covenant with Abraham and Its Historical Setting," *Bibliotheca Sacra* 127 [1970]: 241–56). He explains how apparently conditional texts (e.g., Gen. 12:1; 17:1; 17:9–14) harmonize with this (252–54).

8 Ibid. Psalm 89:30–37 sees the impossibility of the abrogation of the Davidic covenant even through human disobedience and its consequent divine chastening. The covenant will finally be fulfiled through divine action. God even inclines men, that they might be restored (Jer. 31:18; cf. Ps. 80:3, 7, 19 [Heb. text: 80:4, 8, 20]). Men must obey in the right spirit, but must do so as enabled by God (Ps. 119:32–40; Phil. 2:12–13). God's blessing does not produce human merit because humans merit no reward. Their rewards are simply a result of what God has graciously given.

9 Jones, "The Prayer," 493.

10 Cf. discussion of 9:20–27 later in this essay.

11 Jones, "The Prayer," 493.

12 Patrick Harris, "A Biblical Model for Penitential Prayer, Daniel 9:3–19" (M.Div. thesis, Grace Theological Seminary, Winona Lake, Ind., 1986), 51.

13 Cf. Leupold, *Exposition,* 395–99.

[14] In support of a sixth-century dating, see R. K. Harrison, *Introduction to the Old Testament* (Grand Rapids: Eerdmans, 1969), 1110–27; also his "Book of Daniel," in *Zondervan Pictorial Encyclopedia of the Bible*, ed. M. C. Tenney (Grand Rapids: Zondervan, 1975), 2:12–21; Gleason Archer, *A Survey of Old Testament Introduction*, rev. ed. (Chicago: Moody, 1974), 379–403. For a premillennial case, cf. Robert C. Culver, *Daniel and the Latter Days* (New York: Revell, 1954); introduction and Daniel 2, 7, 9, and 12 in Leon Wood, *A Commentary on Daniel* (Grand Rapids: Zondervan, 1973).

[15] E. J. Young, *The Prophecy of Daniel* (Grand Rapids: Eerdmans, 1949), 154–56.

[16] That Darius was "made king" (cf. the hophal form of the verb in Dan. 9:1) could be by God permitting it (cf. Ps. 75:6–7; Dan. 4:35; 5:25–28) or by a human superior. Cf. evidence to distinguish Cyrus from Darius, who was Cyrus's appointee over the Babylonian part of the Persian Empire, in John Whitcomb Jr., *Darius the Mede* (Grand Rapids: Eerdmans, 1959).

[17] Daniel consistently knelt (Dan. 6:10).

[18] Psalm 80:3, 7, 19 (prayer) [in Heb. text, 80:4, 8, 20]; Jeremiah 29:12 (prayer) with verses 12–14 (restoration); 30:3–11, 18–24; 31:7–40 (restoration); 32:17–25 (prayer) and 32:26–44 (restoration). The anticipated "everlasting covenant" (32:40) appears to be the "eternal covenant" of Hebrews 13:20.

[19] Jeremiah did pray, but some passages have God telling him not to pray for Israel because of their hardened rejection (7:16; 11:14; 14:11–12).

[20] Cf. references in n. 18 above and also Psalms 74 and 79.

[21] God calls on people to repent (e.g., 2 Kings 17:13; Isa. 55:6–7; Jer. 25:5; Ezek. 14:6; 18:30). Yet in enabling grace He helps people repent (Ps. 80:3, 7, 19 [in Heb. text, 80:4, 8, 20]; Jer. 31:18). People come as He draws them (cf. John 6:44).

[22] H. C. Leupold, *Exposition of Daniel*, 395–99.

[23] BDB, 680; cf. examples in 2 Chronicles 20:3; Ecclesiastes 1:13, 17; 8:9, 16; Daniel 10:12.

[24] In Daniel 1:2, for example, אֲדֹנָי ("Lord") is in control even when Babylon's king conquers Judah, because He gave Judah's king into Nebuchadnezzar's hand. And in 9:4, אֲדֹנָי is "the great and awesome God."

[25] Hypocrites can simulate these outward practices, as Jezebel in her fast (1 Kings 21:9, 12), or through wrongly motivated actions (Isa. 58:3–7). On the other hand, in the lives of pious ones they are signs of God-honoring devotion and true submission (fasting, Dan. 10:2–3; sackcloth, 2 Kings 19:1–2; ashes in mourning, Job 2:8; Jer. 6:26).

[26] J. F. A. Sawyer, "Types of Prayer in the Old Testament. Some Semantic Observations on Hitpallel, Hithannēn, etc.," Semitics 7 (1980): 131–43.

[27] Sawyer, "Types of Prayer," 131–43. The idea of intercession is specified by a preposition such as בְּעַד (bĕ'ad, "pray on behalf of"; e.g., Gen. 20:7; Num. 21:7; Jer. 7:16). Used alone as in Daniel 9:3, the word usually refers to liturgical prayer in general (cf. 2 Sam. 7:27; 1 Kings 8:54; Pss. 35:3; 80:5; Isa. 1:15; Dan. 9:3, 21 [noun] and 9:4 [verb]). Another indication of the word's general meaning is in Isaiah 56:7 where the temple is twice the "house of prayer" [tĕpillāh]. Prayer in God's temple could diverge into a variety of particular facets. Jonah, while intensely alarmed inside the great fish, illustrates a more restricted meaning: "My prayer (tĕpillāh) came to Thee, into Thy holy temple" (Jonah 2:7 [Heb. text, 2:8]). In such a predicament, the term for prayer must denote the specific aspect of petition. The general meaning of tĕpillāh is similar to προσευχῆς (proseuchēs) in the NT (cf. Eph. 6:18; Phil. 4:6) where other words specify requests (e.g., δεήσεως [deēseōs], Eph. 6:18; Phil. 4:6, and αἰτήματα [aitēmata], Phil. 4:6) (cf. J. B. Lightfoot, St. Paul's Epistle to the Philippians [1953 reprint, Grand Rapids: Zondervan, n.d.], 160). In the LXX פָּלַל (pālal) is usually rendered by προσεύχομαι (proseuchomai) (R. B. Girdlestone, Synonyms of the Old Testament [1976; reprint, Grand Rapids: Zondervan, n.d.], 219).

[28] Johannes Hermann, "εὔχομαι, εὐχή, etc.," TDOT, 2:785.

[29] Hermann, "εὔχομαι," 2:785. Cf. Psalms 28:2, 6; 31:22; 116:1; 130:2; 140:6 for other examples. Zechariah 12:10 refers to a spirit (or Spirit) of grace (חֵן, hēn) and of supplications, i.e., a receptive and repentant attitude, sensitive to the need for grace. God "gives grace to the afflicted" (Prov. 3:34b). Among others, He gave grace to Noah (Gen. 6:8), Abraham (18:3; cf. vv. 17–19), Lot (19:19), Moses (Exod. 33:12–13; 34:9), Gideon (Judg. 6:17), and David (2 Sam. 15:25).

[30] Solomon has *taḥănûnîm* often in prayer for Israel (2 Chronicles 6 = 1 Kings 8). Daniel exemplifies an adeptness in Scripture that fosters naturalness and spontaneity in incorporating biblical wording and concepts in prayer.

[31] For evidence of a Mosaic dating of Deuteronomy, see R. K. Harrison, *Introduction,* 637–62.

[32] Some refer this to the high priest Onias III, murdered in 171 B.C. However, the reference is more reasonably to God (Goldingay, *Daniel,* 210–11; Wood, *A Commentary,* 228; Young, *The Prophecy,* 172, 181). In favor of this, God is the "Prince of the host" (8:11), since the place Antiochus Epiphanes opposes is "His sanctuary," i.e., more probably God's. God instituted the sacrifice (Exodus 29). And in 8:25 it is God that the "horn" (leader) stands against, for the "horn" is broken without human agency, i.e., by the One he opposes, God (cf. Dan. 2:45).

[33] Cf. nn. 8 and 21 regarding God's bringing men to repentance.

[34] André Lacocque, *The Book of Daniel* (Atlanta: John Knox, 1979), 176.

[35] E.g., a pouring out of wrath on Jerusalem yet to come (2 Chron. 34:25; Jer. 7:20) and later reported as recently accomplished (Jer. 42:18; 44:6); cf. BDB, 677.

[36] However, the "great" in "great compassion" (Dan. 9:18) is a different word, רַב *(rab),* "much, many, great."

[37] Ronald J. Williams, *Hebrew Syntax,* 2d ed. (Toronto: University of Toronto Press, 1976), 36; BDB, 879.

[38] Walter C. Kaiser Jr., *A Biblical Approach to Suffering* (Chicago: Moody, 1982), has a detailed description of the horror in Lamentations.

[39] E.g., Sodom and Gomorrah (Deut. 29:23); Admah and Zeboim (Deut. 29:23; Hos. 11:8).

[40] Joyce C. Baldwin, *Daniel* (Downers Grove: InterVarsity, 1978), 166.

[41] Isaiah 11:16 compares a future restoration of Israel with the past one from Egypt. It is very difficult to identify details of Isaiah's description with a historical period before that relating to the second advent of the Messiah.

[42] Cf., for example, n. 8.

[43] In Psalm 65:2 (Heb. text 65:3) "prayer," תְּפִלָּה *(tĕpillāh)* is the general noun for prayer as in Daniel 9:3, 17, 21 (cf. verbal forms in vv. 4, 20). Also in the same verse, a form of the same word for "hear", שֹׁמֵעַ *(shōmēaʿ,* "you who hear") appears in Daniel 9:17 (שְׁמַע [*šĕmaʿ,* "hear"]) and 9:19 (שְׁמָעָה [*šĕmāʿāh,* "hear"]).

[44] Cf. n. 18.

[45] Cf. Rogers, "The Covenant," 248, 255–56.

[46] Cf. nn. 7–8.

[47] Isaiah 65:24 refers to God's determination before man's prayer occurs (cf. Isa. 46:9–10).

[48] General words for prayer as found in Daniel 9:3 (noun) and 9:4 (verb).

[49] Lit., transitive idea, "falling (a tree)" or "causing to fall," מַפִּיל *(mappîl)* as in Daniel 9:18.

[50] As also in Daniel 9:3, 17–18.

[51] C. F. Keil, *Biblical Commentary on the Book of Daniel* (Grand Rapids: Eerdmans, n.d.), 33. Keil sees the cause of Daniel's weariness in his spiritual quest for God's will. This fits with the larger context in which Daniel is weary and in need of angelic strengthening (8:17–18, 27; cf. 10:8, 16–19). It is difficult to conceive of a celestial being as wearied, even when opposed by another celestial creature (10:13). The view also suits the words used: מֻעָף *(muʿāp,* "wearied") and בִּיעָף *(bîʿāp,* "with weariness") (BDB, 419), not עוּף *(ʿûp,* "he flies,") (BDB, 733).

[52] So Wood, *A Commentary,* 245; John F. Walvoord, Daniel, *The Key to Prophetic Revelation* (Chicago: Moody, 1971), 215; Young, *The Prophecy,* 190. These prefer a reference to Gabriel as "being caused to fly rapidly," based on the word meaning "to fly" (see n. 51) rather than the meaning chosen by BDB (419), "weary from winged flight." It is problematic to assume that this angel has wings, like other celestial beings (e.g., cherubim, seraphim; see Goldingay, *Daniel,* 228 n. 21).

[53] Cf. BDB, 326, on חֲמוּדָה (ḥămûdāh, "treasure") and the word as used in Daniel 11:38, 43; Ezra 8:27.

[54] Intensification rather than numerical plurality is the force of the plural form.

[55] To relate the six aspects in 9:24 with the complex of realities God will consummate at the second advent is reasonable. Based on the death of the Messiah at His first advent (cf. Isaiah 53), Israel will see these benefits realized fully at Messiah's second advent (Jer. 31:33–34; Ezek. 37:23; Rom. 11:25–27). Wood's perspective is helpful (*A Commentary*, 247–51): God will restrain the transgression of Israel without denying extension of the same restraint to Gentile sin. He will bring it under His sovereign control and end the enmity of centuries. Not only will He stop transgression, but He will "make an end of sins" through a lasting solution. He tells us how He will do it too: by expiation "to atone for iniquity." "Atone," the usual OT word for atonement, was often used in the sacrifices that pointed to Messiah's future death for sin, referred to here as His being "cut off" (v. 25). The basis for atonement has been laid, but as Romans 11 explains, Israel's national benefits await the second advent. This agrees with much OT prophecy in which the final resolution of Israel's trouble is in a second advent context (cf. n. 15). Fourth, God will "cause righteousness of ages to come in" through a permanent cure. Previously, Israel always fell back into transgression and needed the more permanent solution anticipated in OT prophecies of the second advent. "To seal up vision and prophecy" relates to fulfiling prophetic revelation. Anticipated conditions will become realities for Israel. Daniel's larger perspective provides for Gentile blessing at the second advent, too (cf. Dan. 7:27). "To anoint (consecrate) a holy of holies," as Wood shows, refers to God's restoration of temple operations during the future millennial era.

[56] Cloud imagery linked with a person is a mark of divine presence and authority (E. J. Young, *Daniel's Vision of the Son of Man* [London: Tyndale, 1959], 11). God makes the clouds His chariot (Ps. 104:3) and comes in a cloud (Exod. 34:5; Num. 10:34; Isa. 19:1). At least 70 times God is associated with a cloud (e.g., Exod. 13:21; 2 Sam. 22:12; Job 22:14; Ps. 68:34). His glory cloud appears in the temple (1 Kings 8:10–11; Ezek. 10:3), and He is connected with clouds in Ezekiel 1:4, 28. The NT also associates the Son of Man with deity, as a figure from heaven (e.g., Matt. 24:30; 26:64; Mark 13:26; 14:62; Rev. 1:7). A. J. Ferch, though favoring the view that

the son of man in Daniel 7:13–14 is an angel, admits that before the 19th century, "The majority of interpreting commentators considered Daniel 7:13 to be a prophecy of Christ's second advent" (*The Apocalyptic Son of Man in Daniel 7* [Ann Arbor, Mich.: University Microfilms International, 1979], 36).

[57] The rebuilding of the *temple* in 520–515 B.C. is the focus in the Book of Ezra: 1:2–5; 2:68; 3:6, 8–12; 4:1, 3, 24; 5:2–3, 8–9, 11, 13, 15–17; 6:3, 5, 7–8, 12, 14–16 (temple finally completed), 17, 22.

[58] Cf. n. 55 and Ralph Alexander, *Ezekiel* (Chicago: Moody, 1976), 129–36; Paul Enns, *Ezekiel* (Grand Rapids: Zondervan, 1986), 179–81; Charles H. Dyer, "Ezekiel," in *Bible Knowledge Commentary*, ed. J. F. Walvoord and Roy B. Zuck (Wheaton: Victor, 1983–85), 1:1303–4.

[59] Rebuilding the *city* and its *wall* is emphasized in Nehemiah: 1:2–33; 2:3, 5, 8, 12–13, 15, 17; 3:1, 3, 6, 8, 13–15; 4:1, 6, 15, 17, 19; 5:16; 6:1, 6, 15 (city finally completed).

[60] To supplement the prophetic viewpoint of this essay, see Paul D. Feinberg, "An Exegetical and Theological Study of Daniel 9:24–27," *Tradition & Testament, Essays in Honor of Charles Lee Feinberg,* ed. John S. and Paul D. Feinberg (Chicago: Moody, 1981), 189–220; Harold H. Hoehner, *Chronological Aspects of the Life of Christ* (Grand Rapids: Baker, 1977), 115–39.

[61] Hoehner, *Chronological Aspects,* 117–19. That the "sevens" are composed of years is a natural conclusion based on Daniel's attention to years in 9:1–2, on the phrase "sevens of days" (10:2–3) where "sevens" have to be clarified as referring to days and not years, and the computation through which sevens of years works out as Hoehner shows, with the end of the sixty-two plus seven (= sixty-nine) sevens at the first advent of Jesus Christ.

[62] Hoehner, *Chronological Aspects,* 119–31.

[63] E. G. Young, *The Prophecy,* 208–19.

[64] Hoehner, *Chronological Aspects,* 131–33.

[65] E.g., Genesis 12:1–3; Isaiah 49:6; 51:4; 56:6–7; Zechariah 14:9, 16.

CHAPTER FIVE

Romans 11:2–6

Paul's Use of Elijah's Mt. Horeb Experience

Michael G. Vanlaningham

Paul's use of 1 Kings 19:10–18 in Romans 11:2–6 has an important role in his proof that God has not cast off His people Israel. His main dependence is upon the Massoretic Text rather than the Septuagint. He makes a number of changes in his adaptation of the OT passage, none of which violates the meaning of the OT context. Despite apparent parallels between Elijah and Moses in the OT, the 1 Kings passage does not elevate Elijah to the level of Moses in God's plan. Rather it emphasizes the sovereignty of God at work to preserve a remnant. Paul's theological emphasis in Romans 11:2–6 is upon God's preservation of a remnant of Jews through grace, not human merit. Through this means He guards against the total loss of the people of Israel.

* * * * *

The prophet Elijah has an important place in both testaments, and has attracted moderate attention from NT scholars.[1] One of the references to Elijah that has not attracted as much attention (and rightly so) is Paul's reference in Romans 11:2–6 to the pericope involving Elijah on Mt. Horeb (1 Kings 19:10–18). Though this NT citation of an OT text is not as theologically problematic as other references to Elijah, it nevertheless has a pivotal position in Paul's argument in Romans 11. It supports his case that God has not cast off His people. It therefore deserves careful attention.

This exegetical analysis purposes to examine the textual, hermeneutical, exegetical, and theological details of 1 Kings 19:10, 14, and 18 in their context, and then to determine why Paul used the verses in his *apologia* of Romans 11:2–6 and what the OT verses add to his argument.

TEXTUAL AND HERMENEUTICAL FACTORS

When one examines the MT, LXX, and Paul's citation in Romans 11:3–4, more agreement between Paul's text and the MT is apparent than between either of these and the LXX. Several notable differences between the NT and MT passages occur, however. The following will focus on some hermeneutical implications of these differences.

First, Paul abbreviates 1 Kings 19:10 and 14 by omitting the MT's mention of Elijah's zeal (קִנֵּאתִי קַנֹּא [*qann'ō qinnē'ti*, "I have been very zealous"]), Israel's rejection of the covenant (עָזְבוּ בְרִיתְךָ בְּנֵי יִשְׂרָאֵל ['*āzĕbû bĕrîtkā bĕnê yiśrā'ēl*, "the sons of Israel have forsaken Your covenant"]),[2] the mention of the sword (בְחֶרֶב, *behereb*, "with a sword"), and the rather redundant לְקַחְתָּהּ (*lĕqahtāh*, "to take her [Elijah's life]"). Also the phrase וְכָל־הַפֶּה אֲשֶׁר לֹא־נָשַׁק לוֹ (*wĕkāl–happeh 'ăšer lō'–nāšaq lô*, "and every mouth which has not kissed him") in 1 Kings 19:18 finds no parallel in Paul's citation. With the possible exception of the first omission (Elijah's zeal, *qann'ō qinnē'ti*), no significant theological reason for Paul to have shortened these verses is evident. The points to which Paul refers are quite sufficient for his purposes and do not violate the OT sense.

Second, Paul inverts two phrases from 1 Kings 19:10, 14: נְבִיאֶיךָ הָרְגוּ (*nĕbî'êkā hārĕgû*, "they have killed your prophets")—τοὺς προφήτας σου ἀπέκτειναν *(tous prophētas sou apekteinan)* and מִזְבְּחֹתֶיךָ הָרָסוּ (*mizbĕhōtêkā hārāsû*, "they have torn down your altar")—τὰ θυσιαστήριὰ σου κατέσκαψαν *(ta thysiastēria sou kateskapsan)*. H. A. W. Meyer maintains that the inversion is accidental and has no real significance.[3] Meyer may be correct, but possibly Paul inverted them to de-emphasize the killing of the prophets. Though Paul's situation was always perilous (cf. Rom. 8:36), it was not as critical when he wrote Romans as Elijah's was at the time of the pericope. Perhaps his intent was to avoid drawing a parallel between himself and Elijah, and thus he placed the killing of the prophets first. It is impossible to be certain of Paul's motivation on this point, however.

Third, and perhaps most significantly, is the apparent change by Paul of a future-referring Hiphil perfect first common singular verb וְהִשְׁאַרְתִּי (*wĕhiš'artî*, "I will leave") in 1 Kings 19:18[4] to the aorist κατέλιπον[5] (*katelipon*, "I have left") in Romans 11:4. The shift may not be as significant as one might suppose. While the sparing of the remnant was probably as yet future, the context of 1 Kings 19 shows that God's decision to spare the 7000 had already been made before the interaction in 19:18 with Elijah and that the 7000 even at that point were being preserved.[6] Possibly, then, Paul is emphasizing in Romans this antecedent decision by God to preserve some,[7] and Paul reflects this emphasis with the use of the aorist *katelipon*.[8] Paul's change of tense is not completely *ad hoc* if this interpretation is correct.

Fourth, Paul makes one notable addition to the OT texts, an addition not reflected either in the LXX or the MT. In Romans 11:4 he adds the first person reflexive pronoun ἐμαυτῷ (*emautō̦*, "for myself"). By adding this word Paul does not do great violence to the OT meaning of the passage. In the context of 1 Kings 20 where the figure 7000[9] occurs again in reference to the soldiers under Ahab in his fight against Benhadad, it is evident that God intended to preserve the 7000 soldiers at least in part for His own sake—so that Ahab would revere the true God (20:13, 28). Hence Paul's use of *emautō̦*, along with the other variations from the MT, does no violence to the OT meaning of the text.

EXEGETICAL FACTORS

Two primary procedures appear to have guided the formation of 1 Kings 19:10, 14, 18. One is inter-textual and the other is inner-textual. Both contribute to Paul's reading and use of this OT text in his epistle.

Several scholars draw attention to the remarkable parallels between Elijah's experience at Mt. Horeb and Moses' experiences.[10] Despite these parallels, the writer of 1 Kings probably shows a fundamental disparity between the two individuals, not a correlation. In the exposure he had to God, Moses received encouragement for his work,[11] but according to Robert L. Cohn the interaction of Elijah and God was essentially a decommissioning of Elijah as a prophet.[12] William J. Dumbrell maintains that Elijah did not learn anything in the theophany he experienced, nor was any information communicated to him in the "still, small sound." Elijah was an "accuser of the brethren" rather than an intercessor on behalf of the people as Moses was. Dumbrell suggests that through these differences the author is indicating that Elijah was *not* a new Moses, and that God was not beginning a radically new movement through him. All of this tends to emphasize the point made overtly in 1 Kings 19:18, namely, that God Himself would preserve a faithful remnant that would not worship Baal, and that He would do this sovereignly and graciously apart from any significant involvement by Elijah.[13] Dumbrell writes,

> Israel's future did not depend upon the manifestation of his [Elijah's] particular genius of giftedness. It depended as it always did and would upon the sovereign intervention of Yahweh, who would continue to honour his commitment made at Sinai to Israel, through the instruments and circumstances which he from time to time would choose. . . .[14]

In essence, then, Elijah would not enjoy the prominence in God's plans that Moses did.[15] The differences between Elijah and Moses support the concept of the sovereignty of God to work as He sees fit in the preservation of a remnant apart from human participation. Other factors within the passage itself also point in this direction.[16]

Inner-textual factors also influenced the formation and meaning of 1 Kings 19, the main one being the point mentioned above, the presence of the figure 7000 in chapters 19 and 20.[17] Though Cohn maintains rightly that 1 Kings 17–19 is "an example of a carefully woven literary tissue . . . ," he also maintains wrongly that 1 Kings 20 is ". . . an unrelated war story."[18] Chapter 20 *does* appear to be unconnected with what precedes. However, the promise God made to Ahab that he would be victorious over an enormously superior foe in Ben-hadad suggests literary, theological, and exegetical connections with 1 Kings 19. The most important of these connections is God's gracious preservation of the 7000 soldiers *even though they did not merit God's preservation*. Ahab did not deserve the protection he received from God. This inner-textual factor (the preservation of 7000) may have played an important role in Paul's use of the pericope in Romans 11.

THEOLOGICAL FACTORS

In light of the textual, hermeneutical, and exegetical considerations reviewed above, three theological observations emerge. First, Paul's main point in Romans 11:2–6 is that God was preserving a remnant of Jews, just as He had in 1 Kings. The two situations are analogous (οὕτως οὖν καί ἐν τῷ νῦν καιρῷ . . . [*houtōs oun kai en tǭ nyn kairǭ* . . . , "therefore so also* in the present time," Rom. 11:5]).

Second, He accomplishes this preservation κατ᾽ ἐκλογὴν χάριτος (*kat' eklogēn charitos,* "according to the election of grace," 11:5) and χάριτι, οὐκέτι ἐξ ἔργων (*chariti, ouketi ex ergōn,* "through grace, not from works," 11:6). This preservation of a remnant in Paul's day fits precisely with the preservation revealed in 1 Kings 19:18 and observed in 1 Kings 20:15, where the preservation is entirely through God's sovereign intervention and grace apart from all human merit (since Ahab had none).

Third, some NT scholars maintain that in Romans 11:1–6 the whole nation is in view. The entirety (πᾶς Ἰσραήλ [*pas Israēl,* "all Israel"], 11:26) will be saved in the end.[19] But in Romans, as in 1 Kings, the point Paul makes is that the Jews as a people would be *completely lost* apart from the gracious, sovereign intervention of God.[20] In 1 Kings, the people were lost in Baalism and thus, without God's intervention, lost in the ensuing judgment of God. In Romans 11 also, the people were lost. God preserves a remnant, guarding against the total loss of the people.[21]

CONCLUSION

Paul's use of the Elijah-Horeb pericope in Romans 11 demonstrates his careful reading of the OT (probably the Hebrew *vis-a-vis* the LXX). His use of the OT passage in no way wrests it from its narrative and theological milieu. In applying it to his current situation, Paul shows that there is a very close analogy between his own situation and Elijah's. Some were questioning the validity of Paul's gospel in light of the almost wholesale rejection of it by the Jews. By the use of 1 Kings 19, Paul demonstrates that in fact God's plans for the Jews had not failed. He had not rejected His people. On the contrary, the gracious preservation of a (small) remnant had been squarely within God's sovereign plan throughout history, as seen conspicuously in the statement God made to Elijah on Mt. Horeb.

ENDNOTES

[1] Cf. Walter C. Kaiser Jr., *The Uses of the Old Testament in the New* (Chicago: Moody, 1985), 77–88, and the bibliography in these pages.

[2] It is impossible to say dogmatically why Paul omitted the mention of breaking the covenant. Perhaps he viewed this as a fairly nebulous thing, with the killing of the prophets and destroying of the altars being a more concrete and observable evidence of that breach. But this is speculative.

[3] H. A. W. Meyer, *A Critical and Exegetical Handbook on the Epistle to the Romans* (1886, 6th Funk and Wagnalls ed.; reprint, Winona Lake, Ind.: Alpha, 1979), 428.

[4] For the future force of the verb, cf. Gerhard Hasel, *The Remnant: The History and Theology of the Remnant Idea from Genesis to Isaiah* (Berrien Springs, Mich.: Andrews University, 1972), 169; Norman H. Snaith, "1 Kings," in *The Interpreter's Bible,* ed. George Buttrick (New York: Abingdon, 1956), 3:164; Ernst Käsemann, *Commentary on Romans* (Grand Rapids: Eerdmans, 1980), 299. Though these writers do not justify their interpretation of a future sense with וְהִשְׁאַרְתִּי ("I will leave"), the fact that it is a *waw* conversive with an Hiphil perfect (the *wĕqtl* combination; note the *shewa* with the *waw*, the shifting of the *Mêrĕkhâ* accent to *Milra'*, and the *wĕqtl* combination following the future-referring (imperfective) Hiphil

imperfect יָמִיר in 19:18), as well as being found in God's discourse, support their conclusions. Cf. Bruce K. Waltke and M. O'Connor, *An Introduction to Biblical Hebrew Syntax* (Winona Lake, Ind.: Eisenbrauns, 1990), 456–58, 527–28.

[5] The NA[26] indicates that there is a textual variant with κατέλιπον ("I have left"), most likely due to itacism. The more likely choices are between the imperfect κατέλειπον ("I was leaving"), which has ancient proto-Alexandrian support (P[46] A 1739) and support from the Western F and G, and the aorist κατέλιπον, which has equally strong support from Alexandrian (B), Western (D), and Byzantine texts. The problem probably has to be decided on the basis of intrinsic probability, in which case κατέλιπον is the preferred reading. The context argues for a reading that reflects God's selection as a complete action (the aorist aspect; cf. ἀπόσατο ["rejected"], προέγνω ["foreknew," 11:2]; ἔκαμψαν ["bowed," 11:4]), rather than a background process (the aspect of the imperfect tense). In either case, neither the meaning nor the theology is affected much. What is most surprising is that the LXX text, based on Vaticanus, reads καταλείψεις ("you will leave," future active, second person singular) in 1 Kings 19:18, but Vaticanus in Romans 11:4 reads the aorist κατέλιπον ("I have left," first person singular). More on this point will follow below.

[6] If God's decision had not as yet been made, then 19:18 would hardly function as either an encouragement for or a reproof of Elijah. God corrects Elijah's statement that Elijah was the only one left to God among the entire people. If in fact the 7000 were not already alive and in the process of being preserved, Elijah's statement would be accurate, not in need of revision, and thus would not have evoked God's correction.

[7] C. E. B. Cranfield apparently hints at this interpretation when he says, "Paul writes the first person [κατέλιπον, 'I have left'], adds ἐμαυτῷ ['myself'], and uses the aorist tense, *referring the words to the divine decision*" (*A Critical and Exegetical Commentary on the Epistle to the Romans* [Edinburgh: T & T Clark, 1979], 2:546, emphasis added).

[8] Regardless how one resolves this problem, a more intriguing one exists when considering the reading of the LXX, which has the *second* person singular verb as distinguished from the MT's first common singular or Paul's first person. The *Vorlage* of A and B apparently read

יהשארת (pointed תְ-), not having the final *yod* found in the MT. The Syro-Hexapla (according to James A. Montgomery, *A Critical and Exegetical Commentary on the Books of Kings* [New York: Charles Scribner's Sons, 1951], 318) and Origen (cf. Fridericus Field, *Origenis Hexa plorum* [Hildesheim: Georg Olms Verlabsbuchandlung, 1964], 1:636) also have a second person reading, supporting καταλείψεις while the Lucianic Greek reading is καταλείψω (Montgomery, *Kings* 318). Perhaps a consideration of the context can account for the second person reading. It may be that the 7000 of 1 Kings 19:18 were seen as essentially the same group as the 7000 of 1 Kings 20:15 (LXX 21:15). If this is true, perhaps part of the text history reflects an interpretation in which Elijah had a hand in the preservation of that 7000 under Ahab (cf. the unnamed prophet, usually identified as Micaiah, in 1 Kings 20:13ff., 22ff., etc.). But the reading of the first person by the MT and Paul fits better with the strong contextual emphasis in 1 Kings on God's decision to preserve a remnant apart from human agency, in this case, apart from Elijah's participation.

9 The 7000 of 1 Kings 19:18 has been viewed traditionally by Rashi (cf. C. F. Keil, *I & II Kings* [reprint, Grand Rapids: Eerdmans, 1980], 263–64) and by Jarchi (presumably Yarchi, *aka* Rabbi Abraham Ben-Nathan; cf. Otto Thenius, *Die Bücher der Könige* [Leipzig: Weidmansche Buchhandlung, 1849], 236) as the same group of 7000 found in 1 Kings 20:15. It is doubtful that this is the case, though as Keil (264) points out, "The sameness in the numbers is apparently not accidental. . . ." It is possible that while the two groups were distinct in the mind of the author of 1 Kings, he nevertheless mentioned the same size of the two groups in order to emphasize God's ability and intention to preserve such a group. That God would spare 7000 in 1 Kings 19 is observable in His miraculous and gracious sparing of a different 7000 in 1 Kings 20.

10 Some of the parallels are as follows: While Moses passed 40 days on Mt. Horeb (Exod. 34:28), Elijah took 40 days to get there (1 Kings 19:8); Elijah is in הַמְּעָרָ ("the cave"—note the article), probably an allusion to the location in which Moses found himself in Exodus 33:22; God is said to "pass by" both Moses (Exod. 33:22, עָבְרי, בַּעֲבֹר) and Elijah (1 Kings 19:11, עֹבֵר), and both receive a vision of God (for Moses, see Exodus 34; for Elijah, see 1 Kings 19:11–13). Furthermore, like Moses, Elijah contended on behalf of God against apostates, called for a decision to follow God, and went to Horeb for reassurance. Elijah's theophany shared with the theophany given to Moses and Israel the elements of wind, earthquake, and fire (cf. Exod. 19:9; 20:18–19; Deut. 4:9–10; 5:24–25).

For a discussion of these parallels, cf. Klaus Seybold, "Elia am Gottesberg: Vorstellungen prophetischen Wirkens nach 1. Könige 19," *Evangelische Theologie* 33 (1973): 10–11; William J. Dumbrell, "What Are You Doing Here? Elijah At Horeb," *Crux* 22 (1986): 15–17; Brevard Childs, "On Reading the Elijah Narratives," *Interpretation* 34 (1980): 134–35; Robert L. Cohn, "The Literary Logic of 1 Kings 17–19," *JBL* 101 (1982): 341–42.

[11] Cf. Exodus 6; 19:1–25; 32:7–17; 33:12–23, etc.

[12] Cohn, "Logic" 342–43. Contra A. Sanda, *Die Bücher der Könige* (Münster: Aschendorffsche Verlagsbuchhandlung, 1911), 452; Leah Bronner, *The Stories of Elijah and Elisha: As Polemics Against Baal Worship*, Pretoria Oriental Series, ed. A. Van Selms (Leiden: E. J. Brill, 1968), 26–27; and Burke O. Long, *1 Kings: With an Introduction to Historical Literature* (Grand Rapids: Eerdmans, 1984), 200. Bronner and Long argue from the parallels with Moses and God's appearance to Elijah that this is to be viewed by the reader as a recommissioning of the prophet. They fail to consider the fairly negative nature of the interaction between Elijah and God. But Cohn may go too far in his evaluation. If God were as displeased as Cohn maintains, it would be hard to reconcile that displeasure with His provision of food (1 Kings 19:5–8) and with His theophany. Perhaps it is preferable to say that God was showing Elijah that the significant part of his ministry was over; but this is not the same as Elijah being "fired."

[13] Dumbrell, "Elijah," 15–18. Cf. also R. A. Carlson, "Élie àL'Horeb," *Vetus Testamentum* 19 (1969): 438–39.

[14] Dumbrell, "Elijah," 18–19. Cf. also Gene Rice, *Nations Under God: A Commentary on the Book of 1 Kings* (Grand Rapids: Eerdmans, 1990), 163, who writes, "At Horeb Elijah learns . . . that despite appearances to the contrary, God is in control, . . . that God's timetable may differ from ours, and that the final victory may rest with a future generation and with other leaders God has already chosen."

[15] Cohn ("Logic," 347) maintains also that the miracles Elijah experienced emphasize God's sovereignty and increased participation in the affairs of His people. In 1 Kings 17:22, God acted indirectly through Elijah to restore life to the widow's son; in 18:38, God acts more visibly on behalf of Elijah; and in 19:12ff., the theophany is an even more direct display of God's power. Thus the author presents God's intervention as

increasingly more direct, even to the point of Elijah becoming virtually unnecessary.

[16] There are other points in 1 Kings 19:10–18 worth consideration. Brevard Childs and Gene Rice rightly maintain that the repetition of the questions God asked of Elijah in 19:9 and 13 were reproofs rather than a request for information (Brevard Childs, "On Reading the Elijah Narratives," *Interpretation* 34 [1980]: 134–35; Rice, *Nations Under God,* 158–59). Elijah's response(s) in 19:10 and 14 to God's questions are also informative. The first words of Elijah's responses were קַנֹּא קִנֵּאתִי, which Simon J. DeVries translates as "I have been furiously zealous for Yahweh" ("1 Kings," in vol. 12 of *Word Biblical Commentary* [Waco: Word, 1985], 237). The infinitive absolute frequently carries a strongly emphatic force, as Ronald J. Williams maintains [*Hebrew Syntax: An Outline,* 2d ed. (Toronto: University of Toronto, 1976), 37–38]). Alan J. Hauser and Russel Gregory maintain that Elijah's statement in 19:14 (אִוָּתֵר אֲנִי לְבַדִּי, "and I alone am left") suggests that Elijah had an overinflated view of himself and his role in the fight against Baal, as if he were indispensable (*From Carmel to Horeb: Elijah in Crisis* [Sheffield: The Almond, 1990], 75). Each of these points emphasizes God's sovereignty in the preservation of a remnant.

[17] Cf. 108–9, and esp. n. 9, p. 109.

[18] Cohn, "Logic," 334.

[19] Cf. Peter Stuhlmacher, "Zur Interpretation von Römer 1125–32," in *Probleme biblischer Theologie: Gerhard von Rad zum 70. Geburtstag,* ed. Hans Walter Wolff (München: Chr. Kaiser Verlag, 1971), 557; Johannes Munck, *Christ & Israel: An Interpretation of Romans 9–11* (Philadelphia: Fortress, 1967), 136; Käsemann, *Romans,* 300; Cranfield, *Romans,* 2:547; John Murray, "The Epistle to the Romans," in *NICNT* (Grand Rapids: Eerdmans, 1965), 2:68; James D. G. Dunn, "Romans 9–16," in *Word Biblical Commentary* (Dallas: Word, 1988), 681.

[20] I have attempted to demonstrate elsewhere that πᾶς Ἰσραήλ in Romans 11:26 does not necessarily refer to the nation as a whole (Michael G. Vanlaningham, "Romans 11:25–27 and the Future of Israel in Paul's Thought," *The Master's Seminary Journal* 3 [1992]: 141–74, esp. 158–64). The many uses of the phrase in the LXX support the idea that πᾶς Ἰσραήλ refers only to whatever group of Jews is in the immediate context where the phrase occurs, and usually does not refer to the nation as a whole.

[21] Cf. Hasel, *Remnant,* 171–73; Leon Morris, *The Epistle to the Romans* (Grand Rapids: Zondervan, 1988), 399; C. K. Barrett, *A Commentary on the Epistle to the Romans,* 2d ed., BNTC (London: A & C Black, 1991), 194.

CHAPTER SIX

Romans 11:25–27

The Future of Israel in Paul's Thought

Michael G. Vanlaningham

Ethnic Israel is a dominant theme in Scripture, particularly as it pertains to the future. Paul divulges some key elements in his own Spirit-inspired thinking on this subject in Romans 11:25–27. He looks forward to a time of salvation for the Jewish people by divulging hitherto unrevealed details about their future, i.e., their salvation will follow the bringing in of a prescribed number of Gentiles. Currently beset by a partial spiritual hardening toward God, a significant group of Jews will experience a future repentance and salvation. This will come at some future point in the church age, perhaps as one of the series of events that will compose Christ's second coming. Paul adduces proof of this salvation with two quotations from Isaiah. Through this significant passage God's future program for Israel becomes clearer than before.

* * * * *

Significant contemporary interest surrounds the subject of the Jewish nation. Israel's prominent and permanent place throughout the Bible has been a focus of dispensational theology. A recognition of this prominence is one of the marks distinguishing that system from covenant theology that has often assumed that Israel's privileges and promises have been transferred to the church. The crux of the matter is, Does Israel have a future? The future of Israel is a focal point from both secular and biblical perspectives, a subject that requires understanding for anyone attempting to discern present trends and their relationship to theological themes. Romans 11:25–27 is one of the key Scriptures that teach about this subject. It is worthy of the closest scrutiny in a quest for information on this vital subject.

The following discussion will examine the Romans passage to ascertain Paul's concept of the future of Israel by investigating the hardening of Israel (v. 25a), the identity of "all Israel" (v. 26), the timing of Israel's salvation (v. 26), and the manner of the salvation's accomplishment (vv. 26b–27).

ROMANS 11:25—THE CIRCUMSTANCES SURROUNDING ISRAEL'S SALVATION

An explanatory γάρ (*gar,* "for") links Romans 11:25 closely with 11:24 and the reasoning of the passage up to verse 25.[1] In 11:7–10, Paul has described the divine perspective regarding a hardening that has afflicted the non-elect of Israel, accounting for their rejection of the Messiah. In 11:11–24, Paul has argued that this hardening of Israel has given the Gentile world an opportunity to be recipients of blessings from the Messiah.

While the primary emphasis in this section is the relationship of the salvation of Gentiles and very few Jews, there are hints woven throughout it that Israel "has not stumbled so as to fall" (11:11), that Paul's ministry to the Gentiles would provoke the Jews to envy so that they would seek their own Messiah (11:14), that there would be a restoration of Israel that would be "life from the dead" (11:15), that there was the promise of a spiritual restoration of Jews because of the presence of some who had accepted their Messiah (11:16),[2] and finally, that the Jews could be grafted in once again if they did not persist in their unbelief (11:23).

The explanatory *gar* beginning verse 25 develops the hints of a possible future restoration of the Jews, and how this restoration fits with God's historical plans for salvation of the Gentiles.

The phrase οὐ . . . θέλω ὑμᾶς ἀγνοεῖν, ἀδελφοί (*ou . . . thelō hymas agnoein, adelphoi,* "I do not want you to be ignorant, brethren," v. 25) occurs in other connections in Paul to highlight what he is about to say and to ensure the full attention of his readers (Rom. 1:13; 1 Cor. 10:1; 12:1; 2 Cor. 1:8; 1 Thess. 4:13).[3] In the expression ἵνα μὴ ἦτε [παρ '] ἑαυτοῖς φρόνιμοι (*hina mē ēte [par'] heautois phronimoi,* "that you not be wise in your own estimation," v. 25), the writer reiterates briefly the warning against arrogant thinking toward the Jews on the part of the Gentile believers in the Roman church (cf. v. 20). Ἵνα (*hina,* "That") expresses his purpose in revealing the mystery regarding the hardening of Israel. He was supremely concerned that Gentile believers understand that Israel was not "finished" in the program of God, having been replaced by Gentile believers.[4] Paul opposed a smug attitude in the church against Jewish constituents, especially in light of the Jewish role in God's future plans.[5]

ROMANS 11:25b —THE MEANING
AND IDENTITY OF "MYSTERY"

One of the more difficult points of interpretation in 11:25–27 is the meaning and identification of τὸ μυστήριον (*to mystērion,* "the mystery"). The earliest known uses of the word are in works related to the Greek mystery religions. These denote secret rites or teachings known only by the initiated of a religious cult. Later the word spoke more generally of a secret of any kind. Its only uses in the LXX are eight occurrences in Daniel, where Daniel spoke of an eschatological secret pertaining to what God has decreed for the future (Dan. 2:28). A similar usage was in the Jewish apocalyptic writings, where it also designated a divine secret of God that He alone discloses through revelation at the appointed time. The Jewish background of the word influenced Paul more strongly than the Greek.[6]

Complicating the understanding of "mystery" in verse 25 is the use of the word in the NT to refer to spiritual truths revealed in the OT, but revealed in the OT with varying degrees of obscurity. In the case of the rapture of the church, called a mystery in 1 Corinthians 15:51, no unequivocal OT revelation treated this event (thus making it very obscure, even hidden).[7] No clear explanation of this event occurred prior to its unveiling to Paul and thus to the church.

Some truth related to a mystery may be the subject of revelation in the OT, but the mystery itself is hidden until at God's appointed time it becomes a manifest event.[8] Ephesians 3:4–5 reflects this "present-in-the-OT-but-unclear, then clarified-in-the-NT" use of mystery,[9] as does Romans 16:25–26.[10] Extrabiblical support for this understanding of *mystērion* is in the Dead Sea Scrolls (especially 1QpHab. 7:4, "[To the Teacher of Righteousness] God made known all the mysteries of the words of His servants the Prophets," and CD. 3:12–14, "[God was] revealing to them [the righteous remnant of the Qumran community] the hidden things in which all Israel had gone astray")[11] where the mystery is revelation from God *regarding the clarification of spiritual truths already revealed in the OT.* These parallels illumine Paul's use of *mystērion* in Romans 11:25. The OT had much to say regarding the Messiah and the inclusion of Gentiles in blessings through the seed of Abraham, but God gave further revelation to deepen the knowledge of His people regarding broad OT themes present.[12]

It was not new revelation that Gentiles would be blessed through the seed of Abraham (cf. Gen. 12:3; etc.), nor was it new revelation that God could harden the Jews (cf. Rom. 11:8–9 where Paul cites Deut. 29:4; Isa. 29:10; Ps. 69:22–23). Therefore, neither of these points is identifiable as Paul's mystery in verse 25.

Two viable options for the content of the mystery remain. Possibly what Paul calls the mystery is the way the hardening of the Jews relates to the salvation of the Gentiles. Ridderbos maintains that the mystery pertains to the "back and forth" fashion in which the salvation is effected, beginning first with the Jews, then after the divine hardening, encompassing the Gentiles whose blessings from salvation in turn provoke the Jews to jealousy and consequently salvation in Christ as well.[13] The "back and forth" characteristic applies, but it is discussed in 11:11–24, with verse 25 contributing nothing new to it.[14]

A second option is preferable. What is new both in the context of Romans 11 and in salvation history is the *order* of salvation of the Gentiles and of "all Israel." The salvation of Israel will not occur until the "fullness of the Gentiles has come in."[15] This understanding of *mystērion* has much in its favor. It fits well with the concept of "mystery" as new revelation or as an extensive development and clarification of previously given revelation. What is not new is the blessing of the Gentiles and the hardening of the Jews; what is new (not seen in the OT but revealed here) is the *sequence of salvation* for Jews and Gentiles.[16] This view finds further support in τοῦτο (*touto*, "this"), which probably looks forward to the dependent clause introduced by ὅτι (*hoti*, "that"), which in turn designates the remainder of verses 25–27 as the content of that mystery.[17]

ROMANS 11:25c—THE HARDENING OF ISRAEL

The phrase ὅτι πώρωσις ἀπὸ μέρους τῷ Ἰσραὴλ γέγονεν (*hoti pōrōsis apo merous tō Israēl gegonen,* "that hardness in part has happened to Israel") furnishes the first element of the mystery. The concept of hardening comes frequently in the OT[18] and in the literature of Early Judaism.[19] In the NT, πώρωσις (*pōrōsis,* "hardness") occurs only two other times (Mark 3:5; Eph. 4:18). In both instances it refers metaphorically to hardness of heart (the hard-heartedness of the Jewish witnesses of Jesus' ministry and the hard-heartedness of Gentiles alienated from God, respectively). In 11:25 it means "dullness, insensibility, obstinacy,"[20] conveying the notion of a condition that leaves part of Israel unresponsive to the gospel and excluded from salvation.[21] God is the agent behind the hardening (cf. 11:8, ὁ θεός [*ho theos,* "God"]).

The Extent of the Hardening

The phrase ἀπὸ μέρους (*apo merous,* "in part") expresses the extent of the hardening. The precise meaning and syntactical relationship of this phrase has engendered much debate. One of the problems associated with the phrase is determining whether it is adjectival, adverbial, or temporal in force. There is evidence for an adverbial use in the fact that *apo merous* is roughly like the classical use of phrases such as κατὰ μέρους (*kata merous*, "according to a part") and μέρος τι (*meros ti*, "some part"), and on this basis, according to Tholuck, "cannot well signify anything else but *in part*. . . ." The preposition ἀπὸ (*apo*, "in"), when used with substantives in classical Greek, commonly has an adverbial force. Furthermore, *apo merous* is roughly parallel to the τινες (*tines*, "some, certain ones") of 11:17, and stands somewhat in contrast to πᾶς Ἰσραήλ (*pas Israēl*, "all Israel") of 11:26.[22]

Käsemann maintains that *apo merous* is adjectival and connects it with *pōrōsis*, with the resulting sense "*a partial hardening* has come upon Israel." This connection finds support in 11:7 through the reference to the hardening upon non-Christian Jews alone, leaving Jewish Christianity unaffected by the hardening.[23] Yet this is weak in that Paul apparently deals *extensively* with the numeric expanse of the hardening rather than *intensively* with its severity.

The temporal interpretation of *apo merous* is probably the least defensible. Hodge maintains that the phrase is temporal in Romans 15:24 and that ἄχρι οὗ (*achri hou*, "until") (11:25), which is also temporal, supports the same understanding of *apo merous*.[24] Against a temporal understanding, however, is the emphasis of Paul throughout Romans 11. It is arguably more natural to understand the phrase to refer to numbers rather than time.[25] Also, the position of the phrase and its apparent antithesis to *pas Israēl* speak against such a temporal force.[26] A temporal interpretation of *apo merous* is unlikely in 2 Corinthians 1:14 and 2:5, suggesting that Paul usually intends the phrase to be non-temporal. If he had temporal matters in mind, he possibly would have used a phrase like τὸ νῦν (*to nyn*, "the present") instead.[27]

Although the problem is difficult, the adverbial force has stronger support. A further issue relates to the phrase. Should *apo merous* connect with γέγονεν (*gegonen*, "has happened"),[28] Israēl,[29] or *pōrōsis*?[30] It is preferable to see the phrase modifying *gegonen*, a verb (based on other Pauline usage), but a choice of any of the three options does not affect the essential meaning, since interpreters choosing different connections have reached the same conclusion: only a part of all the people of Israel are hardened.

The Time-frame for the Hardening

A time-frame for this hardening is suggested by the clause ἄχρι οὗ . . . εἰσέλθῃ (*achri hou . . . eiselthē*, "until . . . has come in"). The phrase (*achri hou*) is a shortened form of ἄχρι τοῦ χρόνου ᾧ . . . (*achri tou chronou hō* . . . , "until the time at which . . .").[31] The precise nature of its temporal force has been a subject for strenuous debate. It appears to denote a time after which the hardening of Israel will cease, bringing a change in her spiritual condition. New Testament usage of the phrase elsewhere may overturn this understanding, however. In a number of passages it can plausibly mean "while" or even "during and after,"[32] implying the possibility in the present passage that the hardening of Israel does not stop when the fullness of the Gentiles arrives, but rather that it continues during *and after* the fullness comes in.[33] In other words, *achri hou* may not refer to a new spiritual "beginning" for Israel after a future point (the fullness of the Gentiles); instead, it may refer to prevailing circumstances for Israel *even after the fullness of the Gentiles has come in.*[34]

This view of *achri hou* has been challenged. Murray contends that though it may mean "while" in some contexts, in Romans 11:25 that meaning is unnatural, especially in light of the aorist εἰσέλθῃ (*eiselthē,* "has come in"). He writes,

> In every other instance in the New Testament, whether used with the aorist or future, the meaning "until" is the necessary rendering and indicates a point of eventuation or a point at which something took place (cf. Acts 7:18; 1 Cor. 11:26; 15:25; Gal. 3:19; Rev. 2:25). Hence in Romans 11:25 it would require a departure from the pattern to render the clause other than "until the fulness of the Gentiles will come in". The context makes this the necessary interpretation of the force of the clause in question.[35]

Also opposed to the meaning of "while" for *achri hou* are the verses cited to support that interpretation.[36] The most that can be said from these passages to support the contention of DeCaro, Robertson, and Woudstra is that the hardening of Israel may briefly *overlap* the coming in of the Gentiles' fullness, only to be canceled shortly thereafter. Hence, in Romans 11:25, *achri hou* points to a time (the arrival of the fullness of the Gentiles) after which the hardening of Israel will cease.

Identifying the "fullness of the Gentiles" has been difficult for interpreters. The *Greek-English Lexicon of the New Testament* prefers the meaning "fulfiling" or "fulfilment" in Romans 11:12 (cf. Rom. 13:10 also) but stipulates that some prefer "that which is brought to fullness or completion, full number, sum total, fullness, superabundance of something" in that verse (cf. Rom. 15:29; Col. 1:19; 2:9 also).[37]

Space considerations permit only a presentation of conclusions regarding the use of this word in Paul's writings. In his classic essay on *plērōma,* Lightfoot writes,

Substantially one meaning runs through all the passages hither quoted from St. Paul. In these πλήρωμα *(plērōma)* has its proper passive force [that which is filled, rather than that which fills], as a derivative from πληροῦν *(plēroun,* "to fill") 'to make complete.' . . . It is . . . the full complement, the plentitude, the fulness.[38]

When analyzing Romans 11:25, he adds that the word refers to "the full number, the whole body."[39] But even with this conclusion, the precise meaning of *pēlrōma* in connection with τῶν ἐθνῶν *(tōn ethnōn,* "the Gentiles") in the verse is contested.

The "fullness of the Gentiles" has been interpreted in two ways: qualitatively and quantitatively.

1. In a qualitative sense it refers to the full blessings of the Gentiles. This view finds support in the contrast of 11:12 between to *plērōma* and the spiritual conditions of τὸ παράπτωμα *(to paraptōma,* "the transgression") and τὸ ἥττημα *(to hēttēma,* "loss, defeat"). Neither provides a suitable opposite to *plērōma* if it is understood in an arithmetic sense of "full number."[40]

2. A second view is that the "fullness of the Gentiles" is quantitative, referring to the "full number" or the "numerical whole" of the Gentiles, though it probably does not encompass every individual Gentile. Rather it denotes a large representation of Gentiles from throughout the world. This is the preferred view with several scholars[41] and finds support in Paul's frequent discussion of numbers throughout Romans 11.[42] A few important references from early Judaism reflecting the apparently common belief in an eschatological conversion of a large number of Gentiles add credence to this position.[43]

Deciding between the two options is not easy, but the second has a somewhat stronger case. Even Murray recognizes that *plērōma* does not exclude a numerical connotation and that a combination of the views may be preferable to excluding one or the other.[44] Besides, understanding *plērōma* in a numeric sense with spiritual overtones provides an adequate rejoinder to the objection that to *plērōma* does not provide a logical contrast with to *paraptōma* and to *hēttēma* in 11:12. The better interpretation sees Paul as pointing to the spiritual conversion of a large number of Gentiles.

This conclusion does not resolve all the problems with the phrase "the fullness of the Gentiles," however. Those who embrace a quantitative understanding of the phrase disagree about the manner and time in which this fullness is reached. This issue is closely related to the timing of the salvation of all Israel that is more fully discussed below.

One of the factors in determining the time of the arrival of Gentile fullness is the correct understanding of the verb *eiselthē* (v. 25). Though εἰσέρχομαι *(eiserchomai)* has the basic meaning of "come in/into," "go in/into," "enter,"[45] the term's significance in the present context is not completely clear.

The verb occurs in the Gospels in reference to entering the messianic kingdom or eternal life,[46] so many scholars take the phrase τὸ πλήρωμα τῶν ἐθνῶν εἰσέλθῃ *(to plērōma tōn ethnōn eiselthē,* "the fullness of the Gentiles come in") to refer to the fulfilment of God's purpose in bringing the Gentiles into the messianic kingdom.[47] Yet several reasons make this view unsatisfactory. Though *eiserchomai* ("enter") is used frequently for entering the kingdom or eternal life, the majority of its 194 NT occurrences have no eschatological technical sense.[48] More importantly, Paul uses *eiserchomai* elsewhere only in Romans 5:12 and 1 Corinthians 14:23–24, with neither passage containing eschatological connotations. With a thorough discussion of the timing of the fullness of the Gentiles and the salvation of all Israel yet to follow, this much can be concluded: it is preferable to understand *eiserchomai* in a nontechnical, noneschatological sense. The more defensible sense in 11:25 is the one suggested by Black who says it is better to view Paul's use of *eiserchomai* as parallel to its use in the LXX for the Hebrew בּוֹא *(bôʾ,* "he comes"), which means simply "has come," "has arrived," and so "has been realized."[49] In summary, Paul does not use the verb in an eschatological sense, and the context, while referring to events future to Paul, does not refer unequivocally to the future messianic kingdom or eternity as the other view requires, further proof of which will follow below. The verb refers to the arrival of the fullness of the Gentiles with no allusion to the Gentiles entering the kingdom or eternity.

ROMANS 11:26–27:
THE CIRCUMSTANCES OF SALVATION

The Manner of Salvation

With the phrase καὶ οὕτως *(kai houtōs,* "and thus") (v. 26) Paul changes from the order and time of salvation in 11:25 to consider primarily the manner of the salvation of all Israel in 11:26–27.

Viewing 11:26–27 as instruction about the manner of salvation of the Jews presupposes a modal, non-temporal use of οὕτως *(houtōs,* "thus"), which is problematic. Some scholars maintain the phrase is best understood temporally, resulting in the following sense: "There will be a time of hardening until the fullness of the Gentiles arrives, *and then* all Israel will be saved." Classical Greek usage supports the temporal explanation of *kai houtōs*,[50] as does NT usage in Acts 17:33.[51] In Paul it is probably temporal in 1 Corinthians 11:28; 14:25; 1 Thessalonians 4:17.[52] Further support for the temporal view comes in the deictic *achri hou* (v. 25) as well. The temporal understanding has several important drawbacks, however. The passages from Paul cited as possibly temporal can be as easily (and perhaps more favorably) understood as nontemporal.[53] In Robertson's opinion not a single one of the seventy-three occurrences of *houtōs* in Paul can be viewed as certainly temporal.[54] In addition, in the nine places where Paul writes *kai houtōs* in the same order as 11:26, no temporal understanding is probably justified.[55] On the basis of these observations, a purely temporal force to the phrase is improbable.

The key word in the previous statement is *purely*. A number of credible scholars maintain that though *houtōs* on its own is not temporal, the context virtually infuses such a sense into it in verse 26 because of the strong sequential emphasis surrounding *houtōs*. Therefore, *houtōs* is probably best understood as modal and not primarily temporal, but it is modal with a temporal ambiance.[56] Verses 26–27 are essentially concerned with the manner of Israel's salvation, one aspect of which is its future occurrence.

A further problem associated with *kai houtōs* is determining whether it is retrospective (looking back to what Paul has written in v. 25) or prospective (looking ahead to vv. 26ff.). Jeremias refers *houtōs* back to verse 25 and the hardening of Israel, the salvation of the Gentiles, and the reversal in order of salvation (Gentiles preceding Jews). He says that to construe the adverb with καθώς (*kathōs*, "just as") (v. 26), which follows, is contrary to typical Pauline syntax.[57] But a review of other uses of the οὕτως . . . καί (*houtōs . . . kai*, "thus . . . also") construction, including those in Paul, divulges that they do not shed much light on the problem.[58] Cranfield offers the sanest advice:

> With καὶ οὕτως (*kai houtōs*, "and thus") begins the last of the three parts of the content of the μυστήριον (*mystērion*, "mystery"), the part on which the main stress falls (it is the part which is supported by the OT quotation which follows). The word οὕτως (*houtōs*) is emphatic: it will be in this way, and only in this way, that is, in the circumstances which are indicated by the first two parts of the statement [i.e., (1) πώρωσις . . . γέγονεν (*pōrōsis . . . gegonen*, "hardness . . . has come about"); (2) ἄχρι οὗ . . . εἰσέλθῃ (*achri hou . . . eiselthē*, "until . . . enters")], that πᾶς Ἰσραήλ (*pas Israēl*, "all Israel") will be saved. The οὕτως (*houtōs*, "thus") indicates an inver-

sion of the order in which salvation is actually offered to men according to 1.16. . . .[59]

The Identity of the Saved

Regarding the identification of πᾶς Ἰσραήλ (*pas Israēl,* "all Israel"), there are two basic views.[60] One view, held by John Calvin, refers the expression to the church as the new spiritual Israel, comprised of both Jews and Gentiles. An appeal made to Galatians 6:16 ("the Israel of God") supports this view, but the more probable interpretation of the Galatians passage fails to support this conclusion.[61] A consistent interpretation of Old and New Testaments requires that the two peoples be distinguished from each other.

A second view on the meaning of "all Israel" is better here. "All Israel" in verse 26 must have the same sense as "Israel" in 11:25 ("a hardness has come in part on Israel"). The context requires that *Israēl* be understood to refer to *ethnic* Israel, mentioned in 11:23 ("if they [ethnic Israel] do not continue in unbelief") and 11:30–32 in a contrast between Gentiles and Jews.[62]

Beyond this conclusion four options for the sense of "ethnic Israel" remain.

1. One is that ethnic Israel refers to the elect among the Jews saved throughout the entirety of the church age.[63] This finds support in the progressive salvation of increasing numbers of Jews throughout this age concurrently with the salvation of Gentiles. When the full number of the Gentiles comes in, then the full number of elect Jews will be saved too.[64] According to Horne, to view 11:25–32 as referring to the future salvation of *national* Israel (Israel as a whole, as a nation) disregards the entire thrust of Romans 9–11, a context where Paul adamantly denies that salvation is afforded to the nation (i.e., all ethnic Israel) as such. Horne writes,

> I would state therefore in summary that when Paul states that "all Israel shall be saved" he means to refer to the full number of elect Jews whom it pleases God to bring into his kingdom throughout the ages until the very day when the full number of the Gentiles also shall have been brought in. In keeping with the context, "all Israel" means "the remnant according to the election of grace" (11:5), not the nation in its entirety.[65]

This view has several weaknesses. If "all Israel" is simply the elect from ethnic Israel who are saved along with the Gentiles throughout the age, special revelation to Paul in the form of a *mystērion* (v. 25) is pointless, since it was clear to him and everyone else even superficially familiar with Christianity in the first century that some Jews were being saved. Also militating against this view is the consideration that the salvation of all Israel comes at a particular point in time in the future as indicated by *achri hou . . . eiselthē* (v. 25) as well as by the future σωθήσεται (*sōthēsetai,* "will be saved") (v. 26).[66] To conceive of "all Israel" as elect Jews saved throughout the church age is unconvincing.

2. A second option associated with "ethnic Israel" is to refer it to Israel as a whole. Some scholars maintain that "Israel" in Romans 9–11 denotes the Jewish people as a totality, and not the multitude of individual Jews. The main support of this view is that the saved in "all Israel" consist in both the believing remnant *and* the hardened remainder of Israel. Paul is looking forward to a time when not only the remnant but those of Israel who have strayed will be saved. Furthermore, the concept of "Israel as a whole" finds support in the fact that *pas Israēl* stands in contrast to the λεῖμμα (*leimma,* "remnant") of 11:5 and τινες (*tines,* "some, certain ones") of 11:17.[67]

Several deficiencies in the view are apparent, however. First, "Israel as a whole" is rather ill defined. Several maintain that *pas Israēl* refers to Israel as a whole, but not every individual Jew is included in the salvation.[68] If by this they mean that enough of the individuals in future Israel have exercised faith in Christ to say that the nation or people as a whole are saved, then this is an acceptable view. Otherwise, their definition is incongruous. Second, as will be argued under the third view below, *pas Israēl* was used in the LXX to refer to a group of Jews, with the size of that group left unspecified. Hence, to say that *pas Israēl* means "the people or nation as a whole" may be unjustifiably specific based on LXX usage. Third, this view is shaped by some (e.g., Stendahl and Dunn) to argue that Paul's goal was not to maintain a sense of individualism in the future salvation of the Jews, but to affirm the salvation of the Jewish people as a consolidated group. In Stendahl's case, the salvation of the entire group is distinct from the individuals' exercise of faith in Jesus Christ. This approach is difficult to sustain in light of repeated emphasis on individuals in Romans 9–11.[69]

3. A third option, the strongest of the first three, is that "all Israel" refers to a future group (of unspecified size, though probably a majority) of elect Jews alive at the time of the fullness of the Gentiles. A number of considerations support this. In his helpful study of "all Israel" in 1–2 Chronicles (LXX), Osborne has derived some intriguing observations from a survey of thirty-four uses of the phrase. In his record of the United Kingdom, the Chronicler used "all Israel" to describe the support David had from the Jewish people before his coronation (1 Chron. 11:10; 12:38),

the soldiers of Israel (1 Chron. 19:17), Israel's civic and military leaders (1 Chron. 15:25, 28), and the consolidated kingdom over which David reigned (1 Chron. 14:8).[70]

In relation to the divided kingdom, the phrase was used for the group that was to participate in the crowning of Rehoboam (2 Chron. 10:3) and for Judah alone (2 Chron. 12:1). It was apparently ". . . used specifically for those who are loyal to the king and the cult of Yahweh, and the people from the Northern Kingdom are included if they meet the criterion."[71]

For the period of the fall of the northern kingdom through the exile, "all Israel" was used corporately for the whole nation, whose sins needed to be expiated through sacrifice (2 Chron. 29:24; cf. also 31:1) and for those who were loyal to the the Lord (2 Chron. 35:3).

Osborne concludes,

> This term usually means those people who attach themselves to the Davidic house and to the worship of Yahweh. . . . The term always has the theological meaning of "the people of God." "All Israel" in its final definition is a term signifying the representatives of Israel who attach themselves to the Davidic figure, the king, in an expression of loyalty. This suggests that in Romans 11:26a "all Israel" is a term designating a majority of people loyal to the messiah, the Davidic figure. It is a collective word used for a whole people who may or may not have saving faith. It never has an individualistic connotation.[72]

Osborne's findings require a number of qualifications. First, his final two statements in the otherwise helpful quotation above are in a sense true. "All Israel" is collective, and hence does not always refer (in the OT) to saved individuals. But many passages in 1–2 Chronicles and other OT passages in which "all Israel" occurs, do specify what kinds of individuals make up "all Israel" (i.e., tribal leaders, military leaders, soldiers, etc.). "All Israel" may refer to a group, but individualistic connotations are not absolutely eclipsed.

Second, the picture painted by the OT use of "all Israel" is neither as simple nor as attractive as Osborne makes it.[73] In 1–2 Chronicles *pas Israēl* may refer to those loyal to the king or to the Lord, but in Judges 8:27, for example, "all Israel" played the harlot and pursued idolatry. A further example is 1 Samuel 13:20: "all Israel" was forced to have its tools sharpened by the Philistines. "All Israel" might even be inclined to help dethrone David (2 Sam. 17:13). In 1 Kings 12:16, "all Israel" (here restricted to the northern tribes) rejects Rehoboam as king and stones

Adoram, the king's representative (1 Kings 12:18). These excerpts indicate a more fluid use of "all Israel" than Osborne implies.

Finally, it may be possible to take the diverse uses of "all Israel" and find a common denominator that is more all-encompassing than Osborne's rather incomplete synthesis. As one investigates the many occurrences of "all Israel," a meaning no more technical than "the Jews" emerges—specifically, the Jews who are in the immediate context of the phrase "all Israel."[74] Thus "all Israel" could be the Jews that made up a relatively small group of soldiers (1 Kings 11:16), the Jews who buried Samuel (1 Sam. 25:1), the Jews who were in close proximity to Korah at his demise (Num. 16:34), and the Jews who, with King Rehoboam, apostasized (2 Chron. 12:1). Second Samuel 3:37 is an especially interesting use of *pas Israēl*: "So all the people and all Israel understood that day that it had not been the will of the king to put Abner the son of Ner to death." Note the distinction between "all the people" (πᾶς ὁ λαός *[pas ho laos]*) and "all Israel" (*pas Israēl*). The author could have written simply "all Israel" instead of using both "all the people" and "all Israel," but he apparently wanted to distinguish between those more intimately associated with and in closer proximity to King David, *pas ho laos* (cf. 2 Sam. 3:31–32, 34–36), and a wider group, *pas Israēl*.

4. A fourth option in the meaning of *pas Israēl* in Romans 11:26 is seemingly a more defensible interpretation of the phrase. The above data shows that Paul intended the phrase to convey nothing more than this: "And thus *the Jews* [i.e., as suggested by the context, those who are alive and have faith in Christ at the time of the fullness of the Gentiles] will be saved."[75] Hence, *pas Israēl* contains no hint of the size of the group (a majority, or Israel as a whole), but instead is simply a nonspecific statement that Jews in the future *will* be saved. This group of Jews is probably at least a majority because their salvation was such a consuming hope for Paul and a minority remnant would not have satisfied his longings. But from the wide range of usage in the OT, *pas Israēl* cannot be pressed to yield such a specific understanding.

The Time of Israel's Salvation

The verb *sōthēsetai* provides a natural occasion to consider more fully the time of Israel's salvation and the fullness of the Gentiles. Four opinions regarding when these events take place have surfaced: (1) in Paul's immediate future; (2) throughout the church age; (3) at a time in the more remote future, but still during the church age; and (4) at the second coming. View 2 was discussed above in connection with the first explanation of *pas Israēl* (i.e., that it refers to Jews saved throughout the church age), and was found to be unsatisfactory.

1. The first option is that Paul envisioned the fullness of the Gentiles and salvation of Israel taking place in his own immediate future. Aus offers one of the most articulate defenses of this position. He envisages Paul as anticipating the fulfilment of the many OT prophecies regarding the Gentiles who come to Jerusalem in messianic days. Romans 15:16 portrays Paul as foreseeing that his ministry in Spain would be the fulfilment of these OT prophecies (Isa. 60:1–3, 9; 66:18–20; Ps. 72:8–11).[76] However, Aus's work has several serious methodological flaws. First, he apparently has misread his OT texts (p. 241). He holds that Paul's offering of the Gentiles in Jerusalem would usher in the second coming, but in Isaiah 60:2–3; 66:19–20, it is the second coming that results in the gathering of Gentiles, Jews, and their offerings to Jerusalem. Second, he draws some unwarranted inferences, claiming that in Romans 15:16 the "offering of the Gentiles" is the Gentiles themselves (appositional genitive) because Paul is thinking of the eschatological doctrine of such an offering (pp. 236–37). He fails to demonstrate this eschatological element in Romans 15, however, and is reasoning circularly. He also avers that the "fullness of the Gentiles" in 11:25 and the offering of the Gentiles in Romans 15:16 are "intimately tied" (p. 242), but fails to show clues from either passage to demonstrate the connection.

Third, Aus maintains that Paul's collection for the Jerusalem church (including not only a sizeable amount of money, but also an impressive number of Gentile converts, thus fulfiling the prophetic "gathering" motif) had definite eschatological overtones (pp. 261–62), *though Paul never mentions these when discussing the collection.*[77] One must ask how Aus can discern that these eschatological hopes were important to Paul without Paul ever mentioning them.[78] Fourth, Aus has Paul revising OT motifs so completely as to make them unrecognizable. Instead of the Messiah coming (Isa. 60:2; 66:15–17, 19–20); restoring the nation Israel (Isa. 60:2); gathering Gentiles (Isa. 60:3; 66:18), who in turn gather dispersed Jews to Jerusalem (Isa. 66:19–20), Aus's reconstruction has Paul (a Jew) leading Gentiles to Jerusalem (Rom. 15:16) in hope of bringing about the end (Rom. 11:25c) and the Messiah's return. It is problematic to perceive of Paul as fulfiling any OT prophecies when what he was doing was so diverse from the OT. Finally, Romans 11:14 (σώσω τινάς ἐξ αὐτῶν [*kai sōsō tinas ex autōn,* "and I will save some of them"]) shows Paul's hopes to be high, but probably not so grandiose as Aus suggests. This view is fraught with enough problems to remove it from consideration.

2. See the first view regarding the meaning of *pas Israēl* discussed above.

3. The third view, that the fullness of the Gentiles and all Israel's salvation takes place in the more remote future but during the church age prior to

the second coming, is based on four inferences of the Romans text.
a. In Romans 11:12 and 15, the restoration of the Jews will have an
amazing impact on the world for an indeterminate time following this
restoration.[79] This weighs against the fourth view below, which interprets these events as taking place at the second coming.[80]
b. In Romans 11:23, the key for the "in-grafting" of the Jews is faith.
There is no clear indication in the context of 11:25–27 that this faith is
sparked by observing the second coming of Christ. Rather, faith may be
sparked as it is in Romans 10, through hearing the preached Word of God.
c. The salvation of all Israel entails the forgiveness of sins, which is
based on a covenant, according to 11:26b–27. In the NT the new covenant, of which Paul was a minister (2 Cor. 3:6), is probably the covenant intended in this passage. If the new covenant is in view, it is difficult
(though surely not impossible) to see how the salvation of all Israel and
the fullness of the Gentiles can take place at a time other than during the
church age.
d. Finally, in Romans 11:30–31, the deictic indicators πότε . . . νῦν . . . νῦν
. . . [νῦν] *(pote . . . nyn . . . nyn . . . [nyn],* "formerly . . . now . . . now . . .
[now]") are crucial to a correct understanding of the timing of the fullness and salvation. Dunn rightly sees the *pote/nyn* antithesis as a reference to the salvation-historical division of epochs, with *pote* expressing
the pre-Christ era and *nyn* expressing the arrival of messianic days.[81]
The final disputed *nyn*[82] should not be understood in a manner any different from the preceding two; Gentiles are being saved *now,* during the
present age; Israel is hardened *now,* during the present age; and Israel is
saved *now,* during the present age. No special eschatological sense for
the final *nyn* is justifiable. Therefore, the three occurrences of *nyn* refer
to the gospel era, the interim period before the second coming climaxed
by the salvation of Israel. Corley writes,

> It cannot be stated with precision whether this episode cul-
> minates in the *parousia* or merely precedes it in time; how-
> ever, the time period for the fulfilment of the prophecy has its
> *modus operandi* in gospel proclamation and its *terminus ad*
> *quem* at the return of Christ.[83]

The weaknesses of the third view lie in the nature of the evidence for
it. Its supporting arguments are admittedly inferential, with one of them,
the fourth, relying on a disputed textual variant.
4. A fourth view of the timing of the fullness of the Gentiles and the
salvation of all Israel, one not too distinguishable from the third, is that
these events take place at the very moment of the second coming of

Christ to earth. This is a popular view with interpreters,[84] and a fair amount of evidence has been proffered to support it. The context makes it probable that Paul is looking at the spiritual restoration of Israel as a whole *at the end,* making this salvation an eschatological event in the strict sense. Perhaps this coincides somewhat with Matthew 10:23b, and the conversion of all Israel will occur at the end of the age.[85] Apocalyptic literature in its anticipation that the *eschaton* would follow the repentance of all Israel also supports this explanation.[86] In addition, the future-tense verbs in 11:26–27 (σωθήσεται; ἥξει; ἀποστρέψει [*sōthēsetai; hēxei; apostrepsei,* "will be saved; will come; will turn"]) bolster this view.[87] Further, the quotations from Isaiah, being from eschatological/apocalyptic sections of that book, support a reference to the second coming of Christ. Also, ῥύομαι (*hryomai,* "I deliver") is used in 1 Thessalonians 1:10 to refer to Christ at His second coming; why not here?[88] Finally, the phrase ἐκ Σιών (*ek Siōn,* "from Zion") in 11:26b is probably a reference to the Messiah coming from the heavenly Jerusalem at His second coming.[89]

Several points vitiate this view, however. The future tense verbs may be understood as reflecting a future sense to *Isaiah,* but not to Paul. For Paul these verbs could refer to an already realized fulfilment of the Isaianic prophecies rather than to a fulfilment yet future to Paul.[90] This is Hvalvik's perception when he writes,

> For Paul the Deliverer has already come from Zion (cf. 9.33). This is clearly seen if one compares Rom. 11.28 with 15.8. In 11.26–28 the salvation of "all Israel" is linked with the promises to the fathers (cf. also 9.5), and in 15.8 Paul tells how these promises have been confirmed when "Christ became a servant to the circumcised." This means that God's truthfulness toward his promises is seen in Christ's first coming.[91]

Hvalvik also argues that *ek Siōn* may have been a pre-Pauline reading so that Paul did not change the LXX ἕνεκεν Σιών (*heneken Siōn,* "on account of Zion") to suit his needs.[92] But by the phrase *ek Siōn* Paul may have meant simply that the Messiah would come in His humanity from the Jewish people (Rom. 9:5),[93] or that the place of the Resurrection was earthly Jerusalem.[94] In Paul's other use of *Siōn* (Rom. 9:33) the reference is apparently to Jerusalem.[95] In summarizing the problems against the view that Paul refers to the second coming 11:25–27, Hvalvik notes, "If arguments are given [in support of the second coming], they are few and not very strong."[96] On the other hand, Hvalvik does not respond to all of the evidence to view 3 (e.g., the future tense *sōthēsetai* [v. 26] used by Paul outside his citations from Isaiah) and may be overly severe in criticizing it.

A conclusion about the timing of the fullness of the Gentiles and the salvation of all Israel must rule out the first and second views. A merging of views 3 and 4 is the probable solution. The timing of these events should probably be viewed as taking place during the church age at a specific time future to Paul (and not just future to Isaiah, view 3) and as occurring perhaps several years before Christ's second coming to earth.[97] Furthermore, Israel's conversion serves as a primary prerequisite for the second coming (hence the adjusted View 4).[98] To be more specific than this is to import theological presuppositions not readily supported by the text.

The Scriptural Proof of Israel's Salvation

A consideration of the purpose of the OT citations from Isaiah 59:20–21 and 27:9 (Rom. 11:26b–27) is in order. Hvalvik argues that these verses should not be seen as speaking of the *time* of Israel's salvation, but rather as the ground for the statement καὶ οὕτως πᾶς Ἰσραὴλ σωθήσεται (*kai houtōs pas Israēl sōthēsetai*, "and thus all Israel will be saved").[99] Paul's citation of the two passages from Isaiah are designed to strengthen his case for the restoration of Israel. His use of these verses from Isaiah is important to his argument.

An important change from the LXX in Paul's use of Isaiah 59:20 (alluded to above in the discussion of the fourth view of the timing of the salvation) is the switch from ἕνεκεν (*heneken,* "for the sake of," "to") to the use of ἐκ (*ek,* "from," "out from").[100] Schaller has examined the possibility of a variant Greek OT text that Paul may have been following, concluding that Paul did *not* simply adjust the text to fit it to his purposes, but probably relied on a variant.[101] This is possible (Schaller's arguments are cogent), but it is speculative and does not resolve anything.

In 11:26 Paul draws from Isaiah 59:21a the promise of the new covenant. Rather than continuing to cite the rest of 59:21, which tells of the promise of the Spirit, Paul shifts to Isaiah 27:9, emphasizing a different aspect of the new covenant, namely, the forgiveness of sins. The theme of forgiveness fits better with Paul's argument for the restoration of Israel than a reference to the gift of the Spirit; Paul has emphasized Israel's *paraptōma* and *hēttēma* (11:12) and her ἀπιστία (*apistia,* "unbelief") (11:23), and the need for forgiveness is strong in this chapter. Hence, the shift away from Isaiah 59:21b to Isaiah 27:9 is explicable. So Paul's use of the prophecies of Isaiah fits well with the essential thrust of his argument in Romans 11.

Paul's use of ῥυόμενος (*hryomenos,* "deliverer") is significant to some scholars. Getty notes that whenever Paul uses the verb *hryomai*, he uses it in reference to God (Rom. 7:24; 15:31; 2 Cor. 1:10). No doubt Isaiah used it with God as its referent,[102] suggesting that God, and not Christ, is in view in 11:26. However, the rabbis apparently saw Isaiah 59:20 as messianic (cf. *b.Sanh.* 98a),[103] and it is hard to believe that Paul would have used it referring to any other than Christ.[104]

The phrase ἀποστρέψει ἀσεβείας ἀπὸ Ἰακώβ (*apostrepsei asebeias apo Iakōb,* "will turn ungodliness away from Jacob")[105] is an important link with Romans 4. Hvalvik writes,

> These words in the quotation are significant particularly be-
> cause they form a link to Rom. 4, the great chapter concern-
> ing justification by faith. In 4.5 Paul is speaking about the
> God "who justifies the ungodly (τὸν ἀσεβῆ [*ton asebē,* "the
> ungodly"])" and it is the same God who speaks in the quota-
> tion from Scripture. In 4.7 Paul quotes from Psalm 31.1 the
> word about those "whose sins (αἱ ἁμαρτίαι [*hai hamartiai,*
> "the sins"]) are covered"—it is they who are justified by faith,
> without works. These connecting lines clearly indicate that
> when Paul speaks about the salvation of Israel in 11:25–27,
> he refers to justification of the ungodly and justification by
> faith. Israel's salvation is thus nothing else but salvation *sola
> fide and sola gratia.*[106]

Thus the Isaiah quotations fit well again with Paul's Romans emphasis on salvation from sin and ungodliness by grace through faith.

In 11:27a, the phrase καὶ αὕτη αὐτοῖς ἡ παρ᾽ ἐμοῦ διαθήκη (*kai hautē autois hē par᾽ emou diathēkē,* "and this is the covenant from Me with them") is best understood as referring to the New Covenant of New Testament times. Piper writes that the phrase ". . . certainly refers to the 'New Covenant' which Paul construes as a promise of the salvation of all Israel."[107] This issue does not necessarily bear on the timing of the fullness of the Gentiles or of the salvation of all Israel (surely a salvation that might take place at the second coming would be a "new covenant" salvation). The greater emphasis of Paul's teaching regarding salvation under the new covenant points more to salvation during the church age and through the gospel proclamation of the church than to salvation at the second coming,[108] though all the phases of the latter cannot be completely ruled out.

PAUL'S PICTURE OF ISRAEL SUMMARIZED

In Romans 11 Paul sought to curtail any spiritual arrogance the Gentile believers in Rome might feel in comparing themselves with Jewish believers. He did this by disclosing new revelation he had received regarding the spiritual destiny of the Jews. He pointed out the obvious: a large number of first-century Jews (and, by implication, subsequently throughout the church age) were temporarily hardened. After some future point when a large, divinely determined number of Gentiles will have been saved (probably some time prior to or in conjunction with second-coming events), a (presumably) large number of Jews will be saved through the finished new covenant ministry of Christ. This is apparently what Paul conveys in the three difficult verses, Romans 11:25–27.

A number of issues emerge from the exegetical conclusions of this study. How does the passage relate to suggestions that Paul taught two ways of salvation, one for the Jews and another for the Gentiles? What does this future salvation contribute to the future of *national* Israel? What is the *locus* of the people of God—the church or Israel? What is the contribution of 11:25–27 to theodicy? How does it further an understanding of eschatology as a whole? Further studies will hopefully supply answers to these and other questions.

ENDNOTES

[1] Leon Morris, *The Epistle to the Romans* (Grand Rapids: Zondervan, 1988), 419.

[2] Scholars are divided on the identification of the "first-fruits" (11:16). Some view them as a reference to the patriarchs (Anders Nygren, *Commentary on Romans* [Philadelphia: Fortress, 1951], 397; Morris, *Romans,* 411–12) or to Christ (suggested, though not held by C. K. Barrett, *A Commentary on the Book of Romans* [New York: Harper, 1957], 216). Either of these options is defensible; but it seems preferable to see the first-fruits as a reference to the Jewish remnant of Paul's day (Barrett's preferred view [*Romans,* 216]). Earlier in chapter 11, Paul used himself as proof that God had not permanently cast off all of His people, and supports this contention with an appeal to 1 Kings 19:10ff. Furthermore, ἡ ἀπαρχή *(hē aparchē)* is used by Paul in Romans 16:5 and 1 Corinthians 16:15 for the initial converts of his ministry in a particular area, suggesting that those first-fruits were viewed as a foreshadowing of a greater redemptive work of God in a geographical area (cf. Dan G. Johnson, "The Structure and Meaning of Romans 11," *Catholic Biblical Quarterly* 46 [1984]: 98–99). The figures of the root and the branches complicate the interpretation of 11:16. While the first-fruits may be the remnant,

Nils A. Dahl (*Studies in Paul: Theology for the Early Christian Mission* [Minneapolis: Augsburg, 1977], 151) and C. E. B. Cranfield (*The Epistle to the Romans*, 2 vols. [Edinburgh: T & T Clark, 1979], 2:564) suggest that the metaphor of the root seems to refer to the patriarchs, from whom all Israelites descend. Paul draws upon the continuity of the Israel of his day with the patriarchs as proof of an eventual spiritual restoration for all Israel.

[3] John Murray, "The Epistle to the Romans," in *New International Commentary on the New Testament*, 2 vols. (Grand Rapids: Eerdmans, 1965), 2:91.

[4] Cf. Morris, *Romans*, 419 and n. 108. Barrett (*Romans*, 222–23) takes the tendency of the Gentile to be arrogant toward the Jew as indicating that the Gentile fails to recognize (1) that the acceptance of the gospel implies no merit at all, but faith alone (11:22), (2) that the Gentile's faith is itself the result of God's initiative and mercy (11:16), and (3) that the Gentile's faith and inclusion in the people of God are only one stage in the unfolding of God's all-embracing purpose.

[5] Otto Glombitza ("Apostolische Sorge. Welche Sorge treibt den Apostel Paulus zu den Sätzen Röm 11:25ff," *Novum Testamentum* 7 [1965]: 312–18) emphasizes the apostle's concern about the unity of the church in Rome. He argues that the primary (if not the sole) motivation for Paul's mention of the mystery of Israel's hardening and restoration is that of seeking to keep the Gentiles from becoming arrogant. Glombitza's point is well taken, but the broader context indicates that Paul's objective in Romans 9–11 was also to provide an *apologia* for God and His faithfulness in light of Israel's rejection of the gospel.

[6] Gunther Bornkamm, "μυστήριον, μυέω," *TDNT*, 4:813–14; G. Finkenrath, "Secret, Mystery," *New International Dictionary of New Testament Theology*, 3:501–2. One of the main differences between Jewish and Greek uses of *mystērion* was the ineffability and impenetrableness Greeks ascribed to their mysteries, as well as their disinclination to manifest or explain mysteries to those outside the cult. J. Armitage Robinson points out that the Jewish and Christian concept of *mystērion* involves an unveiling and revealing by God of divine secrets, and that He charges His apostles and prophets to declare them to those who have ears to hear (*St. Paul's Epistle to the Ephesians* [London: MacMillan, 1903], 240).

[7] Markus Bockmuehl, *Revelation and Mystery in Ancient Judaism and*

Pauline Christianity (Tubingen: Mohr, 1990), 170. Robert Gundry hints at the fact that the rapture is new revelation in the NT, not found in the OT (*The Church and the Tribulation* [Grand Rapids: Zondervan, 1973], 14).

[8] Cf. Walter Schmithals, *Der Römerbrief: Ein Kommentar* (Götersloh: Gutersloher Verlagshaus Gerd Mohen, 1988), 403; Werner DeBoor, *Der Brief des Paulus an die Römer* (Wuppertal: R. Brockhaus Verlag, 1967), 268; Herman Ridderbos, *Paul: An Outline of His Theology* (Grand Rapids: Eerdmans, 1975), 46–47; Bornkamm, "μυστήριον," *TDNT*, 4:820; and F. W. Grosheide, *Commentary on the First Epistle to the Corinthians* (Grand Rapids: Eerdmans, 1953), 64.

[9] Ephesians 3:4–5: "And by referring to this, when you read you can understand my insight into the mystery of Christ, which in other generations was not made known to the sons of men *as it has now been revealed* [ὡς νῦν ἀπεκαλύφθη]. . . ." While it has been argued that the particle ὡς carries no comparative sense (i.e., the mystery was not known at all previously as it is now known; cf. C. C. Ryrie, "The Mystery in Ephesians 3," *Bibliotheca Sacra* 123 [1966]: 29), the fact that the OT contains a significant amount of teaching regarding the blessing of Gentiles along with Jews weighs against seeing truth related to the mystery in Ephesians 3 as something entirely new. Though the OT foresaw the future blessing of Gentiles with Jews, it did not predict the joining together of the two groups in one body, the church, as was revealed to Paul according to the Ephesians 3 passage. For an interpretation of ὡς with a comparative force, cf. Harold W. Mare, "Paul's Mystery in Ephesians 3," *Bulletin of the Evangelical Theological Society* 7 (1965): 83–84.

[10] It may be instructive that the other occurrence of "mystery" in Romans (16:25–26) refers most likely to the "Christ event," which cannot be viewed as completely new revelation.

[11] P. T. O'Brien, *Colossians, Philemon* (Waco: Word, 1982), 84; Raymond E. Brown, *The Semitic Background of the Term "Mystery" in the New Testament* (Philadelphia: Fortress, 1968), 24–28; Ralph Martin, *Colossians and Philemon* (London: Marshall, Morgan & Scott, 1974), 71.

[12] Chrys Caragounis, *The Ephesian Mysterion: Meaning and Content* (Lund: C. W. K. Gleerup, 1977), 104 n. 24; Mare, "Mystery," 83–84.

[13] Ridderbos, *Paul*, 358–60. Cf. also William Hendriksen, *Exposition*

of Paul's Epistle to the Romans (Grand Rapids: Baker, 1981), 378; J. Christiaan Beker, *Paul the Apostle: The Triumph of God in Life and Thought* (Philadelphia: Fortress, 1980), 334.

[14] F. A. G. Tholuck, *Exposition of St. Paul's Epistle to the Romans* (Philadelphia: Sorin and Ball, 1844), 388–89; Bruce Corley, "The Jews, the Future, and God," *Southwestern Journal of Theology* 19 (1976–1977): 50.

[15] Nils Dahl, *Studies in Paul: Theology for the Early Christian Mission* (Minneapolis: Augsburg, 1977), 152 and n. 44.

[16] W. D. Davies, "Paul and the People of Israel," *New Testament Studies* 24 (1977–78): 28.

[17] Cf. Max Zerwick and Mary Grosvenor, *A Grammatical Analysis of the Greek New Testament*, vol. 2 (Rome: Biblical Institute Press, 1979), 485.

[18] Cf. especially the hardening of Pharaoh in Exodus 4:21; 7:3; 9:12. See also Psalm 95:8; Isaiah 6:10; 63:17.

[19] *T. Levi* 13:7; 1QS 1:6; 2:14, 26; 3:3; 5:4; CD 2:17–18; 3:5, 11; 8:8.

[20] BAGD, 732.

[21] John Piper, *The Justification of God: An Exegetical and Theological Study of Romans 9:1–23* (Grand Rapids: Baker, 1983), 155–56.

[22] Otto Michel, *Der Brief an die Römer* (Göttingen: Vandenhoeck & Ruprecht, 1966), 280; Tholuck, *Romans,* 388–89; A. T. Robertson, *A Grammar of the Greek New Testament in the Light of Historical Research* (Nashville: Broadman, 1934), 550.

[23] Ernst Käsemann, *Commentary on Romans* (Grand Rapids: Eerdmans, 1980), 313.

[24] Charles Hodge, *Commentary on the Epistle to the Romans* (1886; re-print, Grand Rapids: Eerdmans, 1950), 373. Cf. also R. C. H. Lenski, *The Interpretation of St. Paul's Epistle to the Romans* (Columbus, Ohio: Wartburg, 1945), 719, for a summary of this position (though Lenski does not adopt it himself).

[25] Lenski, *Romans,* 720. For the points supporting a numerical emphasis

of Paul in this context, cf. especially the 7000 of 11:4; the remnant in 11:5; the οἱ λοιποί in 11:7; the phrase τινὰ ἐξ αὐτῶν in 11:14; the "first-fruits" and "root" in 11:16; and the parallel between τὸ πλήρωμα τῶν ἐθνῶν and πᾶς Ἰσραήλ in 11:26.

²⁶ Käsemann, Romans, 313.

²⁷ H. A. W. Meyer, Critical and Exegetical Handbook to the Epistle to the Romans (6th Funk and Wagnalls ed.; reprint, Winona Lake, Ind.: Alpha, 1979), 446–47.

²⁸ This view is maintained by Cranfield, Romans, 2:575; Meyer, Romans, 446; Michel, Römer, 280; Joachim Jeremias, "Einige vorwiegend sprachliche Beobachtungen zu Römer 11, 25–36," in Die Israelfrage nach Römer 9–11, ed. Lorenzo de Lorenzi (Monographische Reihe von "Benedictina," vol. 3; Rome: St. Paul's Abbey, 1977), 195. This view is probably the best based on the other four Pauline uses of the phrase in which ἀπὸ μέρους modifies the verb. Cf. Romans 15:15 (τολμηρότερον δὲ ἔγραψα ὑμῖν ἀπὸ μέρους, "But I have written boldly to you on some points"); Romans 15:24 (ὑμῶν πρῶτον ἀπὸ μέρους ἐμπλησθῶ, "after I have enjoyed your company for a while."); 2 Corinthians 1:14 (καθὼς καὶ ἐπέγνωτε ἡμᾶς ἀπὸ μέρους, "just as you partly did understand us"); and 2 Corinthians 2:5 (λελύπηκεν . . . ἀπὸ μέρους, "someone has caused sorrow . . . in some degree").

²⁹ A. Rese, "Die Rettung der Juden nach Römer 11," in L'Apôtre Paul: Personalte, Style et Conception du Ministère, ed. A. Vanhoye (Leuven: Leuven University Press, 1986), 427; Cranfield, Romans, 2:575; Morris, Romans, 420; Käsemann Romans, 313; de Boor, Römer, 268; Nygren, Romans, 404; Barrett, Romans, 223; and Hendriksen, Romans, 378. This view is supported by the context (11:7, οἱ δὲ λοιποὶ ἐπωρώθησαν), and by the apparent contrast with πᾶς Ἰσραήλ in 11:26. Thus the limits of the hardening are delineated, and Jewish Christianity is not affected by it. Also, Romans 11 says earlier that not all the Jews were hardened, supporting the view that only part of Israel has been affected during this age.

³⁰ Dunn, Romans, 2:679; Corley, "Jews" 52 n. 48. Paul is still looking at the nation as a whole (according to this view), and this unified whole is blinded somewhat. This is the most natural connection of the phrase (it is argued), is a grammatically permissible use of the prepositional phrase as an adverb, and denotes a quantitative limit, indicating that only a part of Israel is affected. While this is a defensible position, it is probably not

the best option for several reasons. First, as it was mentioned above, Paul usually uses ἀπὸ μέρους as a modifier of the verb, not a noun as this view requires. Second, this interpretation is not altogether clear. "A partial hardening" is taken by Dunn, et al., as a reference to part of Israel being affected; but "partial hardening" seems to be understood better as "a hardening of low intensity," and the context suggests that this is probably not Paul's point. Meyer (*Romans,* 446) maintains that the phrase should be understood *extensively* in light of οἱ λοιποί in 11:7, and τινες in 11:17, and not *intensively* as is the sense demanded by a connection with πώρωσις.

[31] Zerwick and Grosvenor, *Analysis,* 2:485.

[32] E.g., Hebrews 3:13, "But encourage one another day after day *as long as* [while] it is still called Today [ἄχρις οὗ τὸ σήμερον καλεῖται]"; Acts 27:33, "And . . . *until* [while] the day was about to dawn ['Άχρι δὲ οὗ ἡμέρα ἤμελλεν γίνεσθαι], Paul was encouraging them all to take some food"; and Luke 21:24, "and Jerusalem will be trampled underfoot by the Gentiles *until* the times of the Gentiles be fulfiled [ἄχρι οὗ πληρωθῶσιν καιροὶ ἐθνῶν]." These verses are suggested by Murray, *Romans,* 2:92 n. 45, though Murray himself does not hold to this understanding of ἄχρι οὗ in Romans 11:25.

[33] In support of this understanding of ἄχρι οὗ, there are at least three passages in which it is used with aorist verbs and could be rendered "while" or "during and after." In Matthew 24:38 ("they were eating and drinking . . . until [ἄχρι ἧς] the day that Noah entered the ark"), the "until" does not signal the cessation of eating and drinking; in fact, Genesis 7:4, 10 indicate that after Noah entered the ark an additional seven days elapsed, during which there is no indication that the godless behavior of Noah's coevals ceased. In Acts 7:17–18 ("the people increased and multiplied in Egypt, until [ἄχρι οὗ] there arose another king over Egypt who knew nothing about Joseph" [Exod. 1:8]), it is apparent from Exodus 1:12 that the ascension of the new king of Egypt did not terminate fruitfulness of the Hebrew people. In the following two examples (1 Cor. 11:26; 15:25) the aorist subjunctive is used as it is in Romans 11:25. In 1 Corinthians 11:26 ("you proclaim the Lord's death until [ἄχρι οὗ] He comes [ἔλθῃ, aorist subjunctive]"), the coming of Christ does not stop the observance of the Lord's Supper, since according to Matthew 26:29 there will be at least one more observance of it with Christ "in [His] Father's kingdom." Finally, in 1 Corinthians 15:25 ("For He must reign until [ἄχρι οὗ] He has put [θῇ, aorist subjunctive] all His enemies

under His feet"), the reign of Christ does not cease at the time His enemies are made His footstool; it continues past that point.

[34] For this understanding of ἄχρι οὗ, cf. Louis A. DeCaro, *Israel Today: Fulfilment of Prophecy?* (Grand Rapids: Baker, 1974), 111–14; O. Palmer Robertson, "Is There a Distinctive Future for Ethnic Israel in Romans 11?" in *Perspectives on Evangelical Theology,* ed. Kenneth S. Kantzer and Stanley N. Gundry (Grand Rapids: Baker, 1979), 219–21; and Marten H. Woudstra, "Israel and the Church: A Case for Continuity," in *Continuity and Discontinuity: Perspectives on the Relationship Between the Old and New Testaments: Essays in Honor of S. Lewis Johnson, Jr.,* ed. John S. Feinberg (Westchester, Ill.: Crossway Books, 1988), 236.

[35] Murray, *Romans,* 2:92 n. 45; cf. also Cranfield, *Romans,* 2:575, who writes, "Paul's meaning is not that Israel is in part hardened during the time in which the fullness of the Gentiles is coming in, but that the hardening will last until the fullness of the Gentiles comes in. The entry of the fullness of the Gentiles will be the event which will mark the end of Israel's hardening."

[36] The support of the verses is not as clear-cut as it might appear. In Matthew 24:38, a serious change took place for the godless after Noah entered the ark, just as happened for the Hebrews when a new Pharaoh ascended the throne of Egypt (Acts 7:17–18) and will happen for the observance of the Lord's Supper after Christ's second coming (1 Cor. 11:26) and for Christ's rule following the subjection of His enemies (1 Cor. 15:25; cf. 15:24).

[37] BAGD, 672.

[38] J. B. Lightfoot, *St. Paul's Epistles to the Colossians and to Philemon* (1879; reprint, Grand Rapids: Zondervan, 1959), 260–61 [transliteration and translation added].

[39] Lightfoot, *Colossians,* 260.

[40] Murray, *Romans,* 2:94–95; Morris, *Romans,* 420.

[41] Cf. Matthew Black, *Romans* (NCB; London: Marshall, Morgan and Scott, 1973), 143, 147; William L. Osborne, "The Old Testament Background of Paul's *All Israel* in Romans 11:26a," *Asia Journal of Theology* 2 (December 1988): 289–90; Lightfoot, *Colossians,* 260; Roger D. Aus, "Paul's Travel

Plans to Spain and the *Full Number of the Gentiles* of Rom. XI:25," *Novum Testamentum* 21 (1979): 232–62; Gerhard Delling, "πλήρης, κ. τ. λ.," *TDNT,* 6:302; Charles Journet, "The Mysterious Destinies of Israel," in *The Bridge: A Yearbook of Judaeo-Christian Studies,* ed. John M. Oestereicher (New York: Pantheon, 1956), 2:84; Anthony A. Hoekema, *The Bible and the Future* (Grand Rapids: Eerdmans, 1979), 142, 144; Zerwick and Grosvenor, *Analysis,* 2:485; Cranfield, *Romans,* 2:575–76; and Lenski, *Romans,* 720.

[42] See note 25 above.

[43] Cf. *2 Bar.* 23:4–5; 30:2; *4 Ezra* 2:38, 40–41; 4:35–36. Both *2 Baruch* and *4 Ezra* were written after, and in response to, the fall of Jerusalem (George W. E. Nickelsburg, *Jewish Literature Between the Bible and the Mishnah: A Historical and Literary Introduction* [Philadelphia: Fortress, 1981], 277–94).

[44] One of the problems with Murray's view (that the fullness of the Gentiles refers to their full blessings) is that it is difficult to determine just what is meant by this. If it does not entail some sort of numerical enlargement, then the statement is meaningless in the present context. Whenever a Gentile finds salvation in Christ, he receives all the blessings to which Christ entitles him, including the promise of glory (Rom. 8:29–30). Paul is referring to more than this as Murray himself concedes. The fullness must involve not only full spiritual blessings, but full spiritual blessings *for a numerically large number of Gentiles.*

[45] BAGD, 232.

[46] Cf. Matthew 5:20; 7:13–14, 21; 18:3, 8; 19:17; 23:13; Mark 9:43–47; 10:15, 23–25; Luke 13:24; John 3:5.

[47] This is the view of Sanday and Headlam, *A Critical and Exegetical Commentary on the Epistle to the Romans* (Edinburgh: T & T Clark, 1902), 335; Morris, *Romans,* 419–20; Cranfield, *Romans,* 2:680–81; Corley, "Jews" 52. Corley maintains that the phrase refers to the completion of the gospel mission among the Gentiles, thus giving a view slightly different from the "Kingdom" view of the other scholars mentioned in this note. But Corley also assigns a semi-technical eschatological force to the verb, and for this reason he is listed here with the others.

[48] Dieter Zeller maintains that the eschatological connotation of

εἰσέρχομαι in the Gospels has no bearing on Romans 11:25 (*Juden und Heiden in der Mission des Paulus: Studien Zum Römerbrief* [Stuttgart: Verlag Katholisches Bibelwerk, 1973], 254).

[49] Black, *Romans,* 147. Cf. Mark 9:28; Luke 7:6; 14:23; Acts 1:13; 3:8; 5:21; 9:12; 13:14, etc. Black does not appear to assign an eschatological sense to the verb, but does not make himself clear on whether or not an eschatological sense is warranted. Cf. also Johannes Munck, *Christ & Israel: An Interpretation of Romans 9–11* (Philadelphia: Fortress, 1967), 132, who says that Paul does not use εἰσέρχομαι in the same eschatological way it is used in the Gospels. However, in Acts 14:22, Luke does use this word with an eschatological sense in quoting Paul ("Through many tribulations we must enter [εἰσελθεῖν] the kingdom of God").

[50] Cf. Xenophon, *Anabasis* 3.4.8; Epictetus, *Dissertationes* 4.8.13 (LSJ, 112).

[51] Käsemann, *Romans,* 313.

[52] Corley, "Jews," 53–54.

[53] On a modal view of οὕτως in 1 Corinthians 11:28, cf. C. K. Barrett, *A Commentary on the First Epistle to the Corinthians* (New York: Harper and Row, 1968), 273 (His translation "*that* [in the previously-mentioned manner] is how he should eat" implies a modal interpretation); in 1 Corinthians 14:25, cf. Charles Hodge, *A Commentary on 1 & 2 Corinthians* (1857; reprint, Carlisle, Penn.: Banner of Truth, 1983), 298; and in 1 Thessalonians 4:17, cf. F. F. Bruce, *1 & 2 Thessalonians,* vol. 45 of Word Biblical Commentary (Waco: Word Books, 1982), 103.

[54] Robertson, "Future," 221.

[55] Romans 5:12; 11:26; 1 Corinthians 7:17, 36; 11:28; 14:25; 15:11; Galatians 6:2; 1 Thessalonians 4:17. As already mentioned, Romans 11:26; 1 Corinthians 11:26; 14:25; 1 Thessalonians 4:17 are disputed, but are probably not temporal as some claim.

[56] Peter Stuhlmacher, "*Zur Interpretation von Römer* 11[25–32]," in *Probleme biblischer Theologie: Gerhard von Rad zum 70. Geburtstag,* ed. Hans Walter Wolff (München: Chr. Kaiser Verlag, 1971), 557. For the opinion that οὕτως is modal with a temporal flavor, cf. Scott Hafemann, "The Salvation of Israel in Romans 11:25–32: A Response to Krister Stendahl,"

Ex Auditu, ed. Robert A. Guelich, 4 (1988): 53; Dunn, *Romans,* 2:681; Bruce Longenecker, "Different Answers to Different Issues: Israel, the Gentiles, and Salvation History in Romans 9–11," *Journal for the Study of the New Testament* 36 (1989): 118 n. 35; and Walter C. Kaiser Jr., "Kingdom Promises as Spiritual and National," in *Continuity and Discontinuity: Perspectives on the Relationship Between the Old and New Testaments: Essays in Honor of S. Lewis Johnson, Jr.,* ed. John S. Feinberg (Westchester, Ill.: Crossway, 1988), 301–3. Even Corley ("Jews" 53–54) maintains that a temporal understanding of οὕτως can include a modal sense, so that the two options need not be mutually exclusive.

[57] Jeremias, "Beobachtungen," 198–99. See Jeremias's treatment for the details. Cf. also, for the same perspective (that οὕτως is retrospective), Dieter Sänger, "*Rettung der Heiden und Erwählung Israels: Einige vorläufige Erwägungen zu Römer* 11.25–27," *Kerygma und Dogma* 32 (1986): 107–8; and Ulrich Wilckens, *Der Brief an die Römer* (EKK, 3 vols.; Zürich: Benziger Verlag, 1980), 2:254–55.

[58] In Luke 24:24 (καὶ εὗρον οὕτως καθὼς καὶ αἱ γυναῖκες εἶπον, "and they found it *thus just as* the women said"), the οὕτως clearly refers to what precedes, as is the case in Ephesians 4:20 (ὑμεῖς δὲ οὐχ οὕτως ἐμάθετε τὸν Χριστόν, καθὼς ἐστιν ἀλήθεια ἐν τῷ Ἰησοῦ, "but you have not *thus* learned Christ, *just as* the truth is in Jesus"); but in Romans 15:20 (οὕτως δὲ φιλοτιμούμενον εὐαγγελίζεσθαι οὐχ ὅπου ὠνομάσθη Χριστός, . . . ἀλλὰ καθὼς γέγραπται, "and *thus* being ambitious to preach now where Christ was named, . . . but *just as* it is written") it refers to what follows. The other NT occurrences of the οὕτως . . . καθώς ("thus . . . just as") construction provide no assured conclusion on the grammatical relationship of οὕτως ("thus") in Romans 11:26.

[59] Cranfield, *Romans,* 2:576 [transliteration and translation added].

[60] These views are presented and summarized well in Charles Horne, "The Meaning of the Phrase 'And Thus All Israel Will Be Saved,'" *Journal of the Evangelical Theological Society* 21 (December 1978): 331–33.

[61] See S. Lewis Johnson Jr., "Paul and 'The Israel of God': An Exegetical and Eschatological Case-Study," in *Essays in Honor of J. Dwight Pentecost,* ed. Stanley D. Toussaint and Charles H. Dyer (Chicago: Moody, 1986), 181–96.

[62] Horne, "Meaning," 331–32.

[63] For the sake of clarity, "church age" (a phrase used several times in the pages that follow) refers to that period of time beginning on the day of Pentecost and concluding at the second coming.

[64] William Hendriksen, *Israel in Prophecy* (Grand Rapids: Baker, 1968), 44.

[65] Horne, "Meaning," 334; cf. Hoekema, *Bible,* 144, 146.

[66] That the salvation of Israel takes place at a specific point of time in the future is argued by Stanley E. Porter, who writes,

In the logic of the argument here, Paul claims that the hardness has come and will last until such time when the fulness of the Gentiles may come (Aorist Subjunctive). . . . The future form [σωθήσεται] is used parallel to the Subjunctive, here designating a logically subsequent event in relation to another projected event . . . , with the added assurance that if the fullness of the Gentiles enters then the salvation of Israel is expected. ("Verbal Aspect in the Greek of the New Testament, with Reference to Tense and Mood," in *Studies in Biblical Greek,* vol. 1 [New York: Peter Lang, 1989], 435)

[67] Cf. Longenecker, "Answers," 96–97; Munck, *Christ & Israel,* 136; Stuhlmacher, "Interpretation," 557; Dahl, *Studies,* 153; BDF, par. 275(4), p. 143; W. D. Davies, "Paul," 16 n. 2; Dunn, *Romans,* 2:681.

[68] E.g., Longenecker and Davies.

[69] E.g., the testimony of Paul himself as proof that God has not rejected His people [11:1]; the first-fruit and the root [11:16]; the individual branches that are broken off [11:17]; and the opening verses of the entire three-chapter section [Rom. 9:1–5] in which Paul expresses intense concern regarding the salvation and condemnation of *individual* Jews (Piper, *Justification,* 38–48, 54).

[70] Osborne, "Background," 285–86.

[71] Ibid., 87.

[72] Ibid.

[73] With the help of *IBYCUS/TLG,* I searched the LXX for the phrase πᾶς Ἰσραήλ (to limit the search and to provide the closest parallels to Romans

11, only the nominative singular was considered), and found 73 occurrences, some of which are mentioned in this second caveat.

[74] The exception to this comes in the geographical references to "all Israel," from Dan to Beersheba (1 Sam. 3:20; cf. also 1 Kings 8:65).

[75] As an aside from this exegetical study, it is interesting to note how this identification of "all Israel" coincides with a premillennial return of Christ to establish on earth a kingdom in which the Jewish people will play the leading role.

[76] Aus, "Travel Plans," 234. Against Aus, and for a more plausible understanding of Paul's missionary plans and expectations, cf. Peter Richardson, *Israel in the Apostolic Church* (Cambridge: Cambridge University Press, 1969), 145–46.

[77] This is Aus's observation ("Traveling Plans," 261–62).

[78] For Paul's statement of his goal for the collection, cf. 2 Corinthians 8:13–15, where he says that the collection is designed to meet pressing physical needs in the Jerusalem church.

[79] Journet, "Destinies," 85.

[80] To be sure, Journet's point can support the view that the second coming is in mind; if Israel is blessed at the second coming, then those blessings can continue to have an impact on the whole earth even into the millennial kingdom (assuming a premillennial eschatology). But the remaining arguments taken together with this one make the second coming difficult to connect with the salvation and fullness if it consists only of a single event.

[81] Dunn, *Romans,* 2:687.

[82] The second νυν of 11:31 has a spotty MS tradition, giving rise to the use of brackets in the NA[26] and the UBS[3c], with a "D" rating in the latter. But there is evidence to suggest that it was the original reading. All three readings (ὕστερον ["afterwards"]; νῦν ["now"]; *omit*) have reasonably strong MS support. Following the critical apparatus of NA[26], ὕστερον is supported by diverse text types: 33 is an excellent MS with largely Alexandrian readings as is the Sahidic; 365 is largely Caesarean or Western. This reading is also ancient, with the Coptic originating in the third or

fourth century and finding wide acceptance in geographically diverse places (Egypt = Sahidic; the West = 365). The omission of νῦν is supported by the proto-Alexandrian and very ancient p⁴⁶ (copied ca. A.D. 200), the later Alexandrian A (from the fourth century), the second corrector of D (Western text), the Western and later F and G (both from the ninth century), and Ψ as well as most Old Latin and many Syriac (Byzantine text-type) MSS. These MSS also indicate a wide acceptance from Egypt to Syria to the West. The inclusion of νῦν has strong MS support as well. The great ℵ is joined by B in a strong proto-Alexandrian reading (and these are ancient as well: ℵ is from the fourth century, B from the fifth). D* is a Western text originating probably in the sixth century—but it has numerous singular readings and should be used with caution in resolving textual problems. The Bohairic apparently was based on a similar Greek text to B, giving Alexandrian readings.

From the MS evidence, νῦν should probably (with great caution) be accepted as original. But when coupled with the transcriptional probability, the caution may be eased somewhat. Of the three readings, the one that may have given rise to the others is probably νῦν. Metzger writes, "The difficulty in meaning that the second occurrence of νῦν seems to introduce may have prompted either its deletion or its replacement by the superficially more appropriate ὕστερον" (A Textual Commentary of the Greek New Testament [Stuttgart: United Bible Societies, 1971], 527). Furthermore, νῦν is also the harder reading (cf. Zerwick and Grosvenor, Analysis, 2:486). From a scribe's perspective, it makes less sense to say that Israel was now being saved when in fact this was not the case. Hence a possible substitution of ὕστερον for νῦν, or else a complete omission. It is difficult to see how the omission could be original since it makes fine sense without any other additions, and is thus less likely to give rise to the other two readings. Also, ὕστερον is cogent by itself as well, making it difficult to see how it could give rise to νῦν.

In light of its solid MS evidence (including antiquity and geographical diversity), the likelihood that νῦν gave rise to the other readings, and the fact that it is the harder reading, the second νῦν of 11:31 should be preferred as the original reading—and with slightly less reticence than Metzger expresses.

---

⁸³ Corley, "Jews," 56; cf. also Robertson, "Future," 227.

⁸⁴ Cf. Bockmuehl, Mystery, 173; de Boor, Römer, 268; Stuhlmacher, "Interpretation," 561; Schmithals, Römerbrief 2:404; Dunn, Romans,

2:682; Munck, *Christ and Israel,* 134, 137; Jacob Jervell, "Der unbekannte Paulus," in *Die Paulinische Literatur und Theologie,* ed. Sigfreid Pedersen (Göttingen: Vandenhoeck & Ruprecht, 1980), 45; W. D. Davies, "Paul," 27; Wilckens, *Römer,* 2:256; Käsemann, *Romans,* 314; Cranfield, *Romans,* 2:578; Daniel P. Fuller, *Gospel & Law: Contrast or Continuum? The Hermeneutics of Dispensationalism and Covenant Theology* (Grand Rapids: Eerdmans, 1980), 188, 190.

[85] Cranfield, *Romans,* 2:557. Dunn (*Romans,* 2:682) avers that the salvation of all Israel will take place at the final salvation, i.e., the redemption of the body and the restoration of all of creation (Rom. 8:19–23; 11:12).

[86] Cf. *T. Dan* 6:4; *T. Sim.* 6:2–7; *T. Jud.* 23:5–24:2; *As. Moses* 1:18; *2 Bar.* 78:6–7; *Apoc. Abr.* 31:1–2. E. Elizabeth Johnson, *The Function of Apocalyptic and Wisdom Traditions in Romans 9–11* (Atlanta: Scholars Press, 1989), 128.

[87] Wilckens, *Römer,* 2:256.

[88] Stuhlmacher, "Interpretation," 561 n. 31.

[89] Corley, "Future," 55; de Boor, *Römer,* 268; Schmithals, *Römerbrief,* 404.

[90] Zerwick and Grosvenor, *Analysis,* 2:485, allege that the future verb ἥξει is a future tense with the perfect sense "has come."

[91] Reidar Hvalvik, "A 'Sonderweg' for Israel: A Critical Examination of a Current Interpretation of Romans 11:25–27," *Journal for the Study of the New Testament* 38 (1990): 93; cf. also Dieter Zeller, *Der Brief an die Römer* (Regensburg: Verlag Friedrich Pustet, 1985), 199.

[92] Cf. the brief discussion of this in the section below on "The Scriptural Proof of Israel's Salvation."

[93] E. Johnson, *Function,* 162.

[94] Hvalvik, "Sonderweg," 95.

[95] In fact, in the NT when Σιών refers to the heavenly Jerusalem, there are modifiers present to make this clear (cf. Heb. 12:22).

[96] Hvalvik, "Sonderweg," 92.

[97] That this conversion is "perhaps several years before the second coming" is suggested by the positive effect the renewed Israel will have on the world (11:12, 15).

[98] With due respect to D. A. Carson, "Matthew," in vol. 8 of *Expositor's Bible Commentary*, ed. Frank E. Gabelein (Grand Rapids: Zondervan, 1984), 487–88, and Robert H. Gundry, *Matthew: A Commentary on His Literary and Theological Art* (Grand Rapids: Eerdmans, 1982), 474, these scholars miss the point in Matthew 23:39 οὐ μὴ με ἴδητε ἀπ᾽ ἄρτι ἕως ἂν εἴπετε. The residents of Jerusalem will not see Christ until their Psalm 118:26-like confession. The order of events is not that they will not see Christ until they see Christ (which, though hopelessly tautologous, is an integral part of the posttribulationism), but that they will not see Christ *until the Jews of Jerusalem acknowledge Him as being from God. After* that acknowledgment Christ will return to the Jewish people, but not before. So their change of heart transpires *before* Christ's return as a necessary prerequisite to it, not *while* He is returning as posttribulationism requires.

[99] Hvalvik, "Sonderweg," 95. Hvalvik probably overstates his point somewhat, however. The ὅταν carries some deictic force, so that a temporal understanding cannot be completely ruled out. But for the most part he is correct. These verses use the OT to show that God will save Israel just as Paul also has said.

[100] Four items differentiate the MT, the LXX, and Romans in these verses. (1) In Isaiah 59:20, compare the phrase וּבָא לְצִיּוֹן גּוֹאֵל ("a Redeemer will come to/for Zion") with the LXX καὶ ἥξει ἕνεκεν Σιὼν ὁ ῥυόμενος ("a Redeemer will come for the sake of/to Zion") and Romans 11:26 ἐκ Σιών . . . ("*from* Zion . . ."). (2) Also compare the MT וּלְשָׁבֵי פֶּשַׁע בְּיַעֲקֹב ("and to those who return from ungodliness/transgression in Jacob") with the LXX καὶ ἀποστρέψει ἀσεβείας ἀπὸ Ἰακώβ ("and he will turn away ungodliness from Jacob") and Romans 11:26b, which reads the same as the LXX. (3) In Isaiah 59:21, the MT reads וַאֲנִי זֹאת בְּרִיתִי אוֹתָם ("and as for me, this is/will be my covenant with them") in comparison with the LXX and Romans 11:27a, both reading καὶ αὕτη αὐτοῖς ἡ παρ᾽ ἐμοῦ διαθήκη ("and this is/will be the covenant with them from me"). (4) In Isaiah 27:9, the MT reads לָכֵן בְּזֹאת יְכֻפַּר עֲוֹן־יַעֲקֹב ("therefore by this the iniquity of Jacob will be covered/atoned for/removed"), and the LXX has ὅταν αφέλωμαι αὐτοῦ τὴν ἁμαρτίαν ("when I remove his sin") in comparison to Romans 11:27b, which reads ὅταν ἀφέλωμαι τὰς ἁμαρτίας αὐτῶν ("when I remove their sins"). On these differences,

Archer and Chirichigno are probably right (if not overly simplistic) in saying, "Thus we have a conflate quotation, with four minor variants *that do not greatly affect the sense. . . .*" A great deal could be said about the variations between the texts and how Paul's emendation of the LXX and MT indicates his thoughts in this passage.

[101] Brendt Schaller, "῞Ηξει ἐκ Σιὼν ὁ ῥυόμενος: *zur Textgestalt von Jesaja 59:20f. in Röm 11:26f.*" in *De Septuaginta: Studies in Honor of John William Wevers on his 65th Birthday,* ed. Albert Piertersma and Claude Cox (Mississaugh, Ontario: Benben Publications, 1984), 205–6.

[102] Mary Ann Getty, "Paul and Israel in Romans 9–11," *Catholic Biblical Quarterly* 50 (1988): 461.

[103] Dunn, *Romans,* 2:682; Wilckens, *Römer,* 2:257; Tholuck, *Romans,* 389.

[104] E. Johnson, *Function,* 128; Zeller, *Juden und Heiden,* 259. One might view 1 Thessalonians 1:10 as support for the second-coming view of the conversion in Romans 11. Since the Lord Jesus Christ "delivers from the wrath to come" and this deliverance is eschatological, then perhaps the salvation of all Israel also should be located at the second coming. But 1 Thessalonians 1:10 refers to those who are already saved and are awaiting His coming, and does not speak of a mass conversion at that time. Furthermore, though the deliverance spoken of in 1 Thessalonians is future, it is based upon the finished work of Christ at His first advent. This fits well with the interpretation given in this essay: all Israel will be saved in the future, but this salvation is based not on the *second* coming of Christ but on His *first* coming.

[105] To whom does Ἰακώβ refer? It is never used in the NT for the church; the reference here must be to Jews. Cf. P. Richardson, *Israel,* 128–29.

[106] Hvalvik, "Sonderweg," 96 [transliteration and translation added]; cf. also Cranfield, *Romans,* 2:578.

[107] Piper, *Justification,* 20; cf. also Black, *Romans,* 148; Corley, "Future," 55.

[108] Cf. 1 Corinthians 11:26; 2 Corinthians 3:6–18

CHAPTER SEVEN

1 Corinthians 3:12

Gold, Silver, Precious Stones

James E. Rosscup

The six materials in 1 Corinthians 3:12 are arranged to denote a descending scale by moving from a unit of three good qualities to a unit of three bad ones. The verse uses pictures to represent what Paul calls "work" in verses 13 and 14. Paul's main point is to encourage building with quality materials that will meet with God's approval and thereby receive eternal reward. Interpreters sometimes restrict the meaning of the symbols either to doctrine, to people, to activity, or to character. The conclusion is that Paul in the symbols combines several things that lead to Christ's good pleasure and a believer's reward. These are sound doctrine, activity, motives, and character in Christian service.

* * * * *

Paul's context that leads into and away from the picture of "gold, silver, precious stones, wood, hay, straw" is filled with spiritual qualities. He says much to distinguish the wisdom of God from the wisdom of the world. He sees a vast difference between the mind-set of the "natural man" and the mind of believers, "the mind of Christ."[1] He distinguishes sharply between the "spiritual" person and the "carnal."[2]

Then, in 3:5–8a, he focuses on the great common privilege that all those who serve God share. They, in common, are all totally dependent on the grace of God for anything of value that they accomplish. Paul is quick to qualify this lest any should leap to an erroneous conclusion that he is teaching that God sees no differences in those who serve Him. Those who *depend* on the grace of God and ascribe the glory to Him are individually *distinct*. God takes notice of the difference in their individual labor and also will make legitimate distinction in the particular reward that He deems suitable for each worker (3:8b).

Having made this point, Paul then portrays the church under two figures: "God's tillage" and "God's building."[3] His "building" picture blends with that of the "temple" in verses 16–17.[4] The "building" also prepares for the figure of Christ as the "foundation" (vv. 10–11). We read Paul's caution to any worker who builds upon that foundation: let him build carefully! Paul, who refers so often to himself as an example,[5] is an example here. He himself built "as a wise [skilled] architect,"[6] wise, that is, in the wisdom of God, which he mentions in chapters 1–4. He was careful to build consistently with the standard, God's grace. He became a good model of dependence on that grace that others should imitate.

Paul is concerned that others build in a way that is consistent with the spiritual quality he has modeled. Any work they do is to be done in a manner that corresponds in nature to the foundation, Christ, and to the standard set by Paul. To be sure, work on both the foundation and the superstructure must be imbued with God's wisdom and grace. It needs quality imparted by the Holy Spirit through the person who works; it must be done by a person who is "spiritual," a worker who has "the mind of Christ" (2:15–16).

THE MATERIALS OF VERSE 12

Now Paul comes to the verse under investigation. A person who works on the foundation may build with "gold, silver, precious stones, wood, hay, straw. . . ." The list of six words joined without connectives is a construction known as asyndeton.[7] We probably register the effect that Paul intends if we understand that the words represent a descending scale.[8] The first three are pictures of a broad category of qualities that are good. The last three combine as a broad category that is bad, in contrast to the first. These two categories reappear in Paul's direct contrast of 2 Corinthians 5:10 when he refers to all believers being manifest before the judgment seat of Christ. There, every one will receive the things done in his body, things "good or bad." As 1 Corinthians 3:13–15 clarifies, "gold, silver, precious stones" are symbols representing *good* materials. On the other hand, the "wood, hay, straw" are pictures of work that is bad in the sense of worthless, φαῦλος (*phaulos,* "bad") as 2 Corinthians 5:10 describes it.[9]

IDENTIFICATION OF THE MATERIALS
WITH THE "WORK"

The six materials of verse 12 are symbols for the same thing that is called "work" in verses 13 and 14. This is logical for two reasons.

1. Both the materials and the "work" are tested by "fire." In this case "fire" is a symbol for Christ's probing, all-searching judgment that scrutinizes every aspect.[10] Many Roman Catholics have interpreted the "fire" to picture a purging fire that the worker must encounter in an

alleged purgatory.[11] Some Catholics have not followed this view. [12] However they differ, it is not convincing that purgatory is the idea Paul intends in his picture of fire.[13] The thought is that of the workers being tested to be approved, not punished to be improved. And the thought of direct *punishment* to the saved person does not appear to be the point. 2. The materials are symbols that equate with "work," because they have the same result. Whether the description is "gold . . . straw" or "work," they "remain" (v. 14) or "burn up" (v. 15). Although "work" that a man has built on Christ the foundation may "burn," Paul makes it very clear that "he himself shall be saved, yet so as through fire" (v. 15). The purpose of the test is to give an *examination* of the worker as to the nature of his "work," not a *condemnation* of the worker as to his person. His salvation is secure, but the man will experience some kind of "loss."[14] It is reasonable to understand that loss, in a context dealing with work and its reward, as a loss with respect to reward. The worker loses (is reduced, diminished in some fitting degree) in reference to the measure of potential reward he might have received for the burned "work" had Christ appraised it as work that "remains."[15]

As in verse 8, God distinguishes each servant in the varying capacity of eternal reward that He judges equitable to that servant's particular degree of faithfulness (cf. 4:2). This is consistent with Jesus' teaching about degrees (capacities, positions, gradations, stations, roles) of reward. In His Parable of the Pounds (Luke 19:12–27) it is clear when one servant receives reward in terms of a capacity over ten cities and another over five cities.

THE MAIN POINT IN THE MATERIALS OR "WORK"

Gold, silver, and precious stones appear often in the OT. They are in different combinations, either all or two of them being together, or one of the three occurring alone. In some instances, as when gold and silver together are refined by fire, the main objective is to separate the pure metal from the dross, for *retention*. They contrast sharply to the waste materials that the refiners dump on a disposal heap. One such example is Proverbs 27:21: "The crucible is for silver and the furnace for gold, and a man is tested by the praise accorded him."[16] This idea fits 1 Corinthians 3 in some degree.

However, metals in the OT also can focus on *value*. In 2 Chronicles 32:27 they are included in a list of examples describing King Hezekiah's great wealth in treasured things. The verse says, "Now Hezekiah had immense riches and honor; and he made of himself treasuries for gold,

silver, precious stones, spices, shields, and all kinds of valuable articles.
. . ." Then verse 29 adds, "For God had given him very great wealth."
The emphasis on value is clear.[17] The theme of value also is quite suitable to 1 Corinthians 3. The things of a worker that survive Christ's
discerning appraisal are aspects in the "work" that Christ judges to be
valuable. They are the "gold, silver, precious stones." But both OT ideas,
retention and *value* worth retaining, fit naturally with 1 Corinthians 3.
With this in mind, the bottom line is "Build with value that will last!"
Each servant's[18] work will draw Christ's verdict answering the question,
"what sort is it?"—i.e., what is its real quality in His true sense of value
(v. 13)?

THE DEFINITION OF THE MATERIALS

Scholars have come to different conclusions on what the six symbols
and the "work" are in a colaborer's life and work. It can be helpful to see
how these writers define Paul's terms. After this articulation, the object
will be to support the explanation that is the most probable.

1. *Some have been persuaded that Paul uses the symbols to portray
doctrine.* Often those who adopt this view limit the meaning only to
doctrine, regarding this as a natural conclusion.[19] The main reasons are
fairly evident.
a. This explanation recognizes a correspondence between Paul's own
work as an example and the work that others do. When Paul laid the
foundation at Corinth, he preached the truth about Christ, making clear
that doctrinal truth about Christ is the foundation for men's faith (cf. 1 Cor.
3:5). Similarly he "planted" or "sowed" the gospel seed in people whose
hearts were fertile, receptive soil for the truth. The recipients, products
of—but distinct from—Paul's message itself, became "God's tillage"
and "God's building." So when Paul cautions another person in verse 10
to be careful how he builds, Paul refers to work that consists of giving
doctrine that is consistent with the sound indoctrination Paul has given.
Along this line, Meyer reasons: "The ἐποικοδομεῖν (*epoikodomein,* "to
build upon") takes place *on* the persons through doctrines. . . ."[20]
b. A second reason adduced in support of the doctrine interpretation
is also near in the context. The "gold, silver" etc. depict the wisdom of
God in contrast to the wisdom of this world (3:18–20). A good antidote
to false thinking (doctrine) is good wholesome doctrine, the truth. The
ideology or philosophy of the world that originates from man's thinking
is met by giving God's perspective or set of values. Job 28:15–19 places
the value of wisdom from God above the preciousness of gold, silver,

and all precious stones. This theme is frequent in the Proverbs. Paul, consistent with this essential thrust, could use the same OT symbols to depict the value of God's wisdom as expressed in pure doctrine.

c. If the materials represent converts (people) who will "remain" or else "burn" (worthy materials = the saved; unworthy = the unsaved), there is difficulty. How can the builder so mislead people that they, his products, finally burn in eternal lostness while he himself attains final salvation in 1 Corinthians 3:15?[21]

Some interpreters complicate the picture further by explaining the materials or work to be specific doctrines. They ingeniously think up their own exact meanings for each of the six symbols in verse 12. Such imagined meanings appear to be arbitrary, contrived and subjective, imposition into the Word rather than exposition of it. One claim is that gold means preaching the truth of Christ's *deity,* silver Christ's *redemptive work,* etc. The notions vary with the interpreter, and reveal more about the advocates' imaginations than about Paul's intention.

2. *Others have the materials symbolize people.* Why people?

a. The foundation itself is Christ, a person, so the superstructure that His colaborers build upon Him can be other persons, "God's building."

b. People are built together into the church in Jesus' figure of Matthew 16:18, Paul's in Ephesians 2:12–21 and Peter's in 1 Peter 2:4–10. In Ephesians 2, the saints are "built upon" the foundation (v. 20) and the building consists of Jews and Gentiles "built together" (vv. 21–22; cf. 1 Peter 2:5, "being built"). If it is people that comprise the work of God in the other passages, it can be people that Paul means in 1 Corinthians 3:12–15.

c. The materials of 1 Corinthians 3:12 are put to the test of fire, which suggests OT verses where people are pictured by gold and silver being tested by fire (Job 23:10; Ps. 66:10).[22]

d. Paul in 2 Timothy 2:20–21 uses "gold and silver" vessels to depic people. These vessels, which are symbols of people in verse 21, are se in contrast to vessels of "wood and earth." There are possible links wit 1 Corinthians 3. The use of gold and silver is one of these, occurring i both texts. Another connection may be the "house," which some take t represent the church (though some view it as the world). One big differ ence is that the materials in 2 Timothy 2 are *vessels,* whereas 1 Corinthians 3 refers to building substances. Still, as 2 Timothy 2 uses the symbols to draw a distinction between people, Paul may intend the same thing by employing "gold, silver, precious stones" in 1 Corinthians 3.

e. Paul sees the Corinthian believers as "my work in the Lord" (1 Cor. 9:1). Paul had begun the work at Corinth, being the converts' "father" in the faith (4:15). If people are his own "work," people can be the "work" of those who continue building on the same foundation.

f. The problem that those favoring the doctrine view sometimes raise against the people view could be resolved. It is the difficulty of viewing the worker himself as saved (3:15) if people who are his "work" finally burn up in God's judgment. Granted, it is hard to grasp how a man can really wind up saved himself if he has so misled the people who comprise his unworthy work and this kind of work burns. Yet salvation is God's unadulterated *gift,* based on Christ's work and purchase (cf. 1 Cor. 6:20; Eph. 1:7). In Ephesians 1:7, it is based on Christ's blood, not any merit of the Christian. It is a boon grounded in redemption, not the colaborer's results (work) in the lives of others. A person can be saved, do work ostensibly for Christ, yet have some ideas that are misguided; or he can be, at times and in some aspects, a poor example that blights, misleads, and discourages others to turn away, even to hell. Later, *he himself* may "straighten up and fly right," but be unable to go back, locate all of those he caused to spurn Christ and the Christian way, and so undo the damage done through his past unworthy work.

And even if an interpreter insists on the doctrine view, imagining that his view avoids this problem, it has not necessarily done so. The same problem applies to the doctrine view. How may a worker himself finally be saved (1 Cor. 3:15) if in some inconsistent instances his work of teaching has misled some persons to their eternal detriment? Actually, whether an interpreter favors the people view or the doctrine view of the materials in 1 Corinthians 3, the final recourse must be to God's amazing grace, which reaches beyond the grasp of finite minds in cases of human failures.

This may or may not ease the view that the six materials are symbols of people a worker has placed upon the foundation or helped through ministry. The people view has still other difficulties, whether it is valid in 1 Corinthians 3 or not. For example, an interpreter does not follow a true analogy to 1 Corinthians 3 when he adduces proof from OT passages where gold and silver depict people tested by fire. Such texts do not combine two things: first, people who *build* with materials, and second, the *materials* themselves representing other people.

For the people view, a problem also attaches to the 2 Timothy 2 argument. That passage explicitly equates persons with the gold and silver; 1 Corinthians 3 does not. Also, the "work" that burns in 1 Corinthians 3 is not so easily identified as people in the fire of God's wrath, hell. One reason for this is that the *saved* are those who are tested in the fire with which 1 Corinthians 3 is dealing. This fire relates to both good work and bad. But elsewhere where Scripture refers to fire in which the *unsaved* are judged, none of the saved go into that fire. It is indicated that they have an altogether different treatment (Matt. 13:42, cf. v. 43; 2 Thess. 1:7–9, cf. v. 10; Rev. 20:11–15, cf. v. 15a).

3. *Others think that the materials symbolize character.* Kennedy put 1 Corinthians 3 with passages that refer to "the hidden realities of human character."[23]

4. *Many see the materials as incorporating a combination of things.* Such interpreters do not mention simply one thing, as doctrine or people. They specifically include two or more of the meanings this discussion has surveyed. For example, Gärtner says that Paul's warning not to destroy God's temple (vv. 16–17) is directed against a worker's having both "false doctrine and a life in conflict with the will of God."[24] Godet saw the materials as "The spiritual life of the members . . . [which] is, in a certain measure, the teaching itself received, assimilated, and realized in practice."[25] Hanson writes that Paul's conception of the work of the ministry as preaching the gospel "is not limited to speaking alone; the minister must preach the gospel by living the life of Christ in the world."[26]

Robertson and Plummer favor seeing fruit in *character* combined with or in persons, ". . . for the qualities must be exhibited in the lives of persons."[27] Pesch observes that the κόπος (*kopos,* "labor") and ἔργος (*ergos,* "work") that lead to the reward (3:8, 13–15) occur elsewhere under other images such as a worker's κάρπος (*karpos,* "fruit") or a στέφανος (*stephanos,* "crown") comprised of his converts (1 Thess. 2:19). To Pesch, 2 Timothy 4:8 reflects the Pauline idea in its reference to a "crown of righteousness." Pesch phrases this as "Christian life-conduct" or "work."[28] Other scholars see still different combinations within the content of the materials that lead to reward or loss of it.[29]

5. *A proposed larger combination.* Those who view the materials as symbols for a combination of Christ-pleasing things appear to be moving in the stream of Pauline evidence. The work involves the building of further doctrinal truth upon the foundation that is Christ. This is in the lives of people who corporately comprise the "building." The process of instilling truth in people entails work in its many aspects of activity. The doctrine and the activity correlate in unity with work in terms of Christlike character which exhibits the doctrinal message and validates itself in lives of inward and outward practicality.

The focus of this discussion now turns to prove that Paul saw the "work" as fruit in attitudes, motives, and other elements of character, not just doctrine and/or activity. Since many interpreters limit the materials or the "work" narrowly, or appear to, it is necessary to develop evidence in detail. Hopefully this will show the consistency of Paul's concept by correlating it in a variety of ways. Much evidence is from 1 Corinthians 1–4, which demonstrates the point effectively since these chapters are the context of 3:10–15.

a. One clue to the content of the materials is reflected by Paul's exhortations. What elements are crucial to him for those who receive the epistle? He exhorts them to a spirit of unity (1:10), centered in the wisdom and the power of God. He wants them to glory in the Lord (1:29, 31), not in man (3:21); desires that they not deceive themselves, evidently by putting their confidence in the world's wisdom (3:17–19); seeks that they view the apostles as ministers and stewards accountable to God for faithfulness (4:1, 2), apparently in the way they minister (as Paul in 3:10), that is, how they do it in God's wisdom and power; longs that they follow him (4:16) in a lifestyle characterized by elements of spiritual life (4:9–13). The aspects that are vital in Paul's exhortations suggest those he is concerned with in their "work."

b. Paul's purpose clauses reflect the things he regards as crucial. In chapters 1–4 he uses eight (or nine, if 1:7 is seen as a purpose idea[30]) purpose clauses.[31] The point for 3:12 is his attention to qualities of life experience. This suggests that the materials are symbols of content, not doctrinal but making up the Christian life that infleshes that doctrine. This embraces the spiritual dimensions, attitudes, character, and values of the Christian life. It refers to the life empowered by God to express the operation of God's kingdom, which Paul longs to find the Corinthian believers demonstrating (4:20).

c. Paul is warning in 3:10–17. Values reflected in warnings in this context may be clues to discovering what men should seek and shun in the "work" that prepares them to receive reward. Paul uses three other warnings in chapters 1–4. In 3:19, he warns against this world's wisdom, which he may connect with "wood, hay, straw" seven verses earlier. In 4:6–17, he warns against a proud, self-exalting spirit in contrast with the apostles' humility in their hardships. He wants believers to follow his example (v. 16), as he faithfully follows Christ (v. 17; 11:1). The heart of his concern is a product consisting of truly Christian character and attitude. Finally, 4:18–21 warns with regard to a Corinthian "puffed up" attitude in the Corinthian church. Paul may decide to visit them with a "rod," i.e., in discipline. He will look for evidence of the power of God's kingdom at work in their lives. Their speech may betray an absence of spiritual power and give evidence of carnal elements such as "envy" and "strife" in 3:3. If the power is conspicuously present in them for God's apostle to see when he comes to "judge,"[32] it will facilitate their approval in the test of the greater judgment by the apostle's God in the future day. The Lord Himself will search each builder's materials looking for the "power"!

d. Paul's words about the materials occur within a contrast. It seems valid to seek the nature of the materials by looking into other contrasts in the context. There are about thirty contrasts in chapters 1–4. In many Paul speaks about elements of the spiritual life or of doctrine and the life that is consistent with it. Omitting the contrasts in this immediate passage (3:11–12, 14–15), about twenty-seven remain. Of these, at least thirteen pertain to the spiritual life, to fruit that pleases Christ or its opposite, based on doctrine.[33] Some other contrasts relate to doctrine or to communicating it. But even these, in Paul's thought, may be closely united to spiritual experience with its enlivened character, activity, and attitudes. An example is 1:17a. God did not send Paul to baptize but to preach the gospel. Is this preaching in word only, or by word in the context of an exemplary life?

One contrast especially suggests the content that is the essence of the materials, giving them quality or the lack of it. It is spirituality and carnality. At their core both involve attitudes, such as unity or disunity (1:10–12; 3:3–4). Paul's counsel in 3:5–9, which leads into the context under discussion, is a direct antidote to the carnality in verses 3 and 4. Since the contrast is in attitudes, the solution (God will reward for good materials rather than bad) must contrast the same spiritual or carnal attitudes.

e. Paul introduces the context of 3:12 by beginning with the vital ingredients of his own example (v. 10). This suggests the kinds of elements he would desire of others who follow his example. In his own work, he preaches Christ's cross as the power and wisdom of God (1:18, 24; 2:1–4). The true wisdom (2:6–10) is made up of things the Spirit of God reveals. Persons who are "mature" or "spiritual" can receive these (2:6, 12–16; 3:1). In 3:3–4, carnality involves *inability* to receive spiritual realities from God but also characteristics of lifestyle that manifest the lack of these. These unspiritual dispositions are exemplified by "envy" and "strife" in exalting human leaders competitively and fostering disunity. Paul does not see doctrine in isolation but in relation to spiritual attitudes. Again, in 3:5–9 Paul trains his spotlight on the matter of attitudes. He emphasizes God's grace and giving the credit to God for any increase He grants.

f. Paul relates what "remains" or "burns" in the builder's work to the necessity of holiness in verses 16 and 17. Holiness must impregnate work valued by God and appraised as "gold," etc. Believers corporately comprise God's "temple." God's temple, as God Himself, is holy. "Holiness befits thy house . . ." (Ps. 93:5; cf. "glory" in 29:9). So work that scores well in God's test of believers consists in elements with the same nature as God's nature, holiness. The indwelling Spirit and spiritual content with Christ-pleasing value are vital. In terms of what Paul says about believers and the Spirit in 2:1–3:4, the work that Christ will approve for reward will be in harmony with the Spirit, a reflection of His own nature and power. The work should, therefore, be fulfiled "in demonstration of the Spirit and of power" (2:4), power that God alone, not man, can supply (2:5). And it must involve receiving and exemplifying in word or deed things that the Spirit has revealed, elements that express "the mind of Christ" (2:9–16).

g. The close unity of 4:5 with 3:10–15 offers a means of defining the content of the materials of 3:12. Both texts speak of the same further judgment. This is reasonable in light of factors that tie the two together. The Lord is the judge in both; both refer directly to a time of Judgment, "the day" (3:13) and "the time" (4:5). A striking resemblance links "the man's work shall be made manifest" (φάνερον [phaneron, "manifest," 3:13) and the Lord "will make manifest (φανερώσει [phanerōsei]) the counsels of the hearts" (4:5). Also, both use ἕκαστος [hekastos, "every man"]. The significance is that the materials Christ will examine at the judgment (4:5) reach inwardly, even to the "counsels of the hearts." This naturally leads one to perceive that in the judgment of 3:12–15 the materials consist of elements that go beyond doctrine and outward activity per se. They also incorporate inward attitudes and motives. Grundmann discerned this. To him, 4:5 and Romans 2:16 show that the "work" involves inward dispositions that each worker must have interwoven in his ministry, as in Philippians 1:15–16 and 2:20–21.[34] This leads Grundmann to see the worker's life-work or produce of 1 Corinthians 3:12 as "fruit for God," involving both inward dispositions and converts.

h. Paul connects "gold . . ." etc. with a building and the colaborer's work that builds. Passages where he uses this figure or words pertaining to building provide evidence of the content he sees in the materials. The word "edify" (οἰκοδομέω [oikodomeō]) is his word in the building figure. He adds the prefix, ἐπιοικοδομέω [epoikodomeō, "I build upon"), to describe building *upon* Christ the foundation (3:10, 12). In passages where he employs the "building" language, Paul emphasizes strongly the qualities of a Spirit-influenced life.

One example is 1 Corinthians 8:1, "love edifies [builds up]." Paul contrasts love to being "puffed up" in pride, the carnal attitude found in 3:3 and 4:6–7. Another instance, among several,[35] is Romans 14:19. Paul exhorts the saints to pursue dispositions that promote peace and "build up" each other. The introductory οὖν (*oun*, "therefore") shows that verse 19 follows logically from previous considerations. These considerations are twofold, marked out by an explanatory γάρ (*gar,* "for") that begins verse 17 and again verse 18. Before that, Paul says that a person is not to exercise his freedom to eat meat if this would destroy another person for whom Christ died. For in such a case what the believer thinks he is at liberty to do may be spoken of as evil. It is not worth insisting on practicing one's freedom where serving his own interests would harm another. At this point, Paul gives the two explanations why a person ought not to insist on asserting his freedom. First, "the kingdom of God is not meat and drink [these are not the decisive concerns of blessedness in the kingdom], but righteousness and peace and joy in the Holy Spirit." These three may bear their ethical, subjective sense—i.e., denoting experiential characteristics— or be taken in their forensic meaning.[36] In either case, experiencing such realities can be closely related to and flow from the forensic facts. Living in the practical good of these not only benefits believers' own spiritual lives, but furnishes them in "things of the building up of one another" (v. 19). Their work has the ingredients that Christ judges to be of value.

Christians should set a high priority on these, because they seek the profit of one another above their own freedom in such cases. Since these values are of crucial importance, Paul adds a second explanation (v. 18): ". . . he that in these things serves Christ is well-pleasing to God and approved by men." These are marks of good quality in the work of building that win favor of both God and men. In view of these reasons for devoting one's life to the advantage of brothers (vv. 17–18), Paul's "therefore" in verse 19 is natural. Since the qualities God deems of worth in His kingdom are "righteousness, peace, and joy," believers ought to "pursue after the things that promote peace." The words that follow "peace" in verse 19, "and things of building up one another," give warrant to understand not only "righteousness" and "joy" immediately from verse 17, but even Paul's more expanded cluster of fruit (Gal. 5:22–23). In the Romans 14 context, peace in particular is most fitting in view of the potential lack of peace among Christians in verses 1, 3, 10, 13a, 15–16, and 20. Believers provoke tensions with one another by exercising a spirit that harps on criticism. They censor and castigate others over differing convictions and practices.

Paul sees the work of building others in Romans 14 expressing itself in the fruit that the Holy Spirit produces. This appears in the context with a sobering reminder. Christians must realize that all will give an account before the judgment seat of God (vv. 10, 12). The building work, the fruit, will be subjected to the test of Christ's evaluation. This should "therefore" (v. 13) prompt a believer not to judge another in a harmful and carnal sense. It ought to direct him toward preventing another from falling (v. 13) and helping build him up in areas valued by Christ (v. 19).

6. *Conclusion about the materials.* The lines of evidence converge on a broad definition of the content of the six building materials. Work on the building has more than doctrine and activity per se interwoven within it. Fruit in the worker's motives and character also give quality to work that is true to Christ the foundation. This is the work that will elicit the approval of Christ when He judges (v. 13). It is the kind of work that will continue to lead to the reward that Christ deems equitable for it. For each worker will receive his own reward according to the standard of his own labor (v. 8).

CONCLUSION

The conclusion is that the materials contrast three qualities that are of such a nature as to bring reward from Christ with three qualities whose nature is such that they will diminish the degree of one's reward. It is best in defining the materials not to limit the meaning to doctrine, people, activity, or character. Paul more probably intended to depict a combination of things in service that Christ can appraise as fitted for reward. These, in the power of the Holy Spirit, are sound doctrine, activity (effort), motives, and character.

ENDNOTES

[1] 1 Corinthians 2:16. English translations are from the *New American Standard Bible* (La Habra, Calif.: Foundation, 1971) and from the King James Version.

[2] Either of two main interpretations fit the view that becomes evident in this study on 1 Corinthians 3:12. Some see the τέλειοι (*teleioi,* "mature") (2:6) as the saved who have grown to spiritual maturity (so S. Toussaint, "The Spiritual Man," *Bibliotheca Sacra* 125 [1968]: 139–46; C. C. Ryrie, "What is Spirituality?," *Bibliotheca Sacra* 126 [1969]: 204–13). A second view is that *teleioi* and πνευματικοί (*pneumatikoi,* "spiritual") are all the saved (so P. J. Du Plessis, *Teleios, The Idea of Perfection in the New Testament* [Kampen: J. H. Kok, 1959]). All the saved are perfect and spiritual ideally and provisionally in view of "the plentitude of salvation . . . and the consummate bounty of redemptive gifts bestowed . . ." (184).

[3] The two metaphors are also combined in God's work with Israel in the OT (Jer. 1:10; 18:9; 24:6; 31:28; 45:4; Ezek. 36:9–10). Bertil Gärtner cites Qumran references where "plantation" occurs with "house" and

"temple" (*The Temple and the Community in Qumran and the New Testament* [Cambridge: U. P., 1965], 27–29). For the two figures in Philo, Hellenism and Gnosticism, cf. Hans Conzelmann, *1 Corinthians*, 1st ed. (Philadelphia: Fortress, 1975), 75 nn. 61–63.

[4] So F. F. Bruce, *1 and 2 Corinthians* (London: Oliphants, 1971), 44–45: in verses 16–17 the building of verse 9 is "more closely defined as a sanctuary . . . for God to inhabit." Gärtner equates "building" and "temple," since "foundation" (v. 11) and "building" (v. 9) make it "perfectly justifiable to regard these more general expressions in the context of temple symbolism" (57f.). Cf. also Gordon D. Fee, *The First Epistle to the Corinthians* (Grand Rapids: Eerdmans, 1987), 140–41.

[5] Cf. 4:16; 11:1; Philippians 3:17; 1 Thessalonians 1:6; 2 Thessalonians 1:6; 3:9.

[6] Ἀρχιτέκτων (*Architektōn*, "Architect") is used only here in the NT. Ancient texts are not highly definitive as to the duties it denoted. In 2 Macc. 2:29 an architect has comprehensive responsibility over all particulars of a building work. This is in contrast to an architect who must be concerned only with one phase of work such as adorning a building. Isaiah 3:3 (LXX) links the ἀρχιτέκτων (*architektōn*, "architect") with positions requiring expertise. Sirach 38:27 distinguishes him from a τέκτων (*tektōn*, "artisan"). Paul intends a wider meaning than today's "architect" who is only a designer of blueprints. For Paul has personally done the construction work, "laid the foundation." In that he combines the word with σόφος (*sophos*, "wise, skilled"), his emphasis is on being an "expert" or "highly qualified workman." Cf. examples where the term denoted a person of special expertise in J. H. Moulton and G. Milligan, *The Vocabulary of the Greek Testament: Illustrated from the Papyri and Other Non-Literary Sources* (Grand Rapids: Eerdmans, 1963), 82.

[7] Asyndeton also occurs in 1 Corinthians 13:4–7, which relates to the excellencies of love, with one connective, δέ (*de*, "but"), and in Galatians 5:22–23, which lists the fruit of the Spirit, among other instances. As A. T. Robertson says, connectives may be left out "as a result of rapidity of thought as the words rush forth, or they may be consciously avoided for rhetorical effect" (*A Grammar of the Greek New Testament in the Light of Historical Research* [Nashville: Broadman Press, 1934], 427, 1177–78). Asyndeton in 1 Corinthians 3:12 is probably intended for rhetorical effect (cf. n. 8).

[8] F. Blass and A. Debrunner suggest that the list "is to be read with animation emphasizing the studied scale of descending value" (*A Greek Grammar of the New Testament and Other Early-Christian Literature* [Chicago: University of Chicago Press, 1961], 421, par. 460 (3); cf. also C. K. Barrett, *A Commentary on the First Epistle to the Corinthians* [London: Adam & Charles Black, 1968], 88). That Paul intended a word-by-word diminuendo does not necessarily follow from his order of listing the symbols. Silver sometimes is put before gold (Acts 3:6; 20:33; 1 Peter 1:18), sometimes after it (Acts 17:29; 2 Tim. 2:20; James 5:3; Rev. 9:20; 18:12).

[9] Some see "wood, hay, straw" as only inferior work, not bad work. William Barclay, in *The Letters to the Corinthians* (Philadelphia: Westminster Press, 1956), 36, refers them not to building up "wrong things" but "inadequate things . . . weak and watered down; a one-sided thing which has stressed some things too much and others too little . . . out of balance; a warped thing. . . ." The two categories of 1 Corinthians 3 could still correspond with the two in 2 Corinthians 5:10, the "good or bad" (ἀγαθόν *[agathon]* or φαῦλον *[phaulon]*). Φαῦλος *(Phaulos)* means "worthless," but in this context not a third category, not really good, not really bad. It is rather the opposite of ἀγαθόν *(agathon,* "good"), and so it is bad, sinful. Reasons that suggest this are: (1) Forms of *phaulos* do mean "worthless," by often in a both/and way, worthless in the sense of bad or bad in the sense of worthless. In its five other uses in the NT, *phaulos* refers to evil, as E. Achilles says (*"phaulos,"* in *The New International Dictionary of New Testament Theology,* ed. Colin Brown [Grand Rapids: Zondervan, 1975], 1:564; also John A. Sproule, "'Judgment Seat,' or 'Awards Podium'?" *Spire,* Grace Theological Seminary, 13 [1984]: 3). The bad works of the unsaved are *phaulos* (John 3:20). The evil deeds of the unsaved are contrasted with the good (*phaulos/agathos,* John 5:29). Jacob and Esau before birth had not committed good *(agathon)* or evil *(phaulon)* in Romans 9:11. (2) The OT (LXX) has *phauloi* as opposite to δίκαιοι *(dikaioi,* "righteous") (Job 9:23), and *phaulē* for an evil woman (Prov. 5:2). (3) Is it legitimate to assume a meaning that necessitates three categories in 1 Corinthians 3:12–15 and 2 Corinthians 5:10 when both texts list *two* units and can be explained reasonably with *two?* (4) The previous context of 1 Corinthians 3:12–15 has a contrast in 3:1–4 between attitudes that are spiritual and those that are carnal.

[10] Christ's judgment will have to be more probing than fire if all whom He judges are to "receive the things done in their bodies" (2 Cor. 5:10).

Paul's idea is similar to that in Revelation 1:14 and 2:23 where Christ's eyes are like a flame of fire and He "searches the minds and hearts."

[11] Origen sees 1 Corinthians 3:15 as the biblical *locus classicus* for purgatory (Contra Celsum 5:15). Favoring purgatory here, cf. E. Lussier, "The Biblical Doctrine on Purgatory," *American Ecclesiastical Review* CXLII (1960): 225–33, esp. 232. Lussier's other verses for purgatory are reasonably explained in other ways: Isaiah 1:25; 6:7; Zechariah 13:9; Matthew 3:2–3, 11; Sir. 2:5. Other texts often cited for purgatory, also adequately interpreted in other ways, are such as 2 Maccabees 12:43–45; Matthew 12:32; and 1 Timothy 1:18.

[12] Johannes Gnilka surveys 3:10–15 at length in the Eastern and Western churches. He thinks 3:15 does not teach purgatory. The fire is God's glory when He comes for the last judgment. Gnilka's denial here does not mean that he sees no evidence *anywhere* for purgatory (*Ist I Kor 3, 10–15 ein Schriftzeugnis für das Fegefeuer?* [Dusseldorf: M. Triltsch, 1955], 128).

[13] Certain factors are against purgatory in 1 Corinthians 3:15. (1) The purpose of the "fire" is not to *purge* but to *test* for reward. The saved were already cleansed through Christ's blood. The "fire" that tests the "work" is not aimed at "improving the character" (Norman Hillyer, "I Corinthians," in *New Bible Commentary Revised* [London: InterVarsity, 1970], 1056). (2) No punishment is in view. Christ bore all of our punishment (Rom. 8:1). His judgment of the saved is to reward for good and diminish reward, not condemn, for bad. "Fire" here affects *all* who do work on the true foundation; it is not exclusively for work that is worthless. (4) The text does not teach explicitly or implicitly a remission of sins at this testing. It does not deal with changing a person's lot but revealing it (cf. v. 13). There is no suggestion of a later improvement after death in a purgatorial fire. (5) J. F. X. Cevetello, arguing that 1 Corinthians 3:15 may mean purgatory "at least indirectly," makes a concession: "In the final analysis, the Catholic doctrine on purgatory is based on tradition, Not Sacred Scripture" ("Purgatory," in *New Catholic Encyclopedia* [15 vols.; New York, 1967], 11:1034). This is significant, though, as John Townsend says, *most* Roman Catholic scholars see purgatory in 3:15 "in one form or another" ("I Corinthians 3:15 and the School of Shammai," *Harvard Theological Review* LXI [1968]: 500).

[14] Ζημιόω *(Zēmioō)* means "to set someone in a disadvantageous position." The disadvantage was "loss," opposed to κέρδος *(kerdos,* "gain")

or "damage," synonymous with βλάβη (*blabē*, "harm"), as in loss of money or goods (A. Stumpff, "ζημία, ζημιόω," *TDNT*, ed. G. Kittel, II [1964], 888–92; W. Arndt and F. W. Gingrich, *A Greek-English Lexicon of the New Testament and Other Early Christian Literature* [Cambridge: University Press, 1960], 339). Context may help decide the idea. The meaning can be "ruin," as by homosexuality (Stumpff, *"zēmia,"* 889) or "punishment." The latter sense is possible in Proverbs 22:3 [LXX], "fools [the naive] . . . are punished"; cf. also 27:12; or 19:19, "A malicious man [man of great anger] shall be severely punished" or else "bear the penalty, be fined," which is a loss to him. Exodus 21:22 has a man being punished by being fined, penalized, not destroyed as a person. Matthew 16:26 refers to a man's losing his soul, a statement with *zēmioō*, just before referring to the Son of Man rewarding every man according to his works (v. 27). The works are not to merit salvation, but manifest the reality of it. Loss of special reward but not salvation is in view in 1 Corinthians 3:15, but loss of the soul (eternal damnation) in Matthew. Luke 9:25 combines two words for loss: "if he gains the whole world but loses (ἀπόλεσας [*apolesas*]) himself or suffers loss (ζημιωθείς [*zēmiōtheis*])." Apparently *zēmioō* in such a connection can be another term for the loss of eternal salvation. Paul's use of *zēmioō* in two other texts besides 1 Corinthians 3:15 does not refer to eternal punishment or forfeiture of the soul. In 2 Corinthians 7:9, Paul rejoiced that the Corinthians did not "suffer loss" by some adverse reaction to his letter (v. 8). He probably meant a setback in their spiritual experience. And in Philippians 3:8, Paul had "suffered loss" in all things for the sake of Christ and salvation in Him, that is, his sense of the *value* (Stumpff, *"zēmia,"* 890) of things on which he might rely for God's acceptance (vv. 5–6). The word is also used for loss (diminishing) of cargo and tackle from a ship but not the loss of people's lives (Acts 27:10, 21). Cf. Jay Shanor, who cites 4th-century-B.C. Greek building contracts where ζημιόω (*zēmioō*) means "to fine" for not completing a job or for taking too long ("Paul as Master Builder: Construction Terms in First Corinthians," *New Testament Studies* 34 [1988]: 469–71).

[15] In view of Paul's usage (cf. n. 13), his idea in 1 Corinthians is more probably "be assigned loss." Cf. Fee, *First Corinthians,* 143. He might mean that the worker is faced with loss of his "work," which burns. But this is redundant. Paul has just stated that the "work" is "burned." However, due to the close continuity between a Christian's "work" and his "reward" for it (cf. 1 Cor. 3:8), diminishment of one leads to reducing. The subject of reward allows the statement in verse 15 to be parallel with that of verse 14, but to state the other result, to round out a contrast.

The man whose work is of the quality that "remains" will receive reward; the man whose work is faulty and "burns" will be assigned loss with reference to the reward in the measure of it he might have had potentially (cf. Barrett, *First Corinthians*). The μισθόν (*misthon*, "reward," v. 14) is relevant to verse 15 and reasonably suggests an accusative of relation with respect to "experience loss" (Stumpff, *"zēmia,"* 890; Robertson and Plummer, *First Corinthians*, 65). The passive *zēmioō* might be read, "he shall be reduced" in respect to reward (so Robertson and Plummer, *First Corinthians*, 65). This is because (1) the man *himself* receives reward in verse 14, and so verse 15 probably conveys the other side of the picture, also relating to the man himself; (2) in 2 Corinthians 5:10, a man *himself* receives the things done in his body, both good and bad. The things are presumably the fitting reward and the loss of reward that are in continuity with the work (C. K. Barrett, *A Commentary on the Second Epistle to the Corinthians* [Grand Rapids: Eerdmans, 1973], 160); (3) the αὐτός (*autos,* "he himself") can be adequately explained. It may be that the person is diminished in respect to his capacity for special reward. Paul contrasts with that the fact that the man himself will be saved, and will be within the general sphere of blessedness/reward, which is the realm of eternal life, glory, the kingdom, the saints' inheritance, etc.

[16] Cf. also Job 23:10; Psalm 66:10; Zechariah 13:9; Revelation 3:18.

[17] Other examples include the following: gold, silver, and precious stones may be combined to stress value (Job 28:15–19; Dan. 11:38; cf. Rev. 18:12); or, only gold and precious stones occur (1 Kings 10:2; 2 Chron. 9:1; Prov. 3:14–15; Ezek. 27:22; cf. Rev. 17:4; 18:16; 21:18–21); or precious stones appear alone (Exod. 28:17–21; 1 Kings 5:17; 6:7; Isa. 54:11–12; Ezek. 28:12–15); or only gold and silver are listed (Gen. 13:2; 24:35, 53; 44:8; Exod. 3:22; Ps. 119:72; cf. Acts 3:6; 2 Tim. 2:20–21); and gold can occur alone (Ps. 19:10). Naturally, these valued objects were used early to build religious things men held to be of great value, whether false gods (Ps. 115:4; Prov. 3:14) or God's dwelling places (often in the Tabernacle, Exodus 25–40, and Temple, 1 Kings 6–7).

[18] This is, first of all, each official minister who leads in the church, and then other Christians who do work according to the example of the leader's model, whether good quality or bad.

[19] Barrett, *First Corinthians*, 89–90; J. Calvin, *The First Epistle of Paul the Apostle to the Corinthians,* Calvin's Commentaries, ed. D. W. Torrance

and T. F. Torrance (London: Oliver and Boyd, 1960), 75; C. W. Turner, "The Metaphors of St. Paul" (Ph.D. thesis, U. of Aberdeen, Scotland, 1956), 70–71; H. A. W. Meyer, *The Epistles to the Corinthians* (Edinburgh: T & T Clark, 1877), 1:92–94.

[20] Meyer, *Corinthians,* 1:94 [transliteration and translation added].

[21] F. Godet, *The First Epistle to the Corinthians* (Grand Rapids: Zondervan, 1971), 1:183; Meyer, *Corinthians,* 1:93; Turner, "The Metaphors," 70.

[22] Cf. also Proverbs 27:21; Zechariah 13:9; Malachi 3:3.

[23] H. A. A. Kennedy, *St. Paul's Conceptions of the Last Things* (London: Hodder and Stoughton, 1904), 205–7.

[24] Gärtner, *The Temple,* 60.

[25] Godet, *First Corinthians,* 1:183–84.

[26] A. T. Hanson, *The Pioneer Ministry* (London: SCM Press, 1961), 85. The same essential view appears in Jay Shanor, "Paul as Master Builder, Construction Terms in First Corinthians" (paper read at Far West Section of the Evangelical Theological Society, April 13, 1985).

[27] Robertson and Plummer, *First Corinthians,* 62; cf. to the same effect W. Grundmann, "Die Ubermacht der Gnade: eine Studie zur Theologie des Paulus," *Novum Testamentum* IV (1960): 267–91, esp. 286–87.

[28] Wilhelm Pesch, "Der Sonderlohn für die Verkundiger des Evangeliums (I Kor 3,8.14f und Parallelen)," *Neutestamentliche,* Aufsätze, Festschrift für Josef Schmid, ed. J. Blinzler, et al. (Regensburg: Friedrich Pustet, 1963), 204–5.

[29] W. Beardsley thinks "work" in 1 Corinthians 3:13–15 is both activity in preaching/teaching to build up the church and the product, fruit by the power of the Spirit as in 2:4–5 (*Human Achievement and Divine Vocation in the Message of Paul* [London: SCM Press, 1961], 52–60). A. C. Gaebelein, an older Bible expositor, says "work" is service which manifests Christlike character, i.e., fruit ("Romans–Ephesians," in *The Annotated Bible,* 9 vols. [New York: Our Hope, 1916], 99).

³⁰ In 1:7a the ὥστε (*hōste*, "so that") + μὴ ὑστερεῖσθαι (*mē hystereisthai*, "you do not lack") could denote purpose, but probably means that having no lack in any gift is the result of the rich endowment in verses 5–6 (Barrett, *First Corinthians* 38; Godet, *First Corinthians*, 1:54; Meyer, *First Corinthians*, 1:19). The emphasis is on what God has given to outfit saints for spiritual experience in church life, corporately or individually. They have been enriched in terms of gifts in "all speech and all knowledge," both of which Paul relates directly to edification, building up other saints, in chapter 14. Paul thinks of each gift as a "manifestation of the Spirit" and in close relation to its effect in experience, that of ministering "profit" (12:7), and so its exercise with a spirit sensitive to building up the church. Whether purpose or result, 1:7a is relevant in an inquiry into how Paul defines the materials for building in 3:12.

³¹ The eight purpose clauses apart from 1:7a are: 1:28, ἵνα (*hina*, "so that") + καταργήσῃ (*katargēsē*, "he might render inoperative"); 1:29, ὅπως (*hopos*, "so that") + καυχήσεται (*kauchēsetai*, "he might boast"); 1:31, ἵνα (*hina*, "so that") + καυχάσθω (*kauchasthō*, "let him boast"); 2:5, ἵνα (*hina*, "so that") + ᾖ (*ē*, "it might be"); 2:12, ἵνα (*hina*, "so that") + εἰδῶμεν (*eidōmen*, "we might know"); 4:6, ἵνα (*hina*, "so that") + μάθητε (*mathēte*, "you might learn"); 4:6, ἵνα (*hina*, "so that") + φυσιοῦσθε (*physiousthe*, "you might be puffed up"); and 4:8, ἵνα (*hina*, "so that") + συμβασιλεύσωμεν (*symbasileusōmen*, "we might reign together"). The point from these that bears on 3:12 is Paul's recurring focus on characteristics of life experience. This points toward viewing the materials and the "work" of 3:12–15 as including the content of the Christian's life.

³² In 4:19, "I shall know," as Godet says, is "the language of a judge proceeding to make an examination, . . . a forewarning of the judgment about to follow (v. 21)" (*First Corinthians*, 1:236). To the same effect, cf. Robertson and Plummer, *First Corinthians*, 92.

³³ The thirteen are: unity, not disunity (1:10); glorifying in the Lord, not in the flesh (1:29, 31); speaking in demonstration of the Spirit and of power, not in mere human speech, wisdom, and power (2:1–4); faith in God's power, not in man's wisdom (2:5); no one knows the Lord's mind, but we have the mind of Christ (2:16); not as to spiritual but as to carnal (3:1); "I judge not myself, but the Lord judges me" (4:3, 4); "we are fools, but you are wise" (4:10); "we are weak, you strong" (4:10); "we are despised, you honorable" (4:10); not to shame but to warn (4:14); not the speech but the power (4:19); the kingdom is not in word, but in power (4:20).

[34] Grundmann, "Die Ubermacht," 69–70; also "Paulus," 286–87.

[35] Other examples: 1 Corinthians 10:23; 14:3–5, 12, 17, 26; 2 Corinthians 10:8; 12:19; 13:10; Ephesians 2:19–22; 3:17; 4:1–16; 1 Thessalonians 5:11.

[36] J. Murray, *The Epistle to the Romans* (Grand Rapids: Eerdmans, 1968), 2:194. Cf. his defense of the ethical, experiential sense, not the forensic, but cf. C. E. B. Cranfield who favors the forensic idea (*A Critical and Exegetical Commentary on the Epistle to the Romans* [Edinburgh: T & T Clark, 1979], 2:718–19.

CHAPTER EIGHT

1 Corinthians 5:5

Deliver This Man to Satan: A Case Study in Church Discipline

Simon J. Kistemaker[1]

Part of understanding the difficult passage in 1 Corinthians 5:1–5 is the interpretation of the words "deliver this man to Satan" in 5:5. To explain this statement correctly, one must establish what the sin is that caused Paul to deliver the declaration. Then one should realize the responsibility of the local church in Corinth to deal with such a situation. The nature of the authority behind the directive needs also to be appreciated. Then details of the disciplinary action itself need clarification. The whole set of circumstances emphasizes how important it is for local churches to implement church disciplinary actions in dealing with sinning members and to use sound principles in doing so.

* * * * *

In his second epistle, the apostle Peter remarks that some things in Paul's letters are hard to understand (2 Peter 3:16). This is surely an understatement. Anyone who has studied Paul's first epistle to the Corinthians knows that a few passages are not only difficult to interpret, they are enigmatic. Among others these include Paul's command to deliver to Satan the man who committed incest (5:5), the sign of authority on the head of a woman because of the angels (11:10), and the reference to the ones baptized for the dead (15:29). We have the text of these verses, but could wish that Paul had incorporated explanatory footnotes along with them.

In this article, we will investigate the context,[2] the significance, and the message of 1 Corinthians 5:5. By studying the text carefully in the setting of the preceding verses, we will gain a better understanding of it and, at the same time, glean some principles for local churches to follow in exercising church discipline. A personal translation of the paragraph of verses 1–5 is in order as a start:

*¹It is actually reported that there is immorality among you
and of such a kind that does not even happen among the Gentiles, namely, that a man has the wife of his father. ²And you
are arrogant! Should you not rather be grieved? Put the man
who practiced this deed out of your midst. ³For even though I
am absent in the body but present in spirit, I have already
judged the man who has so committed this as if I were present.
⁴When you come together and I am with you in spirit with the
power of our Lord Jesus, ⁵in the name of our Lord Jesus deliver this man to Satan for destruction of the flesh that his
spirit may be saved in the day of our Lord.*

THE CAUSE OF CHURCH DISCIPLINE: INCEST

Paul had been told that someone in the church had committed incest
but that the members of the Corinthian church had not censured this
person. In an earlier letter (cf. 5:9) Paul had warned the Corinthians not
to associate with immoral people. Apparently, they had paid little if any
attention to his instruction because when a man had committed incest,
the church failed to act. Now Paul instructs the church to remove this
man and his heinous sin from their midst. Indeed both the man, because
of incest, and the church, because of failure to impose discipline, are
guilty of sin before God.

"There is immorality among you" (v. 1). The information Paul gives
is scant. He has received a report on immorality that pertains to a male
member of the church and the wife of the man's father. We do not know
whether the woman is a Christian or the father is still living. We know
only that the case of incest concerns a man and his stepmother and that
this immoral conduct is of a kind that even the Gentiles condemn.

According to Paul, the members of the church in Corinth were acquainted with this case of incest. The first word in the Greek sentence,
ὅλως (*holōs*), is an adverb that means either "actually," "generally," or
"altogether." It conveys more the concept of thoroughness than of uni-
versality[3] and signifies that the whole story has been reported. Because
it stands first in the sentence, the adverb is emphatic and modifies the
impersonal verb *it is reported.* Paul is not interested in revealing who the
reporter is or how he has received the news. He only states the fact and
does not provide details, except to say that in an earlier letter he had
warned the Corinthians not to associate with immoral people (cf. v. 9).

"A man has the wife of his father" (v. 1). In Jewish circles, the wording *wife of his father* meant "stepmother." Although not physically re-

lated to the son, yet because of her marriage vows to his father, she would plunge the son into sin by having sexual relations with him. God repeatedly told the Israelites, "Do not have sexual relations with your father's wife; that would dishonor your father" (Lev. 18:8; 20:11; Deut. 22:30; 27:20). If a son purposely had sexual relations with his stepmother, the community would have to put him to death by stoning. Would a son be free to marry her if his father had passed away? In the first two centuries of the Christian era, some Jewish rabbis condemned a marriage of a proselyte son and his pagan stepmother while others tolerated it.[4] Is it possible that this tolerance was known among the Jewish people and proselytes in Corinth? Perhaps, but we do not know. In any case, Paul condemns the deed and calls attention to the conduct of the Gentiles in this matter.

Paul fails to point out whether the father of this church member has passed away. He does not describe the stepmother as a widow, but gives the impression that the father is still alive (cf. Gen. 35:22; Amos 2:7). He writes that this sin is "of such a kind that does not even happen among the Gentiles" (v. 1).[5]

The mention of the name *Gentiles* is a means to emphasize the severity of the sin that the church member had committed. The writer alluded to the Gentiles to prod the Christian community to action. He did not want them to let one member put the entire congregation to shame. As one rotten apple in a box of apples can spoil the whole box, one reckless sinner was on the verge of rendering the entire Corinthian church ineffective in its witness to the Gentile community.

Why were the Corinthians negligent in chastising this immoral person and expelling him? Paul's words are biting: "You are arrogant" (v. 2). In the preceding chapter he had stated that some of the Corinthians were arrogant in their talking (cf. 4:6, 18–19). He here addresses all the believers in Corinth, because he knows that the leaders have led the others astray. They have been haughty for some time already and continue to be proud. They think that they are free to decide not to do anything about this wickedness (6:12; 10:23), and they claim to possess superior knowledge (3:18; 8:1–2). In reality, Paul faces the difficulty of trying to reason with people who lack both humility and constraint.

With a rhetorical question that expects an affirmative answer Paul queries, "Should you not rather be grieved?" (v. 2). Having alerted them to a blame that covers the body of the church, he is asking them to begin a period of mourning. The Greek verb πενθέω (*pentheō*, "I grieve") refers to a sorrow for sin that has been committed either by oneself or by others. The OT provides the example of Ezra, who mourned over the unfaithfulness of the exiles. These exiles had returned to Jerusalem and rebuilt the temple. But they had married foreign women belonging to the people around them (Ezra 10:1–6).[6] Ezra expressed grief and sorrow for the laxity these Jewish exiles displayed with regard to marriage.

In a similar manner, Paul tells the Corinthians to enter a period of grieving and thus exhibit repentance with godly sorrow. He desires that they humble themselves repentantly before God and then experience God's forgiveness and love.

THE INITIATIVE IN CHURCH DISCIPLINE

The Corinthians must turn from their pride, show renewed obedience to God's law, and expel the evil man from the church. Hence Paul says, "Put the man who practiced this deed out of your midst" (v. 2; cf. vv. 7, 13). The Greek indicates that the man has committed an act of immorality, not necessarily that he continues to practice it.

The time for church discipline has arrived. This painful process must take place just the same as a surgeon must use a scalpel to remove a malignant tumor from a patient's body. If the Corinthians do not dismiss the immoral man from the church, the Christian community itself will be placed under divine condemnation as outsiders are (v. 13). The church of Jesus Christ is characterized by holiness and must remove the blatant and unrepentant sinner by excommunicating him. Further, removal accompanied by the church's repentance cleanses the body of Christ.

In verses 2 and 3 Paul gives his outspoken judgment on the matter of immorality. For emphasis he contrasts the pronoun *you* in verse 2 with the pronoun *I* in verse 3: "Should *you* not rather be grieved?" (v. 2), and "For even though *I* am absent in body but present in spirit" (v. 3). He realizes that the Corinthians will read his epistle but will not see the physical presence of Paul. He admits that a geographical distance separates him from the recipients of his letter. Paul is in Ephesus in the western part of Asia Minor and the recipients of the epistle are in Corinth in the southern part of Greece. Distance does not mean that Paul's written words can be taken lightly. On the contrary, he is with the church in spirit and in that sense gives personal leadership. In spirit he takes the gavel in hand, so to speak, and chairs the meeting of the local church. Even though he is unable to have access to all the details, he knows that he and the Corinthians have to remove this blemish from the congregation. He does so through prayer on behalf of the Corinthians and through his written epistle.

Paul tells the congregation that he has taken action with respect to the immoral man. He says, "I have already judged the man who has so committed this as if I were present" (v. 3). He does not list a detailed procedure for church discipline, yet we are confident that the practice of confirming the truth by two or three witnesses had to be followed (cf. Matt. 18:15–17).

Notice that Paul has already judged this man. In effect, he needs no additional information because he knows that this affront to God's holiness must be removed. He writes in the perfect tense, "I have already judged," to indicate that he had already made a decision as soon as he heard about the offense. "Because Paul does not speak of an action but of a judgment there is no question here of divine judgment as in the case of Ananias and Sapphira."[7] Paul says, "as if I were present" (v. 3). This clause should be taken with the verb "I have judged," and in Greek precedes the wording "the man who has so committed this" (v. 3). Let no one think that Paul is far removed from the scene and therefore powerless. Paul is not impotent; he wants the church to take action guided by his judgment. In proper assembly, the church must remove the man who has committed the crime.

The wording is quite emphatic in the clause: "the man who has *so* committed this." For the sake of style some translators delete the word *so*. A few translations, however, dutifully transmit it to show Paul's intended emphasis.[8] Paul writes a sequence of three concepts that serve as demonstratives (the man, so, and this deed). In the Greek, he points out that the act of sinning happened in the past and has lasting effects for the church.

The intent of Paul's words is that the members of the Corinthian church must take immediate action to eliminate this evil from their midst. He instructs them to meet in assembly and to do so as if he himself were present. While they are gathered, they should call on Jesus' name, who Himself had promised that where two or three people gather in His name, He will be present (Matt. 18:20). In addition, they should know that Paul himself will be with them in spirit. They ought not to minimize his presence in spirit as if his physical presence would be real and his spiritual presence illusory. No, not so for several reasons.

First, Paul assures them twice that he is with them (v. 3); he is their spiritual father, watches over them, and constantly prays for them. Second, in the Greek he uses the emphatic personal adjective ἐμοῦ (*emou,* "my") with the noun πνεύματος (*pneumatos,* "spirit"). In English idiom, this adjective is deleted. Third, the phrase *in spirit* is synonymous with the phrase *the power of the Lord.* Paul speaks with the apostolic authority

Jesus delegated to him; as a rightfully appointed apostle he wields divine power.

In verses 3, 4, and 5 Paul writes a lengthy sentence that lacks fluency and so reveals his inner tension and agitation. The difficulty we face is the punctuation of this passage. The Greek original indicates that these verses can be construed as one loosely connected sentence: "For I verily, as absent in body, but present in spirit, have judged already, as though I were present, concerning him that hath so done this deed, in the name of our Lord Jesus Christ, when ye are gathered together, and my spirit, with the power of our Lord Jesus Christ, to deliver such a one unto Satan for the destruction of the flesh, that the spirit may be saved in the day of the Lord Jesus" (KJV). This single sentence becomes unwieldy and fails to communicate Paul's intention clearly. We need fitting punctuation to separate the many clauses so as to relate them meaningfully to the individual phrases.

THE AUTHORITY FOR CHURCH DISCIPLINE

Modern translators shorten such sentences and introduce appropriate punctuation. But even then, numerous questions remain, as is evident from the illustrations taken from several versions. How should the phrase "in the name of our Lord Jesus" be construed?[9] In short, this phrase could modify the four[10] clauses italicized in the following excerpts:

1. *I have already pronounced judgment* in the name of the Lord Jesus on the man who has done such a thing. When you are assembled . . . you are to hand this man over to Satan. (RSV)
2. *When you are assembled* in the name of our Lord Jesus . . . hand this man over to Satan. (NIV)
3. I as one who is present have already judged *the one who has done this thing* in the name of the Lord Jesus. When you are assembled . . . such a person should be handed over to Satan.[11]
4. When you and my spirit are gathered together . . . you should, in the name of the Lord Jesus, *hand over to Satan such a man* as this. (*Cassirer*)

Many translators favor the first possibility because Paul, although absent from Corinth in body but present in spirit, speaks with apostolic authority in Jesus' name. His verdict, then, is not a personal opinion, but is pronounced on Jesus' behalf and with His approval.[12]

Conversely, there is wisdom in looking at a phrase closer in the context of the Greek text and linking it to the nearest phrase as a modifier. When church officials would read this epistle in Greek to the congregation, the hearers would have had to link the phrase in question to either the preceding or the succeeding words. As a result, the immediate context could point to either the second or the third of the versions cited above.

Many scholars endorse the second reading: "When you come together in the name of our Lord Jesus and I am with you in spirit with the power of our Lord Jesus."[13] They profess that believers who gather in the name of Jesus know that He is the head and they are the body (Eph. 1:22–23). The objection to this reading is the repetitive phrase "of our Lord Jesus." This phrase occurs with both the nouns *name* and *power,* and therefore makes them indistinguishable.

The third translation conveys the sense that the man committed sexual sin with his stepmother in the name of the Lord Jesus. But this reading meets serious objections. First, because of textual variants it is difficult to decide whether the reading should be "our Lord Jesus" or "the Lord Jesus." Paul almost always speaks of "the Lord" without the addition of "Jesus." Furthermore, he utilizes the designation "our Lord Jesus" throughout this epistle. In light of these observations scholars prefer the reading with the personal pronoun "our."[14] Next, there appears to be an incongruity in the conduct of a Christian son who had illicit intercourse with his Gentile stepmother and invoked the name of Jesus to justify his sin. I suspect that the last name this sinner possibly invoked would be that "of our Lord Jesus." Last, if the third translation were accurate, we would have expected Paul to note the misuse of Jesus' name with scathing rebuke.

The fourth reading seems best. If we take the prepositional phrase "in the name of our Lord Jesus" with the clause "deliver this man to Satan," the sentence conveys Paul's command to the Corinthian congregation to expel the man. Except for the phrase "in the name of our Lord Jesus," verse 4 should be understood as a parenthetical statement. The emphasis, then, falls on Paul's command and the church's execution. The Corinthians must obey Paul and act on the basis of Jesus' authority. Paul says, "[I have already judged], in the name of our Lord Jesus, deliver this man to Satan." He tells the members that when they come together they must take action, for both Paul's spirit and Jesus' power are present.[15] The words *spirit* and *power* are juxtaposed and synonymous so that when the Corinthians act, they are aided by Paul's spiritual presence and Jesus' power.

THE RESULT OF CHURCH DISCIPLINE: EXCOMMUNICATION

"Deliver this man to Satan" (v. 5). I have translated the Greek aorist infinitive παραδοῦναι (*paradounai,* "to deliver") as an imperative. Handing someone over to Satan is akin to the prescription Jesus gave His disciples: treat an unrepentant sinner as a pagan or a tax collector (Matt. 18:17). The command to deliver someone to Satan has a parallel in another epistle where Paul writes about some people shipwrecking their faith. "Among them are Hymenaeus and Alexander, whom I have handed over to Satan to be taught not to blaspheme" (1 Tim. 1:20 NIV).

Paul's command to hand over a person to Satan is the act of excommunication and is equivalent to purging the evil from the church (cf. v. 13). Believers are safe in the hand of God from which no one, not even Satan, can snatch them (John 10:28–29). But if a sinner is delivered to the prince of this world, he faces destruction. He no longer enjoys the protection that a caring Christian community provides. John C. Hurd puts it graphically: "The Church [is] an island of life in Christ surrounded by a sea of death ruled by Satan."[16]

When adrift and deprived of spiritual support, the possibility is not remote that the outcast will come to his senses and subsequently repent. Here are two examples from the OT and the NT, respectively, of individuals who repented and returned to fellowship. Gomer, who as Hosea's sexually immoral wife personifies Israel, exclaims, "I will go back to my husband as at first, for then I was better off than now" (Hos. 2:7 NIV). And the prodigal son repented by confessing that he had sinned against God and against his father. Of his own volition, the son went to his parental home. This Jewish son came to his senses when he worked seven days a week herding pigs for a Gentile and was physically starving. He had broken God's commands, but confessed his sin before God. In the words of the father, the wayward son was dead; but when he returned home, he was alive again (Luke 15:24, 32).

What does Paul mean with the word *flesh* in the clause "for destruction of the flesh" (v. 5)? We understand the term to signify not part of a human body but "the whole person from the material point of view."[17] The translation "sinful nature" (NIV) or "sinful self" (NCV) fails to correspond as the counterpart of spirit in the text and, therefore, is less than satisfactory. Moreover, the text does not warrant the interpretation that destruction of the flesh results in immediate death because, in a subsequent verse, Paul forbids the Corinthians to have table fellowship with such a man (v. 11). Because of the brevity of the clause "for destruction of the flesh," the question of mode or manner remains unanswered. For lack of pertinent detail, we are forced to resort to either of two hypotheses: first, Satan is permitted to destroy a person's sensuality; or second, he weakens man's physical body.

Those scholars who resort to the first hypothesis explain that the term *flesh* pertains to the baser part of man's physical life that causes him to sin.[18] In the hands of Satan, they say, this part of a person's being perishes while his spirit is being saved. Consequently, they do not see Satan in an adversarial role to the cause of Christ, but as a helper. We demur. Satan is permitted to destroy only that which God allows,[19] but he never leads a sinner to repentance and a saving knowledge of Christ. By contrast, he is set on leading a sinner farther away from God for Satan restrains rather than promotes the cause of Christ. Therefore this explanation fails to merit favor.

The second hypothesis is preferred. It holds that in addition to the act of excommunication, God permits Satan to attack and gradually weaken man's physical body (cf. Job 2:5; 2 Cor. 12:7).[20] Paul is not referring to a sudden demise (as e.g., in Acts 5:1–10), but to a slow process of physical decline. During this process the sinner receives ample time to reflect on his condition and repent (cf. 1 Cor. 11:28–30).[21]

The clause on the destruction of the flesh is grammatically subordinate to the main purpose clause, "that his spirit may be saved" (v. 5). Even though the Greek word πνεῦμα (*pneuma,* "spirit") in translation can be capitalized as "Spirit" or refer to man's "spirit," translators understand the term to refer not to the divine, but the human spirit. Nevertheless, one scholar has suggested the interpretation that the Christian community had to expel the incestuous man "to avoid offense to the presence of the Holy Spirit."[22] Certainly Scripture teaches not to grieve or stifle the Holy Spirit of God (cf. Eph. 4:30; 1 Thess. 5:19). But that is not the point of the current passage. We reject the scholarly interpretation for at least three reasons: first, verse 5 contrasts man's flesh and spirit, not human flesh and the Holy Spirit. Next, Paul states that man's spirit may be saved, not that the presence of the Holy Spirit may be kept. And last, in the preceding verses (vv. 3–4) the word *pneuma* occurs twice and refers to man's spirit, not to the Holy Spirit.

The destruction of the flesh serves the purpose of making possible the restoring of the sinner's soul before he dies. The gift of salvation depends on repentance, which takes place during a person's earthly life, not after his death. Scripture clearly teaches us that repentance must take place on earth, not in hell where the rich man implored father Abraham for help. Physical death irrevocably closes the door to a second opportunity for repentance and salvation (Luke 16:19–31).

Yet Paul writes that the man's spirit may be saved on the day of the

Lord, which seems to point to the judgment day.[23] He does not imply that the man will have to wait until the end of time to be saved. Rather, Paul means that in this life the forgiven sinner receives salvation and in the day of the Lord is counted among those who are glorified. "Salvation is primarily an eschatological reality, experienced in the present to be sure, but to be realized fully at the Day of the Lord."[24] Also, the interpretation of the phrase *day of the Lord* is broader than a reference to the end of time when the judgment will take place. It can also mean a unique period during which God's people rejoice in the Lord. The OT prophets understood the phrase to mean a time in which God claims victory over the world and His people triumph with Him (Isa. 2:11, 17–20; Zech. 14:7).

In His infinite wisdom, God brings a sinner to repentance through various means and methods (cf. 11:32; 1 Peter 4:6). He is interested in the salvation of man's soul and earnestly desires that all people come to repentance (2 Peter 3:9).

With respect to the man who committed incest, Paul hopes that even though Satan may destroy the physical body, the man's spirit may be saved "in the day of the Lord" (v. 5). From Paul's epistles, however, we have no positive proof that the man was restored physically or spiritually.[25]

CONCLUSION

When the Israelites entered Canaan and conquered Jericho, Achan transgressed God's command by taking items devoted to God. The people stoned him and thus removed God's wrath against sin (Josh 7:25–26). God calls His people to be a holy people.

In the Jerusalem church, Ananias and Sapphira purposely tried to deceive the Holy Spirit. Peter uncovered their deception, and God removed them from the Christian community by taking their lives (Acts 5:1–10). God wanted the followers of Jesus to honor the truth.

Paul confronted the Corinthians with the incestuous behavior of one of their members. With a direct command he instructed them to expel the man from the church in the name of the Lord. The man's excommunication consisted of being delivered into the hands of Satan. Paul charged the church to purge itself of wickedness and evil and to embrace the virtues of sincerity and truth (v. 8).

If Paul had not acted forcefully to exclude this man from the church, the man's sin would have continued to infect the entire congregation. Indeed, the man's immoral conduct posed a direct threat to the existence of the church itself. The church dwells figuratively in a glass house, and the world is free to observe the people within this house. When the church fails to check a sin that the world condemns, the church has become ineffective because of disobedience and spiritual defilement. The church must deal decisively with sin. It must attempt to bring the offender to repentance and salvation or else resort to excommunication as Paul instructed the Corinthians. In word and deed, the church must exhibit an intense hatred for sin and a genuine desire for holiness. Such holiness demands ardent love for Jesus Christ and total obedience to His commands.

ENDNOTES

[1] This article has been adapted and enlarged from a segment of Dr. Kistemaker's *Exposition of the First Epistle to the Corinthians* (1993), with permission from Baker Book House, Grand Rapids, Mich.

[2] Some issues of textual and exegetical significance in the larger context do not directly impinge on an understanding of verse 5, and so will not be treated. The focus is upon obtaining a grasp of the explicit directive, "deliver this man to Satan."

[3] The *Simple English Bible* has, "It is being told everywhere." By contrast, the *Jerusalem Bible* reads, "I have been told as an undoubted fact."

[4] Str-B, 3:358.

[5] Cicero condemns the crime of incest: *Pro Cluent* 5.11–14.

[6] BAGD, 642.

[7] F. W. Grosheide, "Commentary on the First Epistle to the Corinthians: The English Text with Introduction, Exposition and Notes," in *New International Commentary on the New Testament* (Grand Rapids: Eerdmans, 1953), 121.

[8] KJV, NKJV, NASB, *God's New Covenant: A New Testament Translation* by Heinz W. *Cassirer*. BAGD translates the combination *so* and *this* as "so basely" (597).

[9] In my translation, I have made the phrase "in the name of our Lord Jesus" a part of verse 5.

[10] Hans Conzelmann lists six choices and Leon Morris seven. Consult Conzelmann's *1 Corinthians,* Hermeneia, trans. James W. Leitch (Philadelphia: Fortress, 1975), 97; Leon Morris, *1 Corinthians,* rev. ed., Tyndale (Grand Rapids: Eerdmans, 1987), 84–85.

[11] Jerome Murphy-O'Connor, "I Corinthians V, 3–5," *Revue biblique* 84 (1977): 245; S. D. MacArthur, "'Spirit' in Pauline Usage: 1 Corinthians 5:5," in *Studia Biblica 1978, III. Papers on Paul and Other New Testament Authors,* ed. E. A. Livingstone (Sheffield: JSOT, 1980), 249–56; Gerald Harris, "The Beginnings of Church Discipline: 1 Corinthians 5," *New Testament Studies* 37 (1991): 1–21.

[12] See Gordon D. Fee, "The First Epistle to the Corinthians," in *NICNT* (Grand Rapids: Eerdmans, 1987), 207–8.

[13] E.g., John Calvin, *The First Epistle of Paul the Apostle to the Corinthians,* Calvin's Commentaries series, trans. John W. Fraser (reprint, Grand Rapids: Eerdmans, 1976), 107.

[14] E.g., G. Zuntz, *The Text of the Epistles: A Disquisition upon the Corpus Paulinum* (London: Oxford, 1953), 235–36.

[15] Cf. G. A. Cole, "1 Cor. 5:4 '. . . with My Spirit,'" *Expository Times* 98 (1987): 205.

[16] John Coolidge Hurd Jr., *The Origin of I Corinthians* (Macon, Ga.: Mercer, 1983), 285.

[17] Adela Yarbro Collins, "The Function of 'Excommunication' in Paul," *Harvard Theological Review* 73 (1980): 257; cf. also Eduard Schweizer, "σάρξ, σαρκικός, σάρκινος," *TDNT,* 7:125.

[18] N. G. Joy, "Is the Body Really to Be Destroyed? (1 Corinthians 5:5)," *Bible Translator* 39 (1988): 429–36; A. C. Thiselton, "The Meaning of Sarx in 1 Corinthians 5.5: A Fresh Approach in the Light of Logical and Semantic Factors," *Scottish Journal of Theology* 26 (1973): 204–28; J. Cambier, "La Chair et l'Esprit en 1 Cor. v.5," *New Testament Studies* 15 (1969): 221–32.

[19] Cf., however, T. C. G. Thornton, "Satan—God's Agent for Punishing," *Expository Times* 83 (1972): 151–52.

[20] Colin Brown, among others, states that "physical destruction is not envisaged" ("ὄλεθρος," in *New International Dictionary of New Testament Theology*, 1:466). Morris notes that Paul sees the man's expulsion "resulting in physical consequences" (*1 Corinthians*, 86).

[21] Frederic Louis Godet, *Commentary on First Corinthians* (1889; reprint, Grand Rapids: Kregel, 1977), 257; Morris, *1 Corinthians*, 86.

[22] Yarbro Collins, "Function," 263.

[23] The variants that read "the day of the Lord Jesus" and "the day of our Lord Jesus Christ" do not substantially alter the results of this study. The point is that the reference of the expression is to something eschatological.

[24] Fee, *First Corinthians*, 213.

[25] Cf. E. Fascher, "Zu Tertullians Auslegung von 1 Kor 5, 1–5 (De Pudicitia c. 13–16)," *Theologische Literaturzeitung* 99 (1974): 9–12. Whether 2 Corinthians 3:6–8 is referring to this same individual is uncertain.

CHAPTER NINE

1 Corinthians 6:9 and 1 Timothy 1:10

The Source and NT Meaning of ΑΡΣΕΝΟΚΟΙΤΑΙ, with Implications for Christian Ethics and Ministry

James B. DeYoung

Traditional interpretation of ἀρσενοκοῖται (arsenokoitai, "homosexuals") in 1 Corinthians 6:9 and 1 Timothy 1:10 refers to sexual vice between people of the same sex, specifically homosexuality. Some restrict the term's meaning to "active male prostitute," but stronger evidence supports a more general translation, namely "homosexuals." More recently the definition "homosexual" has been opposed on cultural and linguistic grounds, the claim being that the term "homosexuals" is anachronistic. In addition, criticism of the traditional rendering says the term today includes celibate homophiles, excludes heterosexuals who engage in homosexual acts, and includes female homosexuals. A concern for acts instead of the modern attention to desires was the only factor in the ancient world. The foregoing opposition to the translation of arsenokoitai by "homosexuals" has a number of debilitating weaknesses. Finally, this study argues that Paul coined the term arsenokoitai, deriving it from the LXX of Leviticus 20:13 (cf. 18:22) and using it for homosexual orientation and behavior, the latter of which should be an occasion for church discipline (1 Corinthians 5–6) and legislation in society (1 Tim. 1:8–11).

* * * * *

INTRODUCTION

Coincident with the rise of the gay rights movement in recent years has been an increasing focus on the biblical statements regarding homosexuality or sodomy.[1] As part of this focus, the meaning of the term ἀρσενοκοῖται (*arsenokoitai*, "homosexuals"), used twice by the apostle Paul (1 Cor. 6:9; 1 Tim. 1:10), has received vigorous scrutiny.[2] This issue is particularly crucial to contemporary society since so much of modern ethics is shaped by biblical statements. More particularly, the concern over gay rights and the place of gays or homosexuals in the church and in society require the resolution of biblical interpretation.

This study of historical, linguistic, and literary matters will survey and evaluate recent proposals for the meaning of *arsenokoitai* and present evidence to point to a resolution. Several writers and their positions represent the modern debate on this word. Three authors, Bailey, Boswell, and Scroggs, have provoked considerable discussion and significantly encouraged the wider acceptance of the homosexual lifestyle in society, in the church, and in the ministry.[3]

SURVEY OF NEW INTERPRETATIONS OF *ARSENOKOITAI*

D. S. Bailey

D. S. Bailey was perhaps the trailblazer of new assessments of the meaning of *arsenokoitai*. He takes the term in 1 Corinthians 6:9 as denoting males who actively engage in homosexual acts, in contrast to μαλακοί (*malakoi*, "effeminate"), those who engage passively in such acts.[4] However, he insists that Paul knew nothing of "inversion as an inherited trait, or an inherent condition due to psychological or glandular causes, and consequently regards all homosexual practice as evidence of perversion" (38). Hence Bailey limits the term's reference in Paul's works to acts alone and laments modern translations of the term as "homosexuals." Bailey wants to distinguish between "the homosexual *condition* (which is morally neutral) and homosexual *practices*" [italics in source]. Paul is precise in his terminology and Moffatt's translation "sodomites" best represents Paul's meaning in Bailey's judgment (39). Bailey clearly denies that the homosexual condition was known by biblical writers.

J. Boswell

The most influential study of *arsenokoitai* among contemporary authors is that of John Boswell.[5] Whereas the usual translation[6] of this term gives it either explicitly or implicitly an active sense, Boswell gives it a passive sense.

In an extended discussion of the term (341–53), he cites "linguistic evidence and common sense" to support his conclusion that the word means "male sexual agents, i.e., active male prostitutes." His argument is that the *arseno*-part of the word is adjectival, not the object of the *koitai,* which refers to base sexual activity. Hence the term, according to Boswell, designates a male sexual person or male prostitute. He acknowledges, however, that most interpret the composite term as active, meaning "those who sleep with, make their bed with, men." Boswell bases his interpretation on linguistics and the historical setting. He argues that in some compounds, such as παιδομαθής (*paidomathēs,* "child learner"), the *paido-* is the subject of *manthanō,* and in others, such as παιδοπόρος (*paidoporos,* "through which a child passes"), the *paido-* is neither subject nor object but simply a modifier without verbal significance. His point is that each compound must be individually analyzed for its meaning. More directly, he maintains that compounds with the Attic form *arreno-* employ it objectively while those with the Hellenistic *arseno-* use it as an adjective (343). Yet he admits exceptions to this distinction regarding *arreno-.*

Boswell next appeals to the Latin of the time, namely *drauci* or *exoleti.* These were male prostitutes having men or women as their objects. The Greek *arsenokoitai* is the equivalent of the Latin *drauci;* the corresponding passive would be παρακοῖται (*parakoitai,* "one who lies beside"), Boswell affirms. He claims that *arsenokoitai* was the "most explicit word available to Paul for a male prostitute," since by Paul's time the Attic words πόρνος (*pornos,* "fornicator") and πορνεύων (*porneuōn,* "one committing fornication"), found also in the LXX, had been adopted "to refer to men who resorted to female prostitutes or simply committed fornication."[7]

In the absence of the term from pagan writers such as Herodotus, Plato, Aristotle, and Plutarch, and from the Jewish writers Philo and Josephus, Boswell finds even more convincing evidence for his affirmation that *arsenokoitai* "did not connote 'homosexual' or even 'sodomite' in the time of Paul" (346).[8] He also demonstrates its absence in Pseudo-Lucian, Sextus Empiricus, and Libanius. He subsequently finds it lacking in "all discussions of homosexual relations" (346)[9] among Christian sources in Greek, including the *Didache,* Tatian, Justin Martyr, Eusebius,[10] Clement of Alexandria, Gregory of Nyssa, and John Chrysostom. Chrysostom is singled out for his omission as "final proof" that the word could not mean homosexuality.[11]

Boswell next appeals to the omission of the texts of 1 Corinthians and 1 Timothy from discussions of homosexuality among Latin church fathers (348).[12] Cited are Tertullian, Arnobius, Lactantius, and Augustine. The last named uses "circumlocutions." Other Latin writers include Ausonius, Cyprian, and Minucius Felix. The term is also lacking in state

and in church legislation. By the sixth century the term became confused and was applied to a variety of sexual activities from child molesting to anal intercourse between a husband and wife (353).
Having surveyed the sources, Boswell concludes,

> There is no reason to believe that either ἀρσενοκοῖται *(arsenokoitai)* or μαλακοί *(malakoi)* connoted homosexuality in the time of Paul or for centuries thereafter, and every reason to suppose that, whatever they came to mean, they were not determinative of Christian opinion on the morality of homosexual acts. (353, transliteration added)

It is clear throughout that Boswell defines *arsenokoitai* to refer to male prostitutes. He even goes so far as to conclude that Paul would probably not disapprove of "gay inclination," "gay relationships," "enduring love between persons of the same gender," or "same-sex eroticism" (112, 116–17).

R. Scroggs

Robin Scroggs has built upon the discussion of his predecessors and suggested a new twist to the word. Scroggs believes that ἀρσενοκοῖται is a "Hellenistic Jewish coinage, perhaps influenced by awareness of rabbinic terminology." The term is derived from Leviticus 18:22 and 20:13 where the LXX juxtaposes the two words ἄρσενος *(arsenos,* "male") and κοίτην *(koitēn,* "bed"), and represents the Hebrew מִשְׁכַּב זָכָר *(miškab zākār,* "lying with a male").[13] Yet he believes that Paul did not originate the term, but borrowed it from "circles of Hellenistic Jews acquainted with rabbinic discussions" (108 n. 14). It was invented to avoid "contact with the usual Greek terminology" (108). If this is true, Scroggs observes, it explains why the word does not appear in Greco-Roman discussions of pederasty and why later patristic writers avoided it. It was meaningless to native-speaking Greeks (108).

Scroggs takes the second part as the active word and the first word a the object of the second part, thus differing from Boswell's "learne(discussion" (107). Yet Scroggs understands the general meaning of "one who lies with a male" to have a very narrow reference. With the preced ing *malakoi* (1 Cor. 6:9), which Scroggs interprets as "the effeminate call-boy," *arsenokoitai* is the active partner "who keeps the *malakos* as a 'mistress' or who hires him on occasion to satisfy his sexual desires" (108). Hence *arsenokoitai* does not refer to homosexuality in general, to female homosexuality, or to the generic model of pederasty. It certainly cannot refer to the modern gay model, he affirms (109).

This is Scrogg's interpretation of the term in 1 Timothy 1:10 also.
The combination of πόρνοι (*pornoi,* "fornicators"), *arsenokoitai,* and ἀνδραποδισταί (*andrapodistai,* "slave-dealers") refers to "male prostitutes, males who lie [with them], and slave dealers [who procure them]" (120). It again refers to that specific form of pederasty "which consisted of the enslaving of boys as youths for sexual purposes, and the use of these boys by adult males" (121). Even "serious minded pagan authors" condemned this form of pederasty. He then uses these instances of *arsenokoitai* in 1 Corinthians and 1 Timothy to interpret the apparently general condemnation of both female and male homosexuality in Romans 1. Consequently Paul "must have had, *could only have had* pederasty in mind" (122, italics in source). We cannot know what Paul would have said about the "contemporary model of adult/adult mutuality in same sex relationships" (122).

In relating these terms to the context and to contemporary ethical concerns, Scroggs emphasizes the point that the specific items in the list of vices in 1 Corinthians 6 have no deliberate, intended meaning in Paul. The form and function of the catalogue of vices are traditional and stereotyped. Any relationship between an individual item in the list and the context was usually nonexistent. He concludes that Paul "does not care about any specific item in the lists" (104).[14]

Both on the basis of the meaning of the terms and of the literary phenomenon of a "catalogue of vices," Scroggs argues that the Scriptures are "irrelevant and provide no help in the heated debate today" (129). The "model in today's Christian homosexual community is so different from the model attacked by the New Testament" that "*Biblical judgments against homosexuality are not relevant to today's debate.* They should no longer be used in denominational discussions about homosexuality, should in no way be a weapon to justify refusal of ordination . . ." (127, italics in source).

REACTIONS TO THE NEW INTERPRETATIONS OF ΑΡΣΕΝΟΚΟΙΤΑΙ

D. Wright

In more recent years the positions of Bailey, Boswell, and Scroggs have come under closer scrutiny.[15] Perhaps the most critical evaluation of Boswell's view is that by David Wright. In his thorough article, Wright points out several shortcomings of Boswell's treatment of *arsenokoitai.*[16] He faults Boswell for failing to cite, or citing inaccurately, all the references to Leviticus 18:22 and 20:13 in the church fathers, such as Eusebius, the *Apostolic Constitutions,* Clement of Alexandria, Tertullian, and Origen (127–28). Boswell has not considered seriously enough the possibility that the term derives either its form or its meaning from the Leviticus passages (129). This is significant, for if the term is so derived, it clearly refutes Boswell's claim that the first half of the word *(arseno-)* denotes not the object but the gender of the second half *(-koitai).* The LXX must mean "a male who sleeps with a male," making *arseno-* the object.

Wright also faults Boswell's claims regarding linguistic features of the term, including suggested parallels (129). Though Boswell claims that compounds with *arseno-*employ it objectively and those with *arreno-*employ it as an adjective, Wright believes that the difference between the two is merely one of dialectical diversity: "No semantic import attaches to the difference between the two forms" (131). Wright believes that in most compounds in which the second half is a verb or has a verbal force, the first half denotes its object and where "the second part is substantival, the first half denotes its gender" (132).[17]

It is with Boswell's treatment of the early church fathers that Wright takes special issue because the former has failed to cite all the sources. For example, Aristides' Apology (c. A.D. 138) probably uses ἀρρενομανεῖς *(arrenomaneis),* ἀνδροβάτην *(androbatēn),* and ἀρσενοκοιτίας *(arsenokoitias)* all with the same basic meaning of male homosexuality (133), contrary to Boswell's discussion. Boswell fails to cite Hippolytus *(Refut. Omn. Haer.* 5:26:22–23) and improperly cites Eusebius and the Syriac writer Bardesanes. The latter uses Syriac terms that are identical to the Syriac of 1 Corinthians 6:9 and 1 Timothy 1:10 (133–34).[18]

Next Wright shows how the early church fathers use *arsenokoitai* in parallel with παιδοφθορία *(paidophthoria)* referring to male homosexuality with teenagers, the dominant form of male homosexuality among the Greeks (134). Sometimes this parallelism occurs in the threefold listings of μοιχεία *(moicheia,* "adultery"), πορνεία *(porneia,* "fornication"), and *paidophthoria,* with *arsenokoitai* replacing *paidophthoria* (136). Clement of Alexandria in *Protr.* 10:108:5 cites the second table of the Ten Commandments as "You shall not kill, οὐ μοιχεύσεις *(ou moicheuseis,* "you shall not commit adultery"), οὐ παιδοφθορήσεις *(ou paidophthorēseis,* "you shall not practice homosexuality with boys"), you shall not steal . . ." (150 n. 43, transliteration and translation added).

Another occurrence of ἀρσενοκοιτεῖν *(arsenokoitein,* "commit homosexuality") exists in the *Sibylline Oracles* 2:71–73. It may be, Wright observes, that the word was coined by a Jewish pre-Christian writer in a Hellenistic setting represented by *Or.Sib.,* book 2 (137–38).

Wright also discusses uses of *arsenokoitai* in Rhetorius (6th century) who drew upon the first century A.D. writer Teucer, in Macarius (4th–5th cent.), and in John the Faster (d. 595) (139–40). The last in particular bears the idea of homosexual intercourse, contrary to Boswell.

Wright next replies to Boswell's contention that the term would not be absent "from so much literature about homosexuality if that is what it denoted" (140–41). Wright points out that it should not be expected in writers prior to the first century A.D. since it did not exist before then, that the Greeks used dozens of words and phrases to refer to homosexuality, that some sources (e.g., *Didache*) show no acquaintance with Paul's letters or deliberately avoid citing Scripture, and that Boswell neglects citing several church fathers (140–41).[19]

Boswell's treatment of Chrysostom in particular draws Wright's attention (141–44). Boswell conspicuously misrepresents the witness of Chrysostom, omitting references and asserting what is patently untrue. Chrysostom gives a long uncompromising and clear indictment of homosexuality in his homily on Romans 1:26. Boswell has exaggerated Chrysostom's infrequent use of the term. Wright observes that Boswell has "signally failed to demonstrate any use of ἀρσενοκοίτης *(arsenokoitēs)* etc. in which it patently does not denote male homosexual activity" (144, transliteration added). It is infrequent because of its relatively technical nature and the availability of such a term as *paidophthoria* that more clearly specified the prevailing form of male homosexuality in the Greco-Roman world.[20]

Wright also surveys the Latin, Syriac, and Coptic translations of 1 Timothy 1:10 and 1 Corinthians 6:9. All three render *arsenokoitai* with words that reflect the meaning "homosexual," i.e., they understand *arseno-* as the object of the second half of the word (144–45). None of these primary versions supports Boswell's limited conclusion based on them.

Wright concludes his discussion with a few observations about the catalogues of vices as a literary form. He believes that such lists developed in late Judaism as Hellenistic Jews wrote in clear condemnation of homosexuality in the Greek world. This paralleled the increased concern on the part of moral philosophers over homosexual indulgence. The term came into being under the influence of the LXX (145) so that writers spoke "generally of male activity with males rather than specifically categorized male sexual engagement with παῖδες *(paides)*" (146, transliteration added). If *arsenokoitia* and *paidophthoria* were interchangeable, it is because the former encompassed the latter (146).

In summary, Wright seeks to show that *arsenokoitai* is a broad term meaning homosexuality and arises within Judaism. The views of Boswell,

Scroggs, and others who limit the term to "active male prostitutes" or pederasty are without significant support from linguistic and historical studies.

W. Petersen

More recently Wright's understanding has itself been questioned from a different direction. In a brief 1986 study William Petersen found linguistic confusion in using the English word "homosexuals" as the meaning of *arsenokoitai*.[21] He faulted Wright and English Bible translations for rendering it by "homosexuals" in 1 Corinthians 6:9 and 1 Timothy 1:10.

In a sense Petersen has coalesced Bailey, Boswell, and Scroggs into a single assertion that reiterates, in effect, the position of Bailey. He finds "homosexuals" unacceptable as a translation because it is anachronistic. "A major disjunction" exists between contemporary thought and terminology and the thought and terminology in Paul's time (187–88).

What is this "disjunction"? He bases it on historical and linguistic facts. Accordingly, ancient Greek and Roman society treated male sexuality as polyvalent and characterized a person sexually only by his sexual acts. Virtually all forms of behavior, except transvestism, were acceptable. Christianity simply added the categories of "natural" and "unnatural" in describing these actions. Ancient society knew nothing of the categories of "homosexuals" and "heterosexuals," and assumed that, in the words of Dover quoted approvingly by Petersen, "everyone responds at different times to both homosexual and to heterosexual stimuli . . ." (188).[22]

In contrast to this, modern usage virtually limits the term "homosexual" to desire and propensity. K. M. Benkert, who in 1869 coined the German term equivalent to "homosexual," used it as referring to orientation, impulse, or affectional preference and having "nothing to do with sexual acts" (189).

Petersen then proceeds to cite the *Supplement to the Oxford English Dictionary,* which defines "homosexual" only as a propensity or desire with no mention of acts. Petersen's point is that by using "homosexuals" for *arsenokoitai,* one wrongfully reads a modern concept back into early history "where no equivalent concept existed" (189). Consequently the translation is inaccurate because it "includes celibate homophiles, . . . incorrectly excludes *hetero*sexuals who engage in homosexual acts . . . [and] incorrectly includes female homosexuals" (189, italics in source). Prior to 1869 there was no "cognitive structure, either in our society or in antiquity, within which the modern bifurcation of humanity into 'homosexuals' and 'heterosexuals' made sense" (189).

The foregoing clarifies why Petersen feels that the translation "homosexuals" is mistaken. Yet is it possible that Petersen is the one mistaken, on both historical and linguistic or philological grounds? The next phases of this paper will critically examine Petersen's position.

THE JUSTIFICATION FOR TRANSLATING ΑΡΣΕΝΟΚΟΙΤΑΙ BY "HOMOSEXUALS"

Historical Grounds

A refutation of the foregoing opposition to the translation of *arsenokoitai* by "homosexuals" begins with the historical and cultural evidence. Since virtually everyone acknowledges that the word does not appear before Paul's usage, no historical settings earlier than his are available. Yet much writing reveals the ancient understanding of homosexuality prior to and contemporary with Paul. The goal is to discover whether the ancients conceived of homosexuality, particularly homosexual orientation, in a way similar to present-day concepts.

Petersen, Bailey, Boswell, and Scroggs claim that the homosexual condition, desire, propensity, or inversion—whatever it is called—cannot be part of the definition of the term. They assert this either because the term is limited to acts of a particular kind (Boswell, active male prostitutes; Scroggs, pederasty) or because the homosexual condition was unknown in ancient times (Bailey; Petersen). The following discussion will show why neither of these positions is legitimate. Attention will be devoted to the latter position first with the former one being addressed below under "Linguistic Grounds."

In regard to the latter position, one may rightfully ask, did not the homosexual condition exist before 1869? Is it only a modern phenomenon? Yet if it is universal, as alleged today, it must have existed always including ancient times, even though there is a lack of sophistication in discussing it. Indeed, evidence shows that the ancients, pre-Christian and Christian, not only knew about the total spectrum of sexual behavior, including all forms of same-sex activity (transvestism included), but also knew about same-sex orientation or condition. Petersen admits (190 n. 10) that Plato in *Symposium* (189d–192d) may be a "sole possible exception" to ancient ignorance of this condition. He discounts this, however, believing that even here *"acts* appear to be the deciding factor." However, this is a very significant exception, hardly worthy of being called "an exception," because of the following additional evidence for a homosexual condition.

The *Symposium* of Plato gives some of the strongest evidence for knowledge about the homosexual condition.[23] Plato posits a third sex comprised of a male-female or man-woman (ἀνδρογύνον [andro-gynon, "man-woman"]). Hence "original nature" (πάλαι φύσις [palai physis], 189d) consisted of three kinds of human beings. Zeus sliced these human beings in half, to weaken them so that they would not be a threat to the gods. Consequently each person seeks his or her other half, either one of the opposite sex or one of the same sex. Plato then quotes Aristophanes:

Each of us, then, is but a tally of a man, since every one shows like a flatfish the traces of having been sliced in two; and each is ever searching for the tally that will fit him. All the men who are sections of that composite sex that at first was called man-woman are woman-courters; our adulterers are mostly descended from that sex, whence likewise are derived our mancourting women and adulteresses. All the women who are sections of the woman have no great fancy for men: they are inclined rather to women, and of this stock are the she-minions. Men who are sections of the male pursue the masculine, and so long as their boyhood lasts they show themselves to be slices of the male by making friends with men and delighting to lie with them and to be clasped in men's embraces; these are the finest boys and striplings, for they have the most manly nature. Some say they are shameless creatures, but falsely: for their behavior is due not to shamelessness but to daring, manliness, and virility, since they are quick to welcome their like. Sure evidence of this is the fact that on reaching maturity these alone prove in a public career to be men. So when they come to man's estate they are boy-lovers, and have no natural interest in wiving and getting children but only do these things under stress of custom; they are quite contented to live together unwedded all their days. A man of this sort is at any rate born to be a lover of boys or the willing mate of a man, eagerly greeting his own kind. Well, when one of them—whether he be a boy-lover or a lover of any other sort—happens on his own particular half, the two of them are wondrously thrilled with affection and intimacy and love, and are hardly to be induced to leave each other's side for a single moment. These are they who continue together throughout life, though they could not even say what they would have of one another. (191d–192c)[24]

Should these two persons be offered the opportunity to be fused together for as long as they live, or even in Hades, Aristophanes says that each "would unreservedly deem that he had been offered just what he was yearning for all the time" (192e). Several observations about this text are in order. Lesbianism is contemplated, as well as male homosexuality (191e). "Natural interest" (τὸν νοῦν φύσει [ton noun physei], 192b) reflects modern concepts of propensity or inclination. The words, "born to be a lover of boys or the willing mate of a man" (παιδεραστής τε καὶ φιλεραστὴς γίγνεται [paiderastēs te kai philerastēs gignetai], 192b) reflect the modern claims "to be born this way," i.e., as a homosexual. The idea of mutuality ("the two of them are wondrously thrilled with affection and intimacy and love," 192b) is present. Aristophanes even speaks of "mutual love ingrained in mankind reassembling our early estate" (ὁ ἔρως ἔμφυτος ἀλλήλων τοῖς ἀνθρώποις καὶ τῆς ἀρχαίας φύσεως συναγωγεύς [ho erōs emphytos allēlōn tois anthrōpois kai tēs archaias physeōs synagōgeus], 191d). The concept of permanency ("These are they who continue together throughout life," 192c) is also present. Further mention of and/or allusion to permanency, mutuality, "gay pride," pederasty, homophobia, motive, desire, passion, and the nature of love and its works is recognizable.

Clearly the ancients thought of love (homosexual or other) apart from actions. The speakers in the *Symposium* argue that motive in homosexuality is crucial: money, office, influence, etc. . . . bring reproach (182e–183a, 184b). They mention the need to love the soul not the body (183e). There are two kinds of love in the body (186b) and each has its "desire" and "passion" (186b–d). The speakers discuss the principles or "matters" of love (187c), the desires of love (192c), and being "males by nature" (193c). Noteworthy is the speech of Socrates who devotes much attention to explaining how desire is related to love and its objects (200a–201c). Desire is felt for "what is not provided or present; for something they have not or are not or lack." This is the object of desire and love. Socrates clearly distinguishes between "what sort of being is love" and the "works" of love (201e). This ancient philosopher could think of both realms—sexual acts as well as disposition of being or nature. His words have significance for more than pederasty.[25]

In summary, virtually every element in the modern discussion of love and homosexuality is anticipated in the *Symposium* of Plato. Petersen is in error when he claims that the ancients could only think of homosexual acts, not inclination or orientation. Widespread evidence to the contrary supports the latter.[26]

Biblical support for homosexual inclination in the contexts where homosexual acts are described adds to the case for the ancient distinction. In Romans 1:21–28 such phrases as "reasonings," "heart," "become foolish," "desires of the heart," "lie," "passions of dishonor," "burned in the desire," "knowledge," and "reprobate mind" prove Paul's concern for disposition and inclination along with the "doing" or "working" of evil (see also vv. 29–32). Even the catalogues of vices are introduced (1 Tim. 1:8–10) or concluded (1 Cor. 6:9–11) by words describing what people "are" or "were," not what they "do." Habits betray what people are within, as also the Lord Jesus taught (cf. Matt. 23:28). The inner condition is as important as the outer act; one gives rise to the other (cf. Matt. 5:27).

Petersen errs regarding other particulars too. Transvestism apparently was accepted by the ancients. It was practiced among Canaanites, Syrians, people of Asia Minor, as well as Greeks, according to S. R. Driver.[27] Only a few moralists and Jewish writers are on record as condemning it. For example, Seneca (*Moral Epistles* 47.7–8) condemns homosexual exploitation that forces an adult slave to dress, be beardless, and behave as a woman. Philo also goes to some length to describe the homosexuals of his day and their dressing as women (*The Special Laws* III, 37–41; see also his *On the Virtues,* 20–21, where he justifies prohibition of crossdressing). Even the OT forbade the interchange of clothing between the sexes (Deut. 22:5).

Petersen is also wrong in attributing to Christianity the creating of the "new labels" of "natural" and "unnatural" for sexual behavior. These did not begin with Paul (Rom. 1:26–27) but go as far back as ancient Greece, and even non-Christian contemporaries used them. Plato, the *Test. Naph.,* Philo, Josephus, Plutarch, and others used these words or related concepts.[28]

Linguistic Grounds

The research of Wright and Mendell cited, as well as ancient writers documented above, shows that *arsenokoitai* is a broad term.[29] It cannot be limited to pederasty or "active male prostitutes"; nor can it be limited to acts. It must also include same-sex orientation or condition.

The main difficulty, however, with Petersen's study and that of others before him, lies in the area of linguistics or philology pertaining to the modern term "homosexuals." Petersen has an erroneous concept of dictionaries and meaning when citing the incompatibility of the English and Greek terms.

The preceding historical evidence demonstrates that ancient concepts of homosexuality, though primarily understood as sexual acts, cannot be limited to acts alone. It is plausible, then, that the term *arsenokoitai* may include both acts and orientation or desire—at least in the contexts of

Romans 1, 1 Corinthians 6, and 1 Timothy 1. Paul knew about the immorality of Rome, Corinth, and Ephesus (note the similarity of Eph. 4:17–24 and 5:3–12 with 1 Timothy 1 and 1 Corinthians 6). A subsequent question arises: is the modern term "homosexual" limited to orientation or inclination, excluding acts or behavior? Petersen answers in the affirmative and cites as support both the creator of the word and the meaning he assigned to it, as well as the standard dictionary, *Supplement to the Oxford English Dictionary*. In note 9 (190), however, Petersen acknowledges that *Webster's Third New International Dictionary* (1971) does include a reference to one who "practices homosexuality" and "same-sex sexual activity" after the definitions referring to inclination and preference. He dismisses this as a "popularized, perhaps Americanized usage," as "slang," and as a "corruption of the original meaning." He characterizes Webster's lexicographers as "ignorant of the psychological facts of the case, even though they may be correctly recording the use of the word in popular speech" (190).[30]

Yet Petersen has overlooked several important points or principles.[31] The first one concerns lexicography. Once a word has entered the stream of society it is defined by its entire context—what the users mean by it, regardless of its original definition. Dictionaries reflect usage, including the changes in a word's meaning.

It is apparent that popular and scholarly usage of "homosexuals" today has come to include "same-sex behavior"; indeed this may now be the more prominent definition. If this be so, in light of the breadth of meaning of *arsenokoitai*, "homosexuals" is a closer approximation of its meaning than believed by Bailey, Boswell, Petersen, and others.

A second principle is that words are constantly changing in meaning. *Webster's New Twentieth Century Dictionary of the English Language* (unabridged second ed., 1965) does not include "practice" under the definition of "homosexual" and uses only the words "sexual relations between individuals of the same sex" as the second definition of "homosexuality." Webster's definitions have changed in the span of just six years (compare the third edition cited above). For Petersen to restrict the meaning to an earlier one and to call the later definition a "corruption" is unfortunate.

The meaning of a word may change by being deepened, by being given new value, by taking on a new meaning, or by being given a new concrete application.[32] In the case of "homosexuals," it appears that several of these kinds of changes are occurring because of the increasingly frequent use of the word in different contexts ranging from popular speech to scholarly circles.

A third principle is that words usually mark out a field of meaning. That is, words usually do not have a point of meaning, i.e., a very small area of meaning. The historical-cultural study above shows that homosexuality—or whatever word describes it—existed in various forms including prostitution, pederasty, lesbianism, orientation, and mutuality. The Greeks and Romans employed scores of terms to describe such orientation and behavior. Therefore, it is plausible that such a term as *arsenokoitai* has a broad meaning when its etymology is simply "malebed" or "lying with a male," assuming that the context does not restrict it to a narrower meaning.

A fourth principle stems from the preceding. Since no two words have exactly the same area of meaning, no true synonyms exist within a language and no exact equivalents occur between languages.[33] This allows *arsenokoitai* to be translated "homosexuals" even though it is somewhat imprecise to do so. Terms in two languages can never be exactly equivalent because their contexts can never be identical (given, at least, the time span). They do not share the same area of meaning. It may well be that "sodomists" better represents the idea of *arsenokoitai*, since both terms in their moral and biblical settings represent contexts closer to one another.

It may be that Benkert in 1869 misread or was unacquainted with the history of homosexuality in ancient times. He may have unwittingly altered the whole discussion of the subject by limiting his new term to the homosexual condition.

Petersen asserts that translating *arsenokoitai* by "homosexuals" is anachronistic (the ancients had no concept equivalent to homosexual desire; the English term is limited to homosexual desire), but he is conclusively in error as the above historical-cultural evidence and linguistic principles show. Certain terms such as ἀρρενομανής (*arrenomanēs*, "mad after males"), 4th century A.D., show that there was a "cognitive structure" for the homosexual condition before 1869 (cf. 1 Cor. 6:11, "and such were some of you").

The most that can be said for Petersen's position is that the ancients may not have had a term for exclusive sexual categories (whether a person is "homosexual" or "heterosexual"), whereas moderns do have one or at least may refer to one's *primary* attraction. Hence the contemporary concept of a homosexual may be slightly different from the ancients, who spoke only of what they considered to be a number of *equal* options.[34] Yet some evidence indicates that "exclusively homosexual" persons were identifiable to the ancients (see n. 26 above). Both the Greek and English terms appear broad enough to cover such cases and cannot be limited to acts. Petersen has decidedly overstated the case for both the ancients and the modern era.

Summary of Reactions to the New Interpretations

It is improper to be prescriptive as to the meaning of *arsenokoitai*. It is better to be descriptive. In surveying those who have written on the meaning of the term, Bailey, Boswell, and Scroggs have erred or have been incomplete when they, respectively, define the term as "perverts," "male sexual agents" or "active male prostitutes," and "pederasts." It is more credible that historical and cultural evidence supports the conclusion that the term is broad enough to include both the various forms of homosexual acts and the homosexual condition, inversion or orientation. The studies by Wright and others supply the linguistic evidence for the more general sense of "homosexuals."

As to the assertion by Petersen that the English "homosexuals" should not be used to render *arsenokoitai,* it is evident that the English and the Greek words are sufficiently broad to make them fair and suitable equivalents. Because of usage in various historical and modern contexts, each must include both homosexual behavior and orientation or condition.[35]

SUPPORT FOR THE PAULINE ORIGIN OF ΑΡΣΕΝΟΚΟΙΤΑΙ

Some final questions remain to be answered regarding the source of Paul's term. As Mendell points out, anyone wishing to explain Paul's meaning must answer three questions.[36] Where does he get the word? Why does he use such an arcane word in speaking to his audience? If the word is ambiguous, as Boswell affirms, how can he expect to be understood?

It is a reasonable position that Paul coined the term based on the juxtaposition of the two words *arsenos* and *koitēn* in the LXX of Leviticus 20:13 (cf. 18:22), though absolute proof of this is impossible. It may be suggested that the criteria of style, practice, familiarity with the LXX, and context make this a highly plausible conclusion, however.

Paul has the practice of coining terms, it appears. For example, in 1 Timothy 1:3 and 6:3, Paul used a term he had probably originated. The word ἑτεροδιδασκαλέω (*heterodidaskaleō,* "to teach a different doctrine") does not occur before Paul and only afterward in *Ignatius to Polycarp* 3:1.[37] Hence in the scope of eight verses Paul has possibly coined two terms, though one of them he had used earlier in 1 Corinthians 6:9.

In general, statistics show that Paul probably coined many terms. There are 179 words found in Paul and nowhere else in pre-Christian Greek literature. Of these, 89 occur only one time. Other statistics support the theory that Paul had a creativity in choosing vocabulary.[38]

In addition, Paul displayed considerable dependence upon the LXX. He usually quoted from the LXX rather than the Hebrew of the OT when he quoted the OT. Out of ninety-three quotations of the OT classified by Ellis, Paul used the LXX fourteen times, but only four times did he quote the Hebrew.[39] Obviously Paul was familiar with and used the LXX. More particularly, the NT frequently uses the portion of Leviticus 18–20. The structure and content of these chapters mark them as special. Often identified as the "code of holiness," these chapters (unlike the remainder of Leviticus) are universal in their scope, much the same as the Ten Commandments of Exodus 20 and Deuteronomy 5. The Jews held Leviticus 19 to be a kind of summary of the Torah, a central chapter in the Pentateuch. This respect carried over to the writers of the NT where chapters 18–20 are widely used. They are cited by Christ, Paul, Peter, and James.[40] "You shall love your neighbor as yourself" is from Leviticus 19:18 When Paul alludes to 19:19 in 2 Corinthians 6:14 to illustrate the ban on unequal yoking, he coins a word ἑτεροζυγοῦντες (heterozygountes, "being unequally yoked") that is found nowhere before him. Yet the adjective form ἑτεροζύγῳ (heterozygǭ, "unequally yoked") occurs in 19:19. The LXX probably suggested the coinage to Paul.

Most importantly, both of the contexts where *arsenokoitai* appears suggest that Paul was thinking of the Levitical "code of holiness."[41] First Corinthians 5 has many allusions to Leviticus 18–20. The theme is moral separation, as it is in Leviticus. Topics include distinction from the Gentiles (5:1; cf. 6:1–6; Lev. 18:3, 24–30; 20:23) and future inheritance (κληρονομέω [klēronomeō, "I inherit"], 6:9–10; Lev. 20:23–24). The law of loving your neighbor (Lev. 19:18) is reflected in 6:8. Of the ten vices in 1 Corinthians 6:9–10, only one (drunkards) is not found in Leviticus 18–20. It is feasible, then, that both *malakoi* and *arsenokoitai* come from Leviticus 20:13 and point to the passive and the active same-sex roles. Leviticus 20:13 said that both persons were to be put to death (the penalty is not found in 18:22). The Corinthian list of vices may be a summation of Leviticus 20:23–24 (cf. 18:29–30).

The same observations apply to 1 Timothy 1:10. In the context Paul begins with perversions of teaching regarding the Mosaic Law (vv. 3–8), moves to legislation in general (vv. 9–10), and ends with the gospel (v. 11). With the Law of Moses so dominant, it is not surprising that the list of specific vices corresponds in order to the fifth through the ninth of the Ten Commandments. Since the list uses both single terms and doublets to refer to the Ten Commandments, it is more probable that ἀνδραποδισταῖς (andrapodistais, "slave-dealers") goes with the following "thieves" rather than with the preceding *arsenokoitai*. This militates against Scrogg's narrow sexual definition ("slave-dealers who procure boys as prostitutes," 120) of the term. Hence *pornois* and *arsenokoitai* represent the sixth commandment. The preceding discussion justifies the claim that Paul coined the word in question. No one else in Hellenistic Judaism used the term before Paul. Two questions still remain. Why did Paul coin such a term? It may be suggested that he sought to demonstrate the relation of believers to the Law of Moses, in particular to show that the universal standards of the Law (derived from Exodus 20 and Leviticus 18–20) were still valid. Paul assumed his readers' acquaintance with Judaism: note references to "Satan" (1 Cor. 5:5), the "day of the Lord" (1 Cor. 5:5), "leaven" and "unleaven" (5:6–8), "Passover" (5:7), and judging angels (6:3). He quoted Deuteronomy 17:7 in 5:13. Since Leviticus 18–20 became central to the Day of Atonement, it was natural for Paul to refer to this section of Leviticus (cf. chaps. 16 and 23). The topic of the believer's relationship to the Law or law is the main point in 1 Timothy 1.

Finally, how could Paul expect his Greek readers to understand the term? Compounds involving *arseno-* and *arreno-* and *koitē* abounded. The Greeks were adept at forming compounded Greek words.[42] Therefore Paul coined a word that brought quick recognition.

The word is general, reflecting the passage in Leviticus 20:13. Paul did not use ἀνδροκοίτης (*androkoitēs,* "male having sex with a male"), which would not have suggested a reference to pederasty. His term expressed gender but not gender and maturity; he condemned "males who lie with males of any age."[43] It agrees with the threefold use of ἄρσην (*arsēn,* "male") in Romans 1:27 where Paul condemns same-sex activity.

This theory also explains why the word did not catch on with the secular world after Paul. The Gentiles did not appreciate the biblical context of OT moral legislation. Paul was ahead of and contrary to his time. Perhaps for the same reason "sodomists" and "sodomy" are fading from general secular usage today.

CONCLUSION

It seems quite likely that Paul himself coined a new term that he virtually derived from the LXX of Leviticus 20:13. No other current explanation is as practical as this. If this be true, there are significant consequences, assuming that Paul wrote prescriptively. Obviously he viewed the moral law (derived from Leviticus 18–20; Exodus 20) as authoritative for his Christian audience. Since he and his readers in Corinth and Ephesus knew also about same-sex orientation or condition, sufficient reason exists to apply his term to those today who are inverts or homosexuals in orientation.[44] English translations are justified in their use of words such as "homosexuals" or "sodomists." Besides, these terms should not be limited to acts or behavior. Just as an adulterous orientation or condition is wrong, so is a homosexual one.[45] In addition, it appears that lexicons and dictionaries (e.g., BAGD, *Theologisches Wörterbuch zum Neun Testament, New International Dictionary of New Testament Theology, Exegetical Dictionary of the New Testament*) are too narrow in limiting, explicitly or implicitly, the term to male sexual activity with men or boys.

However, since he referred to behavior in his lists in 1 Corinthians 6 and 1 Timothy 1, he excluded from the kingdom of God all those who engage in same-sex behavior, including forms of pederasty, prostitution, or "permanent mutuality." The term *malakoi* used with *arsenokoitai* probably refers to the passive agent in same-sex activity and comes under similar condemnation.

Other applications follow from the contexts involved. First, homosexual behavior is cause for church discipline in light of the context of 1 Corinthians 5–6. Certain religious bodies that approve a homosexual lifestyle have rejected scriptural authority. In addition, homosexual orientation should be a concern for church counsel and exhortation with a view toward molding a heterosexual orientation.

Second, homosexual behavior is a proper focus and concern of legislation in society and of the sanction of law, according to the context of 1 Timothy 1:8–11. This suggests that "gay rights" is a misnomer. The movement has no legitimate claim to protection by the law.

ENDNOTES

[1] For convenience sake, the term "homosexual" is used to encompass both same-sex orientation and same-sex behavior. The meaning of this term is one of the main considerations of this study.

[2] These times are different from just over a century ago. Then P. Fairbairn (*Pastoral Epistles* [Edinburgh: T & T Clark, 1874], 891) could write of ἀρσενοκοῖται ("homosexuals") that it is a "term for which fortunately our language has no proper equivalent." Unknowingly he thereby touched upon the basis for the contemporary debate and study. The present writer endorses the Pauline authorship of the Pastoral Epistles on the basis of internal and external evidence (see Donald Guthrie, *New Testament Introduction,* 4th ed. [Downer's Grove: InterVarsity, 1990], 621–649, for an extensive discussion and citation of supports of the Pauline authorship).

[3] For example, see Scroggs' (see n. 13 below) influence on M. Olson, "Untangling the Web," *The Other Side* (April 1984): 24–29. For a study suggesting a further prohibition of homosexuality in the OT, see A. Phillips, "Uncovering the Father's Skirt," *Vetus Testamentum* 30, no. 1 (January 1980): 38–43. For a bibliography of other sources dealing with ἀρσενοκοῖται, see the *Wilsondisc Religion Indexes* (New York: H. W. Wilson Co., 1987).

[4] D. S. Bailey, *Homosexuality and the Western Christian Tradition* (London: Longmans, Green, 1975), 38.

[5] J. Boswell, *Christianity, Social Tolerance and Homosexuality* (Chicago: University Press, 1980).

[6] Several translations of 1 Timothy 1:10 are: KJV, "them that defile themselves with mankind"; ASV, "abusers of themselves with men"; NASB, "homosexuals"; RSV, NKJV, NRSV, "sodomites"; NEB, NIV, "perverts"; GNB, "sexual perverts." In 1 Corinthians 6:9 these occur: KJV, "abusers of themselves with mankind"; ASV, "abusers of themselves with men"; NASB, RSV, "homosexuals"; NKJV, "sodomites"; NEB, "homosexual perversion." The RSV and NEB derive their translation from two Greek words, μαλακοί and ἀρσενοκοῖται, which GNB has as "homosexual perverts." NRSV has the two words as "male prostitutes" in the text, and "sodomites" in the footnote. The active idea predominates among the commentators as well; it is the primary assumption.

[7] Boswell, *Christianity,* 344. Yet this was not a word "available to Paul for a male prostitute," for it does not occur at all in any literature prior to Paul (as a search in the *Thesaurus Linguae Graecae* using IBYCUS confirms). If Paul coined the term, it would have no prior history, and all such discussion about its lack of usage in contemporary non-Christian and Christian literature is meaningless.

[8] Again, this would be expected if Paul coined the word.

[9] The key phrase here apparently is "discussions," for Boswell admits later (350 n. 42) that it occurs in quotes of Paul but there is no discussion in the context. Hence the implication is that we cannot tell what these writers (Polycarp *To the Philippians* 5:3; Theophilus *Ad Autolycum* 1.2, 2.14; Nilus *Epistularum libri quattuor* 2.282; Cyril of Alexandria *Homiliae diversae* 14; *Sybilline Oracle* 2.13) meant. Yet Polycarp, who was a disciple of John the Apostle and died about A.D. 155, argues in the

context that young men should be pure. He uses only the three terms πόρνοι, μαλακοί, and ἀρσενοκοῖται from Paul's list. This at least makes Boswell's use of "all" subjective. Apparently Clement of Alexandria *Paedagogus* 3.11; *Stromata* 3.18 also belong here.

[10] Yet Eusebius uses it in *Demonstraionis evangelicae* 1.

[11] Either Boswell is misrepresenting the facts about Chrysostom's use of ἀρσενοκοῖται and its forms (about twenty) in the vice lists of 1 Corinthians 6 or 1 Timothy 1, or he is begging the question by denying that the word can mean homosexual when Chrysostom uses it. Yet the meaning of ἀρσενοκοῖται is the goal of his and our study, whether in the lists or other discussions. Boswell later admits (351) that Chrysostom uses the almost identical form ἀρσενοκοῖτος in his commentary on 1 Corinthians. Although Boswell suggests that the passage is strange, it may be that Paul is seeking to make a refinement in ἀρσενοκοῖται.

[12] Apparently Jerome is a significant omission here, since he renders ἀρσενοκοῖται as *masculorum concubitores,* corresponding "almost exactly to the Greek" (348 n. 36).

[13] R. Scroggs, *The New Testament and Homosexuality* (Philadelphia: Fortress, 1983), 86, 107–8. Independently we came to the same conclusion. Apparently the connection is made in E. A. Sophocles, *Greek Lexicon of the Roman and Byzantine Periods* (from 146 B.C. to A.D. 1100), Memorial edition (New York: 1887), 253.

[14] See discussion, 101–4. He says the same thing about Paul's language in Romans 1:26–27 (128). But this is doubtful. See the more cautious words of P. Zaas, "1 Corinthians 6.9ff: Was Homosexuality Condoned in the Corinthian Church?" *Society of Biblical Literature Abstracts and Seminar Papers* 17 (1979): 205–12. He observes that the words μοιχαί, μαλακοί, and ἀρσενοκοῖται were part of Jewish anti-Gentile polemic. Yet Paul's words at the end of the vice list, "and such were some of you," indicate that "Paul is addressing real or potential abuses of his ethical message, not citing primitive tradition by rote" (210). Wright (see below) disputes Zaas' attempt to associate the term with idolatry (147).

[15] On Boswell's treatment of Romans 1:26–27, the article by R. B. Hays, "Relations Natural and Unnatural: A Response to John Boswell's Exegesis of Romans 1," *Journal of Religious Ethics* 14, no. 1 (spring 1986): 184–215, is an excellent critique.

[16] D. F. Wright, "Homosexuals or Prostitutes? The Meaning of *APΣENOKOITAI* (1 Cor. 6:9, 1 Tim. 1:10)," *Vigiliae christianae* 38 (1984): 125–53.

[17] In an unpublished paper, Henry Mendell, "*APΣENOKOITAI*: Boswell on Paul," effectively refutes Boswell's claims regarding the philology of ἀρσενοκοῖται. He finds the meaning to be general, "a male who has sex with a male" (4–11). The paper is available from the writer of this essay.

[18] Wright's ENDNOTES (148–49) list additional sources in the church fathers.

[19] We also have noticed the same tendency by Boswell to fail to cite all the references to Sodom and sodomy in the Apocrypha and Pseudepigrapha. See J. B. DeYoung, "A Critique of Prohomosexual Interpretations of the Old Testament Apocrypha and Pseudepigrapha," *Bibliotheca Sacra* 147, no. 588 (1990): 437–53.

[20] In light of the claim made by Boswell that the infrequency of ἀρσενοκοῖται points to a meaning lacking homosexual significance, Wright asks pertinently "why neither Philo nor Josephus use παιδοφθορία, nor Josephus παιδεραστία, and why . . . Clement did not use the latter and Chrysostom the former?" (152 n. 71). In a more recent article, "Homosexuality: The Relevance of the Bible," *Evangelical Quarterly* 61 (1989): 291–300, Wright reiterates these same points. He believes the term is general and was "adopted or fashioned" from Leviticus (298). Paul shows a "remarkable originality" in extending the OT ethic to the church (300).

[21] W. L. Petersen, "Can *APΣENOKOITAI* Be Translated By 'Homosexuals'? (1 Cor. 6.9; 1 Tim. 1.10)" *Vigiliae christianae* 40 (1986): 187–91.

[22] K. J. Dover, *Greek Homosexuality* (Cambridge: Harvard University, 1978), 1 n. 1.

[23] We are conscious of the fact that Plato's writings may not reflect Athenian society, or that the speakers in *Symposium* may not reflect Plato's views. However, it is assumed that they do, and with this agrees Dover (*Homosexuality,* 12) and other evidence cited below (n. 25; yet cf. Plato's different view, n. 26).

[24] The translation is that of W. R. M. Lamb, *Plato: Symposium* LCL (Cambridge: Harvard University, 1967), 141–143. Note the reference to "adulteress." If there is a homosexual condition derived from birth or the genes, logically there must also be an adulterous condition derived from birth.

[25] Elsewhere in the *Symposium* we are told that it is the heavenly love to love the male and young men (181c), but this must not be love for boys too young; the latter should be outlawed (181d–e). Such love of youths is to be permanent (181d), lifelong and abiding (184a). Where homosexual love is considered a disgrace, such an attitude is due to encroachments of the rulers and to the cowardice of the ruled (182d—an early charge of "homophobia"?). In Athens it was "more honorable to love openly than in secret" (182d—an ancient expression of "coming out of the closet"). Mutuality was present ("this compels lover and beloved alike to feel a zealous concern for their own virtue," 184b).

For Petersen to label the *Symposium* a "possible" exception to his position is inadequate and misrepresentative. It is a significant witness to Greek society hundreds of years before the time of Christ.

[26] Dover (*Homosexuality,* 12, 60–68) finds homosexual desire and orientation in Plato's works *(Symposium and Phaedrus)* and elsewhere. Philo writes of those who "habituate themselves" to the practice of homosexual acts *(The Special Laws* 3.37–42; cf. *De Vita Contemplativa* 59–63). Josephus says that homosexuality had become a fixed habit for some *(Against Apion* 2.273–75). Clement of Alexandria on Matthew 19:12 writes that "some men, from birth, have a natural aversion to a woman; and indeed those who are naturally so constituted do well not to marry" *(Miscellanies* 3.1). It is addressed in Novella 141 of Justinian's Codex of laws (it refers to those "who have been consumed by this disease" as in need of renouncing "their plague," as well as acts). Pseudo Lucian *(Erotes* 48) and Achilles Tatius *(Leucippe and Clitophon* II.38) speak of it. Finally Thucydides 2.45.2 has, "Great is your glory if you fall not below the standard which nature has set for your sex."

Boswell *(Christianity,* 81–87) cites poets (Juvenal, Ovid), writers (Martial), statesmen (Cicero), and others who describe permanent, mutual homosexual relationships, even marriages. Even emperors could be either gay-married (Nero) or exclusively gay (Hadrian), Boswell says. Scroggs *(Homosexuality,* 28, 32–34) admits that both inversion and perversion must have existed in the past. He discusses possible references to adult mutual homosexual and lesbian relationships, but dismisses them (130–44).

²⁷ See specifics in S. R. Driver, *A Critical and Exegetical Commentary on Deuteronomy* (Edinburgh: T & T Clark, 1895), 250. He observes that the prohibition of cross-dressing in Deuteronomy 22:5 is not a "mere rule of conventional propriety." See also Dover, *Homosexuality,* 73–76, 144.

²⁸ Plato in his last work, in which he seeks to show how to have a virtuous citizen, condemned pederasty and marriage between men as "against nature" (παρὰ φύσιν) (*Laws* 636a–b; 636c; 836a–c; 838; 841d–e). According to *Test. Naph.* 3:4–5 the sodomites changed the "order of nature." The Jewish writers Philo (*On Abraham* 135–137) and Josephus (*Ant.* 1.322; 3.261, 275; *Ag. Ap.* 2.199; 2.273, 275) label sexual deviation as "against nature." Finally, first century moralists such as Plutarch (*Dialogue on Love* 751c–e; 752b–c) spoke of homosexuality as "against nature." Christians clearly did not invent the labels "natural" and "unnatural." See J. B. DeYoung, "The Meaning of 'Nature' in Romans 1 and Its Implications for Biblical Proscriptions of Homosexual Behavior," *Journal of the Evangelical Theological Society* 31, no. 4 (December 1988): 429–41.

²⁹ The philological research by Mendell, in particular, is comprehensive and convincing. He finds Boswell wrong on many points including his observations about the Latin *exoleti* (5); the prevalence of active male prostitution (6); the meaning of κοῖται as a coarse and active word (7); the meanings of compounds of κοίτ- (7–10); the prevalence of ἀρσενοκοῖται in the church fathers (11–18); the law in Roman society (13); the statements of Sextus about Greek law (13); and secular uses (18–19). In appendices Mendell devotes detailed examination to how compounds are formed, including those with κοίτης (25–28), and such compounds in astrological settings (28–29).

Our own philological study confirms Mendell's observations. Mr. Tim Teebken assisted this writer in searching *Thesaurus Lingua Graecae.* The search revealed thousands of occurrences of forms of κοιτ-, μιξ-, and φθορ-. Παιδεραστ-occurs about 200 times, and ἀνδροβατεῖν ("practice unnatural vice"), ἀνδρομανία ("mad after men"), and ἀρρητουργία ("filthy lewdness") and ἀρρητοποιέω ("do unmentionable vice") occur only rarely. Liddell-Scott-Jones, *Greek-English Lexicon,* cites these and other words referring to "unnatural vice."

³⁰ Petersen's reference to the "psychological facts of the case" begs the question. If he is referring to Kinsey and other studies, the "facts" have been disputed. Many psychologists use "homosexual" to cover both orientation and behavior, and have seen many people change from

homosexuality to heterosexuality. These include such psychologists (who have published) as Bergler, Anna Freud, Haddon, Hatterer, Janov, Socarides, Kronemeyer, van den Aardweg, and Keefe. Various groups, such as Homosexuals Anonymous of Reading, Pennsylvania, assist homosexuals in changing their orientation and behavior.

[31] These principles come from J. D. Grassmick, *Principles and Practice of Greek Exegesis* (Dallas: Dallas Theological Seminary, 1974), 143–49, who derives them from such sources as E. Nida, C. S. Lewis, and F. Fisher. See also C. Thiselton, "Semantics of New Testament Interpretation," in *New Testament Interpretation,* ed. I. H. Marshall (Grand Rapids: Eerdmans, 1977), 75–104.

[32] Grassmick, *Principles,* 147–148. See also G. Yule, *The Study of Language* (Cambridge: University Press, 1985), 176–77.

[33] Ibid., 144.

[34] An observation of Mr. Teebken, who assisted in this project.

[35] Although the existence of a homosexual orientation or condition has been assumed, we are not thereby stipulating what is its cause or duration. Neither does Paul. He merely uses a word that covers both what a homosexual is and what he does, and at least for the latter he assigns culpability. Investigations of the cause and duration are beyond the scope of this study.

[36] Mendell, *"ΑΡΣΕΝΟΚΟΙΤΑΙ,"* 20.

[37] Paul also uses rare terms found elsewhere outside the NT only. One such term is ἀνδραποδισταῖς which occurs in 1 Timothy 1:10 and is important to the meaning of ἀρσενοκοῖται. Scroggs defines the former term as "those who steal boys for sexual purposes" and uses it to define the preceding ἀρσενοκοῖται as "pederasts." The word occurs in many pagan writers (e.g., Aristophanes, Plato, Xenophon, Demosthenes, Polybius, Dio Chrysostom). In Philo (*Special Laws* 4.13) it is used generally of a kidnapper who steals people to reduce them to slavery. It appears that Scroggs is again too narrow in his definition and fails to appreciate the structure and OT background of the list of vices of 1 Timothy 1:9–10.

[38] For example, there are 433 words used only in both secular Greek and Paul. Of these, 203 occur but once in Paul. More interestingly, 175 words

occur only in both the LXX and Paul. Of these 31 occur but once in Paul. Of this last group 5 of the 31 are combinations of two words similar in pattern to that of ἀρσενοκοῖται. See R. Morgenthaler, *Statistik Des Neutestamentlichen Wortschatzes* (1973 reprint, Zurich: Gotthelf-Verlag, n.d.), 175–80. The numbers are our calculations.

[39] E. E. Ellis, *Paul's Use of the OT* (Edinburgh: Oliver and Boyd, 1957), 150–52. Some of the remainder of Paul's quotations are in agreement with both the LXX and Hebrew (19 times), and in others he agrees with neither.

[40] Specific citations are available in J. B. DeYoung, "The Old Testament Witness to Homosexuality: A Critical Assessment of the Prohomosexual Interpretation of the OT" (an unpublished paper read at the NW section, Evangelical Theological Society, Portland, Oregon, May 4, 1985), 22–23.

[41] Mendell, *"ΑΡΣΕΝΟΚΟΙΤΑΙ,"* 21–24.

[42] Ibid., 21, 25–28.

[43] Ibid., 6 n. 14.' Ἀνδροκοίτης and its cognate verb are much less frequent (c. 13 occurrences in secular papyri ranging from 30 B.C. to A.D. 140 [most before Paul] and apparently a few others [3?] in the church fathers). There are c. 50 occurrences of ἀρσενοκοῖται, apparently all post-Pauline.

[44] One may cite additional reasons for including "adult-adult mutuality" as well as orientation or condition in Paul's term, as the context and wording of Romans 1:26–27 make clear. See DeYoung, "Nature," 439–40.

[45] It may be that one should distinguish between sexual feelings (amoral) and sexual lust or desire (immoral).

CHAPTER TEN

1 Corinthians 13:11

A Revisit: An Exegetical Update

Robert L. Thomas

About twenty years have passed since this author advanced the interpretation that τὸ τέλειον *(to teleion, "the complete," "the mature") in 1 Corinthians 13:10 referred to the mature body of Christ and that a stage of maturity in the growth of that body marked the termination of revelatory and sign gifts in the ancient church. With a fresh focus on 1 Corinthians 13:11, he now updates the discussion in light of various responses that have questioned the validity of that position. He elaborates on why the substantive cannot mean "the perfect," why it must mean "complete" or "mature," why the context requires such, and answers objections to the view.*

* * * * *

A number of years ago I proposed an interpretation of 1 Corinthians 13:10 that assigned τὸ τέλειον *(to teleion)* the meaning of "complete" or "mature" instead of the more frequent rendering of "perfect."[1] At least three developments show the subject needs a renewed look: (1) a misconstruing or confused statement of my view by others;[2] (2) a continuing claim that biblical exegesis yields no explicit indication of the termination of some spiritual gifts;[3] and (3) a growing personal realization that explanations of the passage have overlooked the important contribution of 1 Corinthians 13:11 to the meaning of *to teleion*. A renewed discussion of the issue can probably do little to remedy whatever it is that causes (1) above, but perhaps a focused treatment of the exegetical nuances related to 1 Corinthians 13:11 and their impact on the meaning of *to teleion* in 13:10 will contribute to a recognition that (2) is wrong in light of the oversight named in (3).

Farnell has conveniently summarized the five main viewpoints regarding the meaning of *to teleion* in 1 Corinthians 13:10: (1) the death of a believer when ushered into Christ's presence, (2) the eternal state,

(3) the completed NT canon, (4) Christ' second advent, and (5) the maturing of Christ's body through the course of the church age.[4] Positions (2) and (4) assign the meaning "the perfect" *to teleion* largely because of the neglect of important factors in 1 Corinthians 13:11. With respect for those who interpret differently, I offer the following as some of these factors.

Reasons Why to teleion *Cannot Mean "the Perfect" in 13:10*

The most common definitions of the English word *perfect* applied to 1 Corinthians 13:10 would probably include:

a. being entirely without fault or defect[5]
b. corresponding to an ideal standard or abstract concept
c. the soundness and the excellence of every part, element, or quality of a thing frequently as an unattainable or theoretical state[6]

Either of these three or a combination of them is the usual notion the average person attaches to the word. All three are qualitative in nature, a characteristic that renders them unsatisfactory renderings of *to teleion*. Four reasons demonstrate this:

1. No other use of *teleios* in Paul can possibly mean "perfection" in the sense of the absence of all imperfection. In fact, the meaning of "perfection" in Greek philosophers—that of a "perfect" man—is absent from the NT.[7] Utopian perfection was a philosophical notion, not a NT idea, for this word.[8] Elsewhere in Paul the adjective is figurative and refers almost exclusively to a grown man (cf. 1 Cor. 2:6; 14:20; Phil. 3:15; Eph. 4:13; Col. 1:28; cf. also Heb. 5:14).[9] One other time, in Colossians 4:12, it means "mature" in the OT sense of wholeness and obedience to God's will, and picks up on Paul's ambition for every man as stated in Colossians 1:28.[10] So six out of the other seven times Paul uses the word, it means "mature." The remaining use is in Romans 12:1 where its meaning is "complete."[11]

This pattern of usage establishes a strong probability that the word includes the sense of maturity in 1 Corinthians 13:10, especially since its other two uses in 1 Corinthians have that sense.

2. In the immediate context of 1 Corinthians 13:8–13, a qualitative word is unsuitable in light of the apodosis of the sentence in 13:10. "Perfect" is not a suitable opposite to ἐκ μέρους (*[ek merous],* "partial"). A better meaning would be "whole" or "complete" as antithetical to *ek merous.*[12]

3. The terminology of 13:11 is most conclusive, however, because it is an analogy with the stages of human life (i.e., νήπιος [nēpios, "child"] and ἀνήρ [anēr, "man"]).

a. This analogy directly impacts the meaning of *to teleion* in 13:10, because it sets up a *teleios/nēpios* antithesis in verses 10–11 that is relative, not absolute, and therefore incompatible with the concept of perfection. The difference between childhood and adulthood is a matter of degree, not one of mutually exclusive differentiation.

b. The *nēpios/anēr* antithesis in verse 11 has the same contextual effect of ruling out the notion of an ideal state as denoted by the translation "perfect."

4. The terminology of 13:12 requires an allusion to degrees of revelatory understanding, not perfection or freedom from imperfection. The verbs βλέπομεν (*blepomen*, "I see") and γινώσκω (*ginōskō*, "I know") correlate with the gifts of prophecy and knowledge and their limited insights compared with the complete understanding that will prevail in the future. This is quantitative, not qualitative, so *to teleion* must have the same quantitative connotation.

Hence both etymological and contextual considerations argue emphatically *against* the meaning "perfect" for *to teleion*.

Reasons Why *to* teleion *Must Mean "Complete" or "Mature"*

Corresponding to the reasons for not translating "the perfect" in 1 Corinthians 13:10 are four considerations that point toward the meaning "complete" or "mature."

1. The idea of totality, wholeness, or completion controls the NT usage of *teleios*. In the present connection, totality took on an added dimension: "Yet in the main the feeling of antiquity . . . was that only an 'adult' can be a 'full' man; hence these senses can overlap in Paul."[13] The thought behind the overlap of "complete" and "mature" in this word's usage is that in the minds of the ancients adulthood represented a degree of completeness that was not, relatively speaking, present during childhood. If ever a clear case for this "overlap" in meaning existed, 1 Corinthians 13:10 is that case. The background of *teleios* not only allows for the overlap; in the circumstances of the context, it also requires the dual concept of "complete-mature."[14]

2. Another reason for this meaning is the consistent sense of the *teleios/nēpios* antithesis in Paul, the NT, and all Greek literature. Whenever in the proximity of *nēpios,* as it is in 1 Corinthians 13:10–11, *teleios* always

carries the connotation of adulthood versus childhood (1 Cor. 2:6 and 3:1; 14:20; Eph. 3:13–14; cf. Heb. 5:13–14).[15] In 1 Corinthians 2:6 Paul speaks of imparting wisdom to τοῖς τελείοις (*tois teleiois*, "the mature"), but he encounters an obstacle because, according to 1 Corinthians 3:1, his readers are *nēpiois* ("*infants*"). In 1 Corinthians 14:20 his command to the Corinthians is to be children (νηπιάζετε *[nēpiazete]*) in malice, but adults (τέλειοι *[teleioi]*) in understanding. In Ephesians 4:13–14, his goal is for all members of Christ's body to attain to the unity of the faith and of the full knowledge of the Son of God, i.e., to a τέλειος ἀνήρ (*teleios anēr*, "mature man"), so that they be no longer νήπιοι (*nēpioi*, "children"). The writer of Hebrews echoes this antithesis in 5:13–14 when he compares elementary teaching to milk that is suitable for a *nēpios* ("child" or "infant") with solid food that is suitable for *teleion* ("the mature").

3. First Corinthians 12–14 has many parallels with Ephesians 4:1–16, a passage that teaches the gradual maturing of the church through the present age. This correspondence is all the more instructive in light of Paul's presence in Ephesus while writing 1 Corinthians. He was probably teaching the Ephesian church the same principles he penned in the Corinthian letter. Then about five years later, as he wrote back to the Ephesian church, he found it necessary to reemphasize and develop further the same truths about growth in the body of Christ that he had instructed them about while present. The similarities between the two contexts include the following:

a. All seven unifying influences listed in Ephesians 4:4–6 are present in 1 Corinthians 12–14 (1 Cor. 12:4–6, 13; 13:13; 14:22). Particularly noticeable are one body, one Spirit, one Lord, one baptism, and one God and Father of all.

b. Emphasis on unity in the body (1 Cor. 12:4–6, 11–13, 24–26; Eph. 4:3, 13) along with the diversity of the body's members (1 Cor. 12:14–26; Eph. 4:11, 16) pervades each passage.

c. The noun μέρος (*meros*, "part") in both passages depicts individual members of Christ's body (1 Cor. 12:27; Eph. 4:16).

d. Corporateness of the body (1 Cor. 12:27a; Eph. 4:15–16) combines with an individualistic focus (1 Cor. 12:27b; Eph. 4:4, 7, 16) as a ruling consideration in both places.

e. The general subject under discussion in Ephesians (Eph. 4:7, 11) is spiritual gifts as it is in 1 Corinthians 12–14.

f. The figure representing the church in both passages is the human body, as it is always when Paul talks about spiritual gifts (1 Cor. 12:12–27; Eph. 4:4, 15–16; cf. Rom. 12:3–8).

g. Edification of the body of Christ is the stated objective in both sections (1 Cor. 14:12, 26; Eph. 4:12, 16).

h. Growth from childhood to adulthood is portrayed in Ephesians 4:13–14 as it is in 1 Corinthians 13:11.

i. The *nēpios/teleios anēr* antithesis is found in Ephesians as it is in 1 Corinthians 13:10–11 (Eph. 4:13–14).[16]

j. Love is the overarching quality in the growth process in both passages (1 Cor. 13:1–13; Eph. 4:15–16).

Since Ephesians 4:1–16 offers a distinct picture of a gradually developing and maturing body of Christ,[17] the probability is strong that Paul intends to convey the same in 1 Corinthians 13:11. Though he may not say explicitly "the complete or mature body" (i.e., the complete body with reference to revelatory activity) in 1 Corinthians 13:10, he had doubtless some time during his extended eighteen-month residence in Corinth taught them verbally (as he did the Ephesian church) regarding this analogy so that it was perfectly clear to them what he was talking about. It remains for the interpreter to clarify what he meant by resorting to another of his writings that is quite relevant to 1 Corinthians.

4. The illustration of 13:11 is hardly suitable to refer to the difference between the present and a period after the parousia.[18] So the analogy of verse 11 must be supplying data supplemental to what is in verse 12.

a. To say that the parousia is in view in verse 11 is to see Paul as using his own adult status to illustrate a perfection that follows the parousia. Yet in Philippians 3:12, he views himself as incomplete in his current state as an adult (τετελείωμαι [*teleleiōmai*, "I am brought to completeness"] a pf. tense; cf. γέγονα [*gegona*], 1 Cor. 13:11, which has a present force: "now that I am a man"[19]). In fact, in the very next verse, 1 Corinthians 13:12, he disclaims such a completed state by noting that currently he is among those whose present state is that of conspicuous limitations.[20] This state of incompletion in Paul as an adult negates any possibility that his adulthood of verse 11 is intended to correspond to the state of completion in verse 12. It is also contrary to Pauline Christian humility as reflected elsewhere in the apostle's writings that he would choose such an illustration (e.g., 1 Cor. 15:9; Eph. 3:8; 1 Tim. 1:15).

b. The nature of the transition from childhood to adulthood is not sudden as will be the change at the parousia. It is a gradual process.[21] Adolescence is a transitional period between childhood and adulthood.

c. By nature the process described by κατήργηκα (*katērgēka,* "I render inoperative") in 13:11 indicates an altered condition that continues. It is a dramatic perfect.[22] It indicates "a change of state which still continues; the emancipation from childish things took place as a matter of course, . . . and it continues."[23] If Christ did not return before a permanent body of NT revelation was finished, a degree of completion would arrive that would render unnecessary a continuation of the revelatory process involving the revelatory gifts.

d. The difference between childhood and manhood is a very feeble illustration of the vast difference between the Christian's present state and that which will exist after the parousia.[24]

Reasons Why 13:8–13 Requires the Completion-Maturity-Concept

1. The purpose of the paragraph of 1 Corinthians 13:8–13 is to establish the eternality of love. This is proven by the beginning ("love never fails," v. 8) and end ("the greatest of these is love," v. 13) of the paragraph.

2. Between these two points the writer shows the eternality of love by two sets of contrasts: (a) one between the duration of revelatory gifts that may or may not extend until Christ's return (13:10–11) and the triad of faith, hope, and love that will definitely extend to the time of Christ's return (13:13a); and (b) one between the triad of faith, hope, and love that continue until Christ's return (13:13a) and love alone that will remain after Christ's return (13:13b).

3. These two sets of contrasts emphasize the secondary character of the revelatory and confirmatory gifts from a temporal standpoint, and the supreme importance and lasting character of love because of its eternality. Love lasts longer than these gifts; it even lasts longer than faith and hope with which it is so closely associated until Christ's second advent.

Objections to the Completion-Maturity Explanation

The objections to this position seem to be about six in number, though no extensive response to the completion-maturity view has yet appeared:[25]

1. *Objection:* Verse 11 is merely an illustration or an analogy and its meaning must be explained in light of the meaning of verse 12, which refers to Christ's second coming.[26]

Response: If verse 11 says something different from verse 12, it must be allowed to have its distinctive contribution. Paul was not just padding his discussion when he inserted verse 11. To interpret verse 11 in light of the meaning of verse 12 is to rob this verse of its distinctive contribution, thereby robbing Scripture of an aspect of its meaning.

2. *Objection:* Verse 12 has τότε (*tote,* "then") to link it with ὅταν (*hotan,* "when") of verse 10.[27] Verse 11 has no such temporal indicator.

Response: Verse 11 *does* have temporal indicators, i.e., the two occurrences of ὅτε (*hote,* "when"). Such a temporal indicator picks up the *hotan* of verse 10 even more specifically than the *tote* of verse 12, which does not limit the temporal reference of the *hotan* in verse 10, but is antithetic to the two occurrences of *arti* in verse 12.

3. *Objection:* The idea of the maturity of the body of Christ is nowhere present in the context.[28]

Response: Maturity is in the context, in 13:11. See also 14:20 where individual maturity is in view. In 1 Corinthians 2:6 and 3:1 individual maturity is also in focus. It is not a matter of maturity not being in the context; it is rather a question of the maturity of what, individuals or the corporate body? Verse 11 most naturally refers to corporate maturity because of the singular number used in the analogy of verse 11 compared to the plurals in verses 9, 12. Paul has a proclivity for going back and forth between talking about the corporate aspect of the body of Christ and the individual members of that body. He does the same in the broader context here (12:12, 27; cf. Eph. 4:13–14).[29] The presence of maturity in the context forces a choice between individual and corporate maturity. The nature of the discussion and the added input from Ephesians 4:1–16 tips the scale in favor of corporate maturity.

The criticism of this maturity-view, which notes that the context does not speak about the immaturity of individual believers,[30] rests on a misunderstanding of the view. The view looks at the immaturity of the total body during its earlier years, not explicitly that of individuals. It was the temporary nature of these gifts that marked the infancy of the body of Christ, not of single members of that body.

Maturity is also implied in the emphasis on edification of the body in 1 Corinthians 14:12, 26 (cf. 12:7). Edification equates with building up, which is equivalent to growth—the same as maturing according to Ephesians 4:13–16. So maturity shows itself contextually in yet another way: through the emphasis on edification that is found in 1 Corinthians 12–14. It is a factor in the passage under study.

4. *Objection:* The context says nothing about the completion of Scripture.[31]

Response: Here is another superficial objection. Completion is in the context. Note the four occurrences of *ek merous* that require an opposite—"completion": 13:9 (twice), 13:10, and 13:12. It is not a matter of completion's not being in the context; it is rather a question of the completion of what. The completion spoken of in verse 12 is unobscured cognitive sight to replace the limited prophetic revelations and unlimited knowledge to replace partial revelations through the gift of knowledge. Those partial revelatory gifts were the means used by the Spirit in bringing the NT Scriptures—among other revelations—to the church. So a termination of revelatory gifts coincided with the completion of the NT. Verse 12 does not speak of seeing God face to face,[32] which would be a qualitative condition that is inappropriate to this context. This would break the continuity of the earlier part of the paragraph where revelatory gifts are in view. Verse 12 must refer to unlimited prophetic sight and knowledge. What is not in this context is a contrast between perfection and imperfection. It is not talking about a qualitative set of conditions, but a quantitative one.

5. *Objection:* The idea of completion or maturity replaces the reference to Christ's return that is clearly in the context.[33]

Response: The maturity concept does not "replace" Christ's return; it supplements it. It adds to it another possible eventuality. Uncertain as he was about the time of Christ's return, Paul left open the possibility that before Christ's return the body of Christ might reach the requisite stage of maturity where the revelatory and sign gifts were unnecessary (13:11). But he also indicated the possibility of Christ's advent before the church reached that stage (13:12).

6. *Objection:* It is a misguided emphasis to focus on verse 11 to explain the meaning of *to teleion*. It is like letting the tail wag the dog to allow an analogy to dictate the meaning of the argument as a whole and the plain statement of verse 12b.[34]

Response: The completion-maturity explanation does not focus on verse 11 alone, but it does give the verse its deserved place as part of the explanation.

An unwillingness to let 13:11 have its natural sense leads inevitably to viewing the analogy to human development as ambiguous.[35] It is obviously going to appear ambiguous if it means something different from what the interpreter wants it to say. By allowing verse 11 to inject the element of maturity into the discussion, one has not allowed the analogy to have precedence over the argument as a whole. He has rather taken into account an indispensable ingredient of the argument. Just as it would be wrong to let the analogy of 13:11 exclude the reference to the second coming in 13:12, it is also wrong to let the reference to the second coming exclude the graphic analogy that expresses another possibility regarding the cessation of prophecy, tongues, and knowledge. The verse cannot be treated as excess baggage that gets in the way of a preconceived interpretation.

So far, the maturity-completion view stands without one unanswerable objection because the proposed weaknesses of the view rest on misunderstanding or have adequate responses.

Paul and the Future of Prophecy, Tongues, and Knowledge

Paul knew of an earlier period when God spoke directly to His prophets, a period that had come to an end with the prophets Haggai, Zechariah, and Malachi, being followed by the 400 silent years (cf. Matt. 23:35, 37; Heb. 1:1–2). He also knew that the close of the OT canon coincided with the cessation of OT prophecy (e.g., Luke 24:44) long before the first advent of Christ.[36] He was conscious that he was now in the midst of a new period during which God was speaking directly to His apostles and prophets, resulting in inspired utterances that, in part, were taking their place alongside the OT canon as inspired Scripture (cf. 1 Cor. 14:37; 1 Thess. 5:26; 2 Peter 3:15–16). One possibility he foresaw was that this period of prophecy could come to its conclusion before the second advent of Christ just as OT prophecy had come to its conclusion four hundred years before the first advent of Christ. Such a cessation would be like the gradual development from childhood to manhood. When the church reached an appointed stage, it would no longer need revelatory and sign gifts. It would expectedly come to a close with the completion of a new canon of an unknown number of writings that resulted from NT prophecy, to serve as a companion to the OT canon. Because of Paul's strong anticipation of Christ's imminent coming, this was a secondary expectation, however, and was added in verse 11 according to the mode of customary Pauline digression.

Paul also knew the possibility that Christ's second coming could be very soon, even within his own lifetime (1 Cor. 15:51–52; 1 Thess. 4:15–17). Had this happened, the period of NT prophecy would have halted abruptly as the members of the body of Christ were transformed immediately into the image of Christ (cf. 1 John 3:2). This would automatically culminate a new completed body of Scripture to serve future generations, because the body of Christ would no longer be on earth to receive more revelation. This principal expectation is reflected by the *gar* that connects 13:12 with 13:10.[37]

The apostle did not know which of these would occur first, a stage of relative completeness marking adulthood in comparison to childhood or a stage of absolute completeness that will characterize those in the immediate presence of Christ. So through inspiration of the Spirit he portrayed his uncertainty by choosing terminology and illustrative material that were compatible with either possibility. He knew that the partial would be replaced by either the mature or the complete, and perhaps by first one and then the other.

The best he could do to emphasize the eternality of love was a double contrast:[38] (1) a contrast between revelatory and sign gifts that may or may not characterize the entire church age on the one hand, and on the other, the qualities of faith, hope, and love that would definitely characterize the entire period; and (2) a contrast between the triad faith, hope, and love that continue to the parousia on the one hand, and on the other, love alone that will survive and continue following the parousia.

It is interesting to compare the ways Paul states the disappearance of faith and hope at the parousia. In 2 Corinthians 5:6–8, faith is juxtaposed with sight, and one is associated with being absent from the Lord and the other with being present with the Lord. Faith will be replaced by sight when Christ returns. According to Romans 8:24–25 Christians await what they hope for, but once it arrives, hope has no further place. When Christ the believer's hope appears, hope will have no further function.

The disappearance of the revelatory gifts is described in terms that are very different. "They will be rendered inoperative" (Καταργηθήσεται *[Katargēthēsetai]*, vv. 8 [twice], 10) in the same way as adult maturation has rendered inoperative and keeps on rendering inoperative (perfect tense, κατήργηκα *[katērgēka]*) the characteristics of childhood (v. 11). This is hardly an exclusive reference to the parousia as is the case with the disappearance of faith and hope. Prophetic sight and knowledge will be infinitely increased at that time so that they are no longer partial. This will be the prevailing state. If the revelatory gifts were unquestionably to extend to the parousia, no rendering inoperative of those gifts is appropriate; they would simply be replaced by universal knowledge for all.

Regardless of what the future might hold, Paul was confident of one thing: "love never fails . . . and is the greatest of these." It will stand the test of time and eternity.

This overarching "fruit of the Spirit" is the supreme quality, for which sensible Christians are very thankful. They may differ in their interpretations of this or that passage, but they have the privilege of continuing to love one another, no matter what. I am grateful for this opportunity of once again voicing in love what I deem to be the truth about a very important text of the NT: *to teleion* in 1 Corinthians 13:10 refers to maturity in the body of Christ, and consequently furnishes a very good exegetical basis for concluding that revelatory and sign gifts granted to the body of Christ ceased functioning in early church history.

ENDNOTES

[1] Robert L. Thomas, "Tongues . . . Will Cease," *JETS* 17, no. 2 (spring 1974): 85–89; idem, *Understanding Spiritual Gifts* (Chicago: Moody, 1978), 106–13, 199–204.

[2] E.g., see note 30.

[3] Wayne A. Grudem ("The New Testament Gift of Prophecy: A Response to My Friends" [unpublished paper presented to the Forty-fourth Annual Meeting of the Evangelical Theological Society in San Francisco, November 21, 1992], 18) has called 1 Corinthians 13:10 an "immovable stumbling block" for the view that the gift of prophecy has ceased.

[4] F. David Farnell, "When Will the Gift of Prophecy Cease?" *Bibliotheca Sacra* 150 (April–June 1993): 191–93. In his defense of view (5), Farnell agrees with the position advocated in the present discussion.

[5] Grudem ("Response," 15) continually injects the qualitative notion as the meaning of ἐκ μέρους (13:10): "This . . . [is a statement] about the imperfect nature of our activity of prophesying" ("Response," 17) and "He states quite clearly that these imperfect gifts will last until the time of Christ's return" ("Response," 18). On the contrary, ἐκ μέρους speaks of the gifts' partial nature, not their imperfection in quality. Grudem is in conflict with himself at this point. In 1982 he wrote that the phrase refers to quantitative rather than qualitative imperfection (Wayne A. Grudem, *The Gift of Prophecy in 1 Corinthians* [Washington: University Press, 1982], 148–49 n. 59). Now in speaking of the same phrase a referring to "the imperfect *nature*" [italics added] ("Response," 17; cf also p. 17 n. 24), he unfortunately appears to have switched to a qualita tive sense for the same phrase.

[6] *Webster's Ninth New Collegiate Dictionary,* 872.

[7] Gerhard Delling, "τέλος, τελέω, κ. τ. λ.," *TDNT,* 8:77.

[8] Ibid., 8:69–72.

[9] R. Schippers, "τέλος," in *New International Dictionary of New Testament Theology*, 2:62.

[10] In Colossians 4:12 *teleioi* is "a term evidently chosen to counteract the gnostic aspiration to 'perfection' by their regimen and cult" (Ralph Martin, *Colossians and Philemon*, NCB [Grand Rapids, 1973], 134).

[11] Grudem erroneously uses Matthew 5:48 and Romans 12:2 to illustrate the meaning of "perfect" for τέλειος ("Response," 14–15). "Complete" is a better English word for these two passages because the concept behind τέλειος is the Hebrew תָּמִים or שָׁלֵם, "wholeness," not the philosophical connotation of perfection in a qualitative or ultimate sense as the word "perfect" implies (Delling, "τέλος," 8:74, 76–77).

[12] Delling, "τέλος," 8:75.

[13] Delling, "τέλος," 8:76. Oepke notes the concept behind childhood in ancient times: "Antiquity primarily sees in the child the element of immaturity or childishness" (Albrecht Oepke, "παῖς, παιδίον, κ. τ. λ.," *TDNT*, 5:642). The opposite of this state is maturity. Νήπιος was used for small children between the ages of 1 and 10 (Georg Bertram, "νήπιος, νηπιάζω," *TDNT*, 4:912). The goal of human development was τέλειος ἀνήρ. As the adult sets aside the nature of a child, so the Christian with the coming of τὸ τέλειον sets aside the γνῶσις that is essential during the stage of the νήπιος (ibid., 919). Ἀνήρ indicates an adult man as distinct from a boy (Albrecht Oepke, "ἀνήρ, ἀνδρίζομαι," *TDNT*, 1:361, 363).

[14] Robert L. Reymond, *What About Continuing Revelations and Miracles in the Presbyterian Church Today* (n.p.: Presbyterian and Reformed, 1977), 31–36, and Walter J. Chantry, *Signs of the Apostles, Observations on Pentecostalism Old and New* (Edinburgh: Banner of Truth, 1976), 50–54, capture the overlapping meaning of *teleios,* but weaken their position by a refusal to apply 13:12 to the situation following the parousia. John R. McRay, "*To Teleion* in I Corinthians 13:10" *Restoration Quarterly* 14 (1971): 172–174, also notes the twin meanings of the term, but concludes that 1 Corinthians 12–14 must be explained on the basis of the entire argument of Ephesians, particularly the Jewish-Gentile issue that is prominent in that book (174–83). Reymond and Chantry refer verse 12 to the completion of the NT canon, but McRay refers it to the final stages of Paul's work among the Gentiles (183). Both positions differ from that defended in the present study.

[15] Archibald Robertson and Alfred Plummer, *A Critical and Exegetical Commentary on the First Epistle of Paul to the Corinthians*, 2d ed. (Edinburgh: T & T Clark, 1914), 297–98; Thomas Charles Edwards, *A Commentary on the First Epistle to the Corinthians* (London: Hodder and Stoughton, 1885), 349.

[16] "In Eph. 4:13 . . . the ἀνὴρ τέλειος is the adult . . . in contrast to the νήπιος of v. 14" (Gerhard Delling, "πλήρης, πληρόω κ. τ. λ.," *TDNT*, 6:302).

[17] Du Plessis notes that τέλειος in Ephesians 4:13 is characterized in three ways: (1) Growth is involved. A body-building process or a dynamic development transpires throughout the period of the church's existence. (2) The dynamic is corporate in nature. Though composed of many members, the body of Christ grows as a unit. (3) Since the image of τέλειος is in the character of an exhortation, it is maturity progressively realized in the present state of the church's existence (Paul Johannes Du Plessis, *ΤΕΛΕΙΟΣ, the Idea of Perfection in the N. T.* [Kampen: J. H. Kok, 1956], 188–93).

[18] Robertson & Plummer, *1 Corinthians*, 297.

[19] A. T. Robertson, *A Grammar of the Greek New Testament in the Light of Historical Research* (Nashville: Broadman, 1934), 900, 971.

[20] Thomas, "Tongues . . . Will Cease," 85. In fact, in verse 12 he refers to himself personally (i.e., in the singular) as currently having only partial knowledge (γινώσκω).

[21] Farnell, "When . . . Cease?" 193.

[22] Cf. Robertson, *Grammar,* 896.

[23] Robertson & Plummer, *1 Corinthians*, 298; cf. Frederic L. Godet, *Commentary on St. Paul's First Epistle to the Corinthians*, 2 vols., trans. Rev. A. Cusin (1957; reprint, Grand Rapids: Zondervan, 1986), 252.

[24] Robertson & Plummer, *1 Corinthians*, 297.

[25] The relevant quotations of Wayne Grudem and Gordon Fee from which these objections are lifted include the following: (1) "This view fails to recognize that vs. 11, which speaks of Paul in the first person and in the

past, is merely an illustration, and our understanding of what it illustrates must conform to vs. 12, which speaks of believers generally ('we') and in the future ('shall know'). And only vs. 12 has *tote* which links it clearly to the *hotan* in vs. 10. Vs. 11 illustrates not the maturity of the church (an idea which is nowhere discussed in this context) but the fact that something complete or perfect replaces something incomplete or imperfect" (Grudem, *1 Corinthians*, 215 n. 60). "Whereas Christ's return is mentioned clearly in 1 Corinthians 13:12, no verse in this section mentions anything about the completion of Scripture . . . or the 'maturity' of the church (whatever that means—is the church really mature even today?). All of these suggestions [including the one about 'maturity'] bring in new elements not found in the context to replace one element—Christ's return—which clearly is right there in the context already" (Wayne A. Grudem, *The Gift of Prophecy in the New Testament and Today* [Westchester, Ill.: Crossway, 1988] 238–39).

(2) "The precise reference of the word *[teleios]* must be determined by the individual context, and there, as we have seen, the context indicates that 'when the perfect comes' refers to the time of Christ's return" (Grudem, *New Testament*, 236).

(3) "Such views [i.e., those that see 'when the perfect comes' as some time before Christ returns] all seem to break down at 1 Corinthians 13:12, where Paul implies that believers will see God 'face to face' 'when the perfect is come'" (Grudem, *New Testament*, 238).

(4) "This view has nothing to commend it except the analogy of v. 11, which is a misguided emphasis at best" (Gordon D. Fee, *The First Epistle to the Corinthians* [Grand Rapids: Eerdmans, 1987], 645 n. 23).

(5) "Even though Paul says '*we* know in part,' the emphasis is not on the immaturity of the Corinthians, but on the relative nature of the gifts" (Fee, *1 Corinthians*, 645 n. 24).

[26] Grudem, *1 Corinthians*, 215 n. 60; Fee, *1 Corinthians*, 654 nn. 23, 25.

[27] Ibid.; cf. also Grudem, "Response," 15.

[28] Grudem, *New Testament*, 238–39; Fee, *1 Corinthians*, 645; cf. also Grudem, "Response," 14.

[29] 1 Corinthians 12:12: "For just as the body is *one* and has *many members*, and *all the members* of the body though they are *many* are *one* body, so also is Christ." 1 Corinthians 12:27: "Now you are [such a thing as the] *body* [an anarthrous collective term] of Christ and *members individually*." Ephesians 4:13–14: "until *we all* attain to the unity of the

faith and of the full knowledge of the Son of God, to a mature *man,* to the measure of the stature of the fullness of Christ, that *we* may be no longer children, tossed about and carried around by every wind of doctrine through the trickery of men in craftiness to the deceit of error . . ." [italics added].

[30] Fee, *1 Corinthians,* 644–55, whose criticism of the mature-body view is off-target when he says that the contrast between immaturity and maturity "will not do since the contrast has to do with the *gifts* being 'partial,' not with the believers themselves."

[31] Grudem, *New Testament,* 238–39.

[32] Contra Grudem, *New Testament,* 238.

[33] Grudem, *New Testament,* 236, 238.

[34] Ibid.; Fee, *1 Corinthians,* 645 nn. 23, 25.

[35] E.g., "the ambiguity of the first analogy [childhood and adulthood]," Fee, *1 Corinthians,* 644.

[36] Cf. Robert L. Thomas, "The Spiritual Gift of Prophecy in Rev. 22:18," *Journal of the Evangelical Theological Society* 32, no. 2 (June 1989): 215.

[37] C. K. Barrett, *A Commentary on the First Epistle to the Corinthians,* Harper New Testament Commentary (New York: Harper & Row, 1968), 306.

[38] Grudem's proposed single contrast—"when Christ returns, prophesy will cease" ("Response," 18)—is too simplistic to account for all the exegetical data of the passage.

CHAPTER ELEVEN

Ephesians

Prayer's Strategic Role

James E. Rosscup

*Ephesians in general and its "armor" passage (6:10–20) in particular
devote a major focus to the importance of prayer in Christian life and
ministry. The power in the armor is essential if believers are to win the
battle against Satan and his demonic forces. The parts of the armor
denote different spiritual aspects of Christian living that are also essential. None of the above can be appropriated without prayer modeled
according to the principles of Scripture. Eleven considerations show
prayer to be inseparable from victory in spiritual warfare. The uses of
"all" in Ephesians 6:18 are a call to an "all-out" commitment to prayer
and remind Christian soldiers of its crucial importance.*

* * * * *

The urgent exhortation of Ephesians 6:10 presses home to each Christian: "be strong in the Lord." Each one must live in that power of God's
armor (Eph. 6:10–13). Through this means alone can the believer successfully encounter the Devil and his demonic associates, who seek to
prevail. A life based on such *power* finds expression in the six *parts* of
the armor that the Christian should implement (6:14–17). The power
represented by the armor relates vitally to *prayer* (6:18–20). The writer
himself models prayer for his readers (1:15–23; 3:14–21). Later, he
calls on *them* to pray in all things and for him as they realize God's
power in their lives and demonstrate it in implementing the armor. In
the two long passages of Paul's model, prayer is strategic in the realization of the wealth of Christians in Christ. Further, it is strategic in
the closing of the epistle as it climaxes the call to live in God's power,
possessing His whole armor and letting that power permeate every
part of the armor.

This study spotlights the summons for Christians to use the power of
God's armor. The parts of the armor specify the elements of that power,
and prayer imparts effectiveness to the armor.

Rereading all thirteen of Paul's epistles with a special eye for references to prayer is a rich experience. Checking these references against a list found in the Society of New Testament Studies monograph by Gordon P. Wiles (*Paul's Intercessory Prayers* [Cambridge: University Press, 1974], Appendices I and II) has also been helpful. Wiles includes lists classified into categories of prayer: doxology, praise, blessing, cursing, worship [actually, worship should be involved in all things in life], hymns, thanks, boasting, petition for self, intercession, and general prayer (297–99).

This writer's count of references to categories of prayer combined with Wiles' lists showed 56 verses in Romans and 42 in 1 Corinthians. The third highest total was in Ephesians with 31 verses. Romans has a total of 433 verses, and Ephesians only 155. Romans covers ten and a half pages in the *New American Standard Bible,* and Ephesians three and a half pages (Iowa Falls: World Bible Publishers, 1973). Despite being only about one-third the length of Romans, Ephesians has proportionately more than 55 percent as many verses directly related to prayer. Colossians also emphasizes prayer, devoting over 20 verses to it. Yet Colossians does not have as many separate longer passages on prayer as Ephesians (cp. Col. 1:9–14 with Eph. 1:15–23; 3:14–21; 6:18–20).

The relation of Ephesians 6:18–20 to the armor passage just before it in 6:10–17 is significant. This study will examine the nature of the connection between the two sections.

PRAYER AS EXEMPLIFIED IN EPHESIANS 6:10–20

Before he *exhorts* the readers to pray, Paul provides them with an *example* by modeling prayer for them. He blesses and praises God (Eph. 1:2–3, 6, 12, 14). Then he injects two bursts of intercession for them in chapters 1 and 3 while describing the spiritual wealth Christ has conferred on believers. The bounty that grace has bestowed, amounting to "all spiritual blessings" (1:3), leads Paul to these prayers. He is anxious for his readers to realize in daily practice the style of life such amazing riches make possible (1:15–23; 3:14–21).

Each intercessory labor exhibits features that Paul pled for before God. They are key items on his "prayer list." Both prayers reveal facets of paramount import for Christian living. They are also examples of how all Christians can make their prayers relevant in spiritual matters, whether for personal needs or for other Christians. The intercessions exemplify a passionate concern for spiritual progress, just as Paul prays elsewhere that Christians may please God "in all respects," being fruitful in every good work (Col. 1:10). In the Colossians passage, Paul prays that God will fill believers with the knowledge of His will, His power,

His steadfastness, His joy, and thanksgiving to Him (vv. 9–12). His burden is for them to be vitally concerned over spiritual matters. It is not for a physical relief from a broken arm, a new job, or sleep as a solution to insomnia. Though the latter burdens are also very important, they should intertwine with the things Paul puts on his epistolary prayer lists. Christians should cast *all* their care upon God (1 Peter 5:7). Yet the life-shaping issues that Paul makes prominent should gain the pervasive place in their prayers. Sadly, they are all too frequently missing from a prayer bulletin, or pop up only here and there.

Does that sound familiar? Where imbalance exists, pastoral leaders must labor to remedy the imbalance through loving teaching, personal example, and emphases that draw together the different elements that are urgently needed in prayer.

In Ephesians, after his focus on wealth and a modeling of what prayer should be, Paul devotes his final three chapters to a lifestyle that matches this wealth. He emphasizes the need for it to be expressed in practical relationships. He shows how believers for whom he prays can translate their riches into a "walk" that reflects positive responses to what he has prayed for. Fond of that word "walk," Paul mentions it in 2:2, 10, returns to it in 4:1, then keeps it before the recipients through regular repetition (4:17; 5:2, 8, 15). Believers can behave in a manner consistent with the high privileges God has granted them. They can display this in a walk (or behavior) of unity (4:1–16), holiness (4:17–32), love (5:1–7), light (5:8–14), and carefulness to be filled with the Spirit (5:15–6:9). These are all descriptions of the same life, and are simultaneously true of a believer.

The five participles in 5:19–21 reflect what accompanies being "filled by the Spirit" (5:18). They include speaking to one another in edification, singing, rejoicing, giving thanks, and showing submission to other Christians. Paul narrows his focus in 5:22–6:9 to specific groups. Wives are to live in the submission of a Spirit-filled life true to the unity, holiness, love, and light, expressing this toward their husbands. Husbands are to love their wives, children to obey their parents, and parents to model the Christ-life to their children. Servants and their masters are to fulfil what is good to one another.

A "walk" of this many-splendored nature is "worthy" (4:1)[1] of the wonderful calling that Paul describes in chaps. 1–3. Such conduct manifests the benefits that Paul highlighted in his own prayers for the believers in earlier parts of the epistle.

Paul has more to say when he arrives at the last of his crucial words in the letter (6:10). He draws this walk befitting such great wealth into a focus that realistically characterizes what form it takes in the world believers face. It is a *hostile* world. All the decent things that God stands for are pitted against the ugly evils used by those who march under the black banner of "the prince of the power of the air" to oppose God and His people (2:2). Those whom God called to the wealth (chaps. 1–3) and the walk (chaps. 4–6) are in a deadly warfare (6:10–20). To cope with this, Paul urges the *power,* the *panoply,* and the *prayer.* The third item is the principal focus of this discussion.

THE POWER IN THE ARMOR

To be victorious, believers need the power of being "strong in the Lord and in the strength of His might" (v. 10). They must have "the weapons of righteousness for the right hand and the left," as 2 Corinthians 6:7 describes. Or, as 2 Corinthians 10:4 defines, "The weapons of our warfare are not of the flesh but mighty before God. . . ." Nothing other than *God's power* is able to win, a theme frequent in Scripture, and the power is intermeshed with prayer.[2] For Christians go up against the ranks of devilish legions in the heavenlies and across international areas who influence and target believers to attack (6:12). These are demonic powers. The Devil is ready to take advantage of any opening to assail those in Christ's church (4:27). They are desperately in need of "strength" (6:10), because they are in peril in having to contend with the enemy's *methodeia* (μεθοδεία), his "cunning stratagems" (v. 11).

How do Christians secure the only power sufficient to win against sinister odds so great? They appropriate weaponry that God supplies. They "put on" or "take." This is in a welcoming trust, receiving what God makes available in grace to be utilized. "I take, He undertakes" has been a winning theme for Christ's people in conflict. Believers made strong in the Lord and in the strength of His might receive ability to stand their ground as spiritual soldiers, no matter what onslaught the Devil and his hordes may mount. They can stop the forces of wickedness personally as individuals and corporately as a church.

They are to "stand, therefore" (v. 14). In the imperative "stand," Paul presses his main exhortation in this section on warfare. "Receive" in verse 17 is subordinate to this in the flow of thought, though coordinated with "stand," and expresses a trustful receptivity toward God who is sufficient to make the stand effective.

As part of the unified Word of God, Ephesians 6:10–20 repeats much of what Jesus taught in His Upper Room Discourse.[3] There, John 15:7–8 fulfils a vital service in teaching a close relationship between a *Word*-filled life and a *prayer*-filled life and its fruitfulness. Paul, a good disciple of Jesus, is saturated with His mind (cf. 1 Cor. 2:16) and reflects it in many facets of Ephesians 6:10–20. See Exhibit C (all exhibits located at the end of this chapter).

THE PARTS OF THE ARMOR

Six pieces[4] of military equipment make up the panoply or list of armor.[5] These are drawn from Paul's knowledge of Scripture and sensitivity to Roman military dress in connection with this. See Exhibit A. He must regard the *few* parts of armor that he specifies as representative of *all* aspects in the Christian life. Many key words that surprisingly do not appear here are strategic elsewhere in the letter—e.g., grace, love, joy (5:20), goodness (5:9). God's grace is abundant in all of His provisions (e.g., 1:3–14; 2:8–9). So is love (1:4–5; 2:4–6; 4:14–16; 5:2; 6:23). Paul also refers earlier to humility, gentleness and patience (4:2), holiness (4:24), and kindness (4:32).

Paul begins his list of key elements in 6:10–18 with two that characterize the "fruit of light" against facets of darkness (5:9). These two are the belt of *truth* and the breastplate of *righteousness* (6:14–15). A third word in 5:9, *goodness,* has been prominent in the context as well (4:28–29; 6:8).

Why does Paul put truth *first?* Other Scriptures sometimes mention it before righteousness (Isa. 48:1; Zech. 8:8), but righteousness also appears before truth (Eph. 4:24; 5:9; 1 Tim. 6:11). Word order with such terms is flexible. Truth is certainly appropriate, wherever it occurs. The Christian has entered the realm of God's truth by being identified with Him in opposition to all influences blossoming from the Devil's lie. So truth is as fitting as any word to begin the armor. Standing for truth against the tempter's falsehood was the issue for the first man and woman in the *creation* context (Gen. 3:5). Truth was again the crux for Jesus in His *conflict* with the tempter before His public ministry (Matt. 4:1–11). Truth was also the issue when the deceiver captured Ananias and Sapphira in the infant *church* (Acts 5:3). Truth is ever the point that the unsaved miss when they listen to the Father of Lies (John 8:44).[6] Truth is the point of issue in the Christian's struggle against the Devil and those who peddle his lies (1 John 4:1–6).

The call to put on armor comes in a context that has made a practical stance in truth crucial (e.g., 4:15, 24). Truth works as a defensive weapon in the battle, standing staunchly against what is false. But it also takes the offensive in ministering positively to help and foster growth in others (4:3, 15, 25, 28). Truth adds fragrance to life through whatever is "pleasing to the Lord" (5:9–10). In Philippians 4:8, truth is first in a list of six positive qualities.

Why does Paul in naming parts of the human body begin with the girded loins? It is because belting the armor securely permits freedom in movement of the feet and legs. And as they are free and able to keep good balance, agility, and speed, so it goes with the upper part of the body (cf. John 8:32, "the truth shall make you free"). The Christian stays upright. Everything in life depends on a basic commitment to God's truth (cf. 4:21, 24). With truth, a believer makes a viable stand against the enemy.

The second piece of armor, righteousness, is often linked with truth in God's Word.[7] Righteousness is a matter on which the Spirit of truth (John 16:13) convicts the unsaved (John 16:8–11). This is the same Spirit as in the armor passage (Eph. 6:17–18). Righteousness is the absolutely necessary benefit that God has imputed once for all to everyone who believes (Rom. 3:21–5:21). It is also a character quality He continually imparts in practical living (e.g., Rom. 6:1–22; 8:1–17).

The third piece of armor, after truth and righteousness, is fittingly "the preparation of the gospel of peace." In the gospel, people agree with God's truth, by which they take their stand against error and stand in unity; they also stand for righteousness that is pitted against unrighteousness. In the gospel a person believes to righteousness (Rom. 10:10). The same gospel ministers to confer peace with God (Rom. 5:1)— amity in place of enmity—and just as surely, the gospel fosters the peace of God (Phil. 4:7). The center of that gospel is Christ. He *is* the believer's peace (Eph. 2:14). He also *established* peace (v. 15), and He *preached* peace (v. 17). Those who have received His gospel message are to live as peacemakers (Matt. 5:9). In this, they bear witness to how God gives peace with Himself, bidding others who hear to be reconciled (2 Cor. 5:19–21). They also can have a daily, peaceful composure that reflects God's sufficiency to cope with any circumstance (Phil. 4:6–7). One of the slickest tricks the Devil employs—i.e., one of his arrows in Ephesians 6:16—is to gain an advantage (Eph. 4:27) and replace peace by creating discord in a believer's heart or between believers.

The "preparation" of the gospel of peace for the feet may refer to a firm foundation, the solid footing (Ps. 18:36) that provides stability (Pss. 18:33; 37:31; Hab. 3:19).[8] Or, better, it can mean a God-imparted, steadied composure that flows from such a gospel to give one the ability (or, preparedness) to stand true to the gospel.[9]

How fitting that after truth, righteousness, and the preparation of the gospel the fourth weapon is the shield of faith (Eph. 6:16). Faith is the instrument by which the unsaved came into salvation ("through faith," 2:8). Faith continues to be of paramount importance in the lives of the saved. Paul writes, "We walk by faith and not by sight" (2 Cor. 5:7). Though he does not include "love" as in his armor passage in 1 Thessalonians 5:8, what he says here is consistent with his point that faith "works through love" (Gal. 5:6). To Paul, love and faith go together (Eph. 6:23). He would concur with John that faith is the victory that overcomes the world (1 John 5:4–5). He also agrees with Peter (1 Peter 5:8) that steadfast resistance to the Devil is by faith.

Here in Ephesians 6, faith is a spiritual shield, no doubt because it defensively wards off fire-tipped arrows that the Devil's emissaries shoot at Christ's soldiers. The Devil and his demons often use people to inflict hurt, or they can work directly on a believer. Arrows of all sorts strike at God's people—arrows that wound by disunity (Eph. 4:2–3); unholy anger in thought or words (4:25ff.); sexually permissive thoughts, words, or acts (5:3–7); the temptation to indulge in drunkenness (cf. 5:18a); attitudes that assault joy, thanksgiving, and submission (5:19–21); unloving attitudes and acts instead of a husband's Christ-like love (5:22ff.), and on and on. The arrows of the enemy are many.

Faith is crucial, then. No wonder the Christian needs it to resist these attacks. Pastors as well as those in their flocks face the same danger. God offers them the same weaponry. By faith, believers such as those in Hebrews 11 have not only staged defensive victories, but have made offensive advances to carry out God's cause. In Ephesians, most references to faith deal with positive advances.[10]

After the above four weapons comes the piece of armor called "the helmet of salvation" (6:17). This may mean the helmet of protection that salvation is, because the wealth is illimitable (chaps. 1–3, especially 1:3). Or, Paul may mean the helmet as the protection that salvation supplies. Either idea points to salvation as protective. Salvation is deliverance; salvation means deliverance. God in Christ supplies deliverance in the *past* sense, eternally clearing Christians from the penalty sin would exact. He also gives deliverance from sin's power in the *present* process of struggles (Rom. 7:14–25; 8:1–39). And He will yet effect deliverance in the *prospective* anticipation, for He promises finally to set them free from the very presence of sin. Some day they will no longer have a sin principle within. They will be redeemed in the grandest completeness, glorified, totally monopolized by God's holiness (Rom. 8:30; Phil. 3:21; 1 John 3:2).

Paul is not through with the armor. Finally, he urges believers to take up a weapon in trustful receptivity. It is "the sword of the Spirit, which is the word of God" (Eph. 6:17). The Word with its gospel is in a wonderful sense the Spirit's sword. The Spirit gave it in inspiration of Scripture. He penetrated believers' hearts with conviction (John 16:8–11) when He gave them the new birth (John 3:3–7). He uses the Word to nourish

Christian growth, and ministers the Word through them in witness to the lost as well as in edifying other believers. Here, faith wards off the enemy arrows by the Word that the Spirit utilizes. As in John 15:7–8, Paul draws a close tie between God's Word and prayer. The Word is the sword *of the Spirit* (Eph. 6:17), and Christians are to pray *in the Spirit* (v. 18). The Spirit teaches the Word that is God's will (cf. John 14:26; 1 Cor. 2:12–13), and helps the saved to achieve God's will in prayer (cf. Rom. 8:26–27).

It is important to observe that Christ Himself is every part of the armor to Christians (cf. Exhibit A). He is the *truth* (John 14:6; Rev. 19:11), the truth and the Son that sets them free (John 8:32, 36). He wears a girdle of truth in Isaiah 11:4–5. He also is their *righteousness,* whether imputed or imparted (cf. 1 Cor. 1:30), and He has "put on righteousness like a breastplate" (Isa. 59:17; cf. 11:4f.). He is their *peace* (Eph. 2:14) and the "good news," the gospel. He is the *Faithful* One toward whom faith is directed (Rev. 19:11).[11] He is their *salvation* (Ps. 27:1), and has worn "a helmet of salvation on His head" (Isa. 59:17). So He has covered the believer's head in the day of battle—and that is relevant to Ephesians 6:10–17—evidently with a helmet (Ps. 140:7). He is the *Word of God* (John 1:1; Rev. 19:13) that the Spirit ministers. His mouth as the ideal Servant speaking His Word is "like a sharp sword" (Isa. 49:2). Christ is the armor, and when Paul writes of this armor in a composite sweep, *personalizing* it, he says, "But put ye on the Lord Jesus Christ, and make not provision for the flesh to fulfil its lusts" (Rom. 13:14). Christians put on Christ when putting on the new man (person), who is created in righteousness and holiness of the truth (Eph. 4:24), created to good works (2:10).

Can anything be more important than this in the life to which God has called Christians? Can anything be more urgent than showing forth *Christ,* their "full armor," to the glory of God?

THE PRAYER WITH THE ARMOR

Christ's being the essence in each spiritual aspect of the armor has a very close association with prayer. Prayer lays hold of *Him* in that Christians are to "be strong in the *Lord* . . ." (v. 10). The kind of prayer that thus draws on Him is prayer deriving its purpose, commitment, passion, values, and priority by the Word.[12] Paul brings out the cruciality of praying like this. Furthermore, other parts of the Word attest to it. Consider the following points that show this.

First, Paul underscores how vital prayer is by his own modeling. He does this in blessing and praise (1:2–3, 6, 12, 14) and twice in being moved to intercession for others (1:15–23; 3:14–21). His prayer model reflects how the Word from God filled with blessings naturally returns in prayer to the God who blesses.

Second, in 6:17–18 Paul's words about the armor connect without a break to the urgency of praying. Praying relates, being vital for every part of the armor. Although the armor passage does not mention prayer until 6:18–20, the rest of Scripture demonstrates prayer to be a saturating element in the armor, as reflected in Exhibit B1 (cf. also Exhibit B2). That prayer should saturate each part of the armor—each aspect of life— is evident in Paul's fourfold use of the word "all" in verse 18. For example, Christians should be "praying at all times in the Spirit." The "all times" would include all the times they express truth, righteousness, and the rest of the positive qualities.

Third, Scripture often lets readers look in on believers praying that God will strengthen them or exulting over His power realized through prayer (Ps. 138:3; Acts 4:29–31). God's warriors live by power when they "Put on the gospel armor, each piece put on with prayer"—as the song "Stand Up, Stand Up For Jesus" urges.[13]

Fourth, many examples in the Word of God emphasize the close tie with victories in battle or in other threats to prayer. Jehoshaphat and his people prepared through offering praise, and God overwhelmingly gave them triumph against invading masses (2 Chronicles 20). Daniel and his friends prepared to face a threat of death through a night vigil in prayer (Dan. 2:17–23). Jesus faced His trials, saturating His lifestyle with prayer (Mark 1:35; Luke 5:16; 6:12; Heb. 5:7). Paul practiced in much prayer, both by night and by day (1 Thess. 3:10). Scores of other such examples emerge in the case files Scripture supplies.

Fifth, as Lincoln notes, prayer "in the Spirit" (v. 18)—the Holy Spirit— links closely with the Word that the Spirit makes effective as a cutting edge, "the sword of the Spirit" (v. 17).[14] The two, God's Word to men and men's scripturally oriented prayers to God, combine in numerous passages (John 15:7, 16; Acts 6:4; cf. Eph. 1:18; Phil. 1:9; 4:6–8; Col. 1:9–10; 1 Tim. 4:5; 1 John 5:14–15; Jude 3, 20). Paul in the Ephesian letter has prayers that interweave references to riches consistent with the Word he spells out in context. For example, he has burst out in blessing (1:3) and praise (1:6, 12, 14), and prayed that the readers might realize the practical benefit of the riches in the Word (1:15–23; 3:14–21). In chaps. 1–3, he "frames" everything he writes in prayer, as Lincoln expresses it.[15] And in 6:18, prayer "in the Spirit" is, as Lincoln defines, "inspired, guided and made effective through the Spirit."[16] This is the Spirit who has been active in sealing believers (1:13–14), is building them as a household of God (2:22), and has revealed truth to them (3:5).

This Spirit of prayer strengthens them with power (3:16), preserves unity among them (4:3), and fills them (5:18). This Spirit, whose sword of power and penetration is the Word (6:17) through whom prayer will be fulfiled (v. 18), obviously fosters prayer that Christians will prevail in God's will in every spiritual aspect of the armor (cf. Exhibit D, 241–43). This Spirit consistently assists the saints to pray κατὰ θεόν (*kata theon,* "according to God," Rom. 8:26–27), i.e., according to His will that His Word expresses.

Sixth, as noticed earlier, every facet that comprises the armor portrays what Christ manifests He is as He lives His will through the saints (cf. Exhibit A). Jesus, now in His people, wants to live out the grand values He so faithfully demonstrated while on earth (cf. Gal. 2:20). He displayed in character and in action living portraits of practical truth, righteousness, and every spiritual aspect of the armor. He worshipfully bathed His every move in prayer to the Father. This is clear at strategic phases of His life (e.g., Mark 1:35; Luke 3:21; 5:16; 6:12; 9:18).[17] Let those who testify with Paul, "To me to live is Christ" (Phil. 1:21), show themselves to be "strong in the Lord," as Ephesians 6:10 says. Let them wage the warfare against Christ's enemies in Christ-like prayer. By being strong in the *Lord,* they can show they are in touch with *Him,* the Commander of the troops. They put on the armor *of God,* maintaining contact in prayer *with God.*

Seventh, the correlation prayer has with the armor is evident in other examples besides those from Jesus' life. Scripture flashes some of these before its readers in newsreel episodes. The acts of the earliest Christian wearers of the armor records this example.[18] They were waging this warfare before and during the time of the writing of Ephesians. Grundmann captures this when he writes,

> Every great decision in the apostolic period, and in the whole life of early Christianity is sustained by persistent prayer. . . . This persistence . . . is determined . . . by looking to Jesus. . . . As the Son, He sought to do the Father's work in an ever new experience of unity with the will and intention and nature of the Father, to receive power for this purpose, and to realize that He was hidden in the Father's hand. . . .[19]

The book of Acts, then, illustrates the inseparability of prayer and the armor (e.g., 2:42; 3:1; 4:24–31; 6:4).

An eighth factor leaves an impression in Ephesians. It recalls the way the power of God and prayer to God enclose the armor passage (6:10–13, 18–20). Paul's model prayers attest the close coordination between power and prayer. He *climaxes* his own prayer in 1:15–23 by pleading God's power for the believers. In 3:14–21, he *commences* his intercession with prayer for power. He seeks power from God, for "power belongs to God" (Ps. 62:11). It is good always to remember in warfare that the Lord is the one by whom "I am saved from my enemies" (Ps. 18:3). He is the God who "trains my hands for the battle" (Ps. 18:34). Such power from the God of power comes through prayer to Him. So Markus Barth captures the conspicuous point of the matter: "Nothing less," he says, "is suggested than that the life and strife of the saints be one great prayer to God. . . ."[20]

Even a ninth factor bids for attention. Paul requested his readers to pray for power in his preaching—power released through forthright boldness (6:19–20). And if power for Paul emanated from prayer, then power for other believers to live successfully must also trace its efficacy to prayer—prayer to God. The closet is crucial to the combat.

In the tenth place, each part of the armor interpenetrates with the whole and synchronizes with all the other spiritual aspects. For example, combatants for Christ live "truth" only with an accompanying commitment to live by "righteousness." Nearby in 5:9, truth and righteousness join *together* as parts in the composite "fruit of light." Goodness does also. This is consistent with the exemplary Messiah who is girded with truth and righteousness (Isa. 11:4). Likewise, Christians do not fulfil their soldiery with truth and righteousness apart from the "preparation" of the gospel of peace. And they do not "fight the good fight of faith" (cf. 1 Tim. 6:12) without wielding the shield of faith. Nor can any of these ethical qualities work in battle apart from the benefit that God gives in His "salvation," a veritable "helmet." Nor do believers war a good warfare detached from the Word of God that is the input in truth and righteousness and furnishes the "preparation" that the gospel assures. Likewise, each spiritual aspect that comprises the armor interrelates with the Spirit. He does His work in men, stirring the very breath and content of real prayer (cf. Exhibit D).

A question might arise as to why the writer (in 6:10–17) holds in reserve any mention of praying until verse 18? A natural answer is that he wanted first to allow descriptions of "the whole armor" (v. 11) to be put before the soldiers as a composite unity. He does not want to interrupt his listing. Once he gets through with all six aspects of armor, however, he bears down hard on prayer, because prayer is to permeate "the whole armor," every facet of it.

An eleventh point is relevant. Consider how believers should intercede for "all the saints" (v. 18). For them, appropriate prayer will be involved with whatever details are strategic to the saints for whom they pray. Among the items in such an involvement will inevitably be prayer that they live according to spiritual values denoted by the armor, matters like truth, righteousness, readiness of the gospel, faith, realities of salvation, and the Word of God. Relevant prayer should also focus on spiritual aspects in wielding the Spirit's sword, through which believers can manifest sensitivity to the other saints' needs. This relates to whatever helps them to stand and even drive back the enemies in verse 12 by God's power.

Prayer has a strategic role, then, in effectiveness for the conflict that believers face.

And what of ourselves? Do we fancy that we somehow will win in the battle where these early Christians could not, though we belittle prayer among our priorities? Do we possess power gained through some driving energy, polished skills, or trusted methods? Are we capable in ourselves where people of prayer before us have sensed an urgent need to throw themselves on God? How much more candid could Paul be than in Ephesians 6:10–20? We make fools of ourselves, setting ourselves up for mediocrity, emptiness, and disaster, if we do not insist to be much in prayer whatever the cost.

The prayer to which Paul summons Christians is marked in verse 18 by the repeated "all." What he is calling for is an "all out" commitment to prayer. "All" is a word that should arouse soldiers to a state of urgency.

Prayer is for all situations ("in every prayer"). Prayer can take various forms, such as praise, blessing, thanks, confession, petition, intercession, and affirmation, to name a few. In the last of these, Christians affirm something like "I love Thee, O Lord, my strength" (Ps. 18:1).

Prayer is for all seasons ("at all times"). Scripture illustrates prayer at every conceivable time.[21] Spurgeon saw praying seven times a day in Psalm 119:164 as "at every touch and turn."[22] Seven denotes a completeness in resorting to prayer, as habitual prayer recurs. Prayer at all times would permeate every part of the armor as a Christian lives in truth and righteousness during these times.

Prayer is all in the Spirit. Where proper, prayer is in the Spirit's power (v. 10), faithful to the Word, which is His sword (v. 17; cf. John 15:7). Prayer in the right pattern draws from the Word its motives, which the Spirit produces in the believer. It gains its guidance from the Spirit and in every way can be touched with commitment to the Spirit's purposes.

Prayer is in all steadfastness. Paul uses two words to express this. One is translated as "being on the alert" (from ἀγρυπνέω, *agrypneō*). It refers to keeping awake, maintaining a watchful sensitivity. Alertness is essential in prayer so as to grasp what to pray in timely effectiveness and not be "asleep at the switch." The person praying is to keep this vigil "with all perseverance" (from προσκαρτέρησις, *proskarterēsis*). This is a quality of steadfast endurance, literally a "holding fast to." Early American cowboys, who took drastic measures to keep alert and hold fast to their work while guarding cattle at night exemplify this idea. They would rub tobacco juice in their eyes to make them smart, keep them open, and help the riders stay at their vigil even when weary. They did this in the interests of their boss and for the safety of the animals. Will we remain constantly steadfast in prayer for the high interests of our Lord and for the benefit of people, who are much more important than cattle?

Prayer is for all the saints. Christians in various collective ways can pray for many saints and conceivably, all-told, for every one of them. Paul's letter has *all* saints in the church in view as Christ's building (Eph. 2:11–21), body (3:1–13), and bride (5:29–30). No *one* believer can necessarily know all the saints, certainly not all the needs arising at all times, even in a local fellowship. Paul probably intended a corporate coverage as all believers become involved. And all individuals can pray sensitively about all the Christians they can be responsibly aware of and mention in a disciplined use of opportunities.

Paul also emphasizes his own sense of urgency for others' prayer (vv. 19–20). Every pastor ought to have many praying "on my [i.e., his] behalf." Prayer for Paul is for him to have boldness with clarity in proclaiming the greatest message, the gospel.[23] It is crucial for any who speak God's Word to have prayer for God's help, whether they speak to many or to one. The Word going forth with God's power can pierce as "the sword of the Spirit" (v. 17; cf. Heb. 4:12).

Such is the vital place of prayer in Christian life and ministry. God has made His moves to steer us to this priority. He could say as one says in the game of checkers when he has made his own move: "It's *your* move." And even when we make our move in prayer, we are taught by God's Word that *He* can be making *His* move again, working in us. Let us make the right move. We can do it the way God has made clear through Paul in Ephesians.

Exhibit A: God or Messiah Is Every Part of the Armor

The Image	The Spiritual Aspect	Scripture: God or Christ
Belt	Truth	cf. Isa. 11:5; John 14:6; 1:9
Breastplate	Righteousness	Isa. 59:16–17; cf. 11:5
Shoes	Gospel	Mark 14:9, death and passion of Jesus, the content of the gospel: John 14:6; Acts 5:42; 8:35; 11:20; 17:18; Rom. 5:6, 8, 21; 8:34; 10:4; 1 Cor. 1:23–24; 2:2; 2 Cor. 5:19; Gal. 1:16; Eph. 3:8 (cf. D. R. Jackson, "Gospel . . .," *Zondervan Pictorial Encyclopedia of the Bible, 2:780–781;* G. Friedrich, "εὐαγγέλιον," *TDNT, 2:728, 730)*
	Peace	Eph. 2:14–16 Christ *is, made,* and *preached* peace
Shield	Faithfulness (as object of men's faith)	Gen. 15:1; 2 Sam. 22:3, 31, 36; Pss. 3:3; 5:12; 7:10, 13; 18:2, 30; 35:2; 84:9 (Messiah); 144:1–2; Prov. 30:5
Helmet	Salvation (deliverance)	Ps. 27:1; Isa. 59:17 (cf. v. 16); 1 Cor. 1:30; 1 Thess. 5:8 (helmet of the hope of salvation, cf. Gal. 5:5)
Sword	Word *(rhēma)*	Gospel, whole message Jesus or His servants speak, or a relevant part of it (Matt. 4:4); John 3:34; 5:47; 6:63, 68; 12:47–48; 17:8; Acts 5:20 ("all the words of this Life"); Rom. 10:8, 17 (gospel or whole word as the word of Christ); Eph. 5:26 (the word that God uses in sanctification, washing members

of His church); 1 Peter 1:25;
1 Thess. 4:15; 1 Cor. 7:10 (words
of the Lord cited by Paul)

Exhibit B1: Aspects of the Armor Related to Prayer

Key Words in Warfare	Ephesians 6	Biblical Relation to Prayer
Power	v. 10	Pss. 119:28b; 138:3; Acts 4:24–31
Deliverance from evil	vv. 11, 13, 16–17	Ps. 119:41; Matt. 6:13; Rom. 10:13
Truth	v. 14	Pss. 25:5; 69:13; 119:43; John 17:17
Righteousness	v. 15	Pss. 5:8; 71:2; Phil. 1:11
Gospel	v. 16	Rom. 10:1; Col. 4:2–4
Witness	vv. 19–20	Acts 4:24–31; Col. 4:2–4
Peace	v. 15	Ps. 4:6–8; Phil. 4:6–7; 1 Thess. 5:23; 2 Thess. 3:16
Faith; Victory	v. 16	Pss. 55:23; 119:42; 143:8; James 5:15; 1 John 5:4–5
Word of God	v. 17	Ps. 119:17–18, 26, 32–40
Spirit of God	vv. 17–18	Eph. 6:18; Jude 20

Exhibit B2: Spiritual Aspects in Ephesians Related to Prayer
(a partial list of prayers by believers or others on their behalf)

1:1; 5:17; 6:6	will of God	cf. Ps. 143:8, 10; Col. 1:9; 1 Thess. 3:11; Philem. 22
1:2	grace	Acts 4:29–31; 2 Thess. 3:18

1:4; 5:2, 25, 33	love	Eph. 3:17–19; Phil. 1:9; 1 Thess. 3:12
1:6	praise	A part of prayer (e.g., Psalms 145–150)
1:7	forgiveness	Psalm 51
1:8; 5:15	wisdom, insight	Eph. 1:17–18
1:13	salvation	Rom. 10:13; Ps. 143:9
1:16; 5:20	thanks	A part of prayer (Col. 1:12)
1:16	mention of saints in prayer	In Paul's prayer
1:18	hope	In Paul's prayer
1:19; 6:10	power	Eph. 3:16; Col. 1:11; Ps. 138:3
2:10	good works	John 15:7–8; Phil. 1:11; 2 Thess. 2:17
3:7	one's spiritual gift	Eph. 6:19–20
3:9	mystery (gospel)	Eph. 6:19–20; Col. 4:3
3:12	boldness	Heb. 4:16; Eph. 6:19–20
3:17	faith	1 Thess. 3:10
3:19	fullness	Eph. 3:19
3:21	glory	Eph. 3:21
4:1; 5:15, etc.	walk	Col. 1:10
4:2	patience	Col. 1:11
4:24	holiness	1 Thess. 3:13

4:24; 6:15	righteousness	Ps. 5:8
4:25; 6:14	truth	Ps. 25:5
4:27	giving Satan no opening	Matt. 6:13
4:29; 5:4	wholesome speech	Phil. 1:9; Col. 1:10
5:9	fruit	John 15:8; Phil. 1:11
5:10	learning what pleases the Lord	Col. 1:10
5:18	filling	Eph. 3:19; Phil. 1:11
5:19	joy	Col. 1:11
6:12	victory vs. satanic hosts	Luke 22:31–32; John 17:15
6:14–15	truth, righteousness and peace (cf. earlier)	
6:17	Word of God	John 15:7
6:18	steadfastness	2 Thess. 3:5

Exhibit C: Spiritual Essentials in John 13–17 and Ephesians 6:10–20

Key Words	John 13–17	Eph. 6:10–20
Power from God	15:4–5, ability	v. 10
Prayer related to the Word	15:1, 16	vv. 18–20

Presence of Evil One	13:2; 17:15	vv. 11, 13, 16; cf. 2:2; 4:26
Protection from Evil One	17:15	vv. 10–17, esp. 11–13, 16
Truth	14:6, 17; 16:26, etc.	v. 14
Righteousness	cf. 17:15, 19	v. 15
Peace	14:27; 16:33	v. 15
Faith	14:1, 10–12; 16:9, 27, 30	v. 16
Salvation	14:6; 17:3	v. 17
Word of God	14:21; 15:3, 7	v. 17
Spirit of God	14:26; 15:26; 16:9–11, 13–15	vv. 17–18

Exhibit D: Prayer in the Spirit
(how prayer in the Spirit [6:18] relates to spiritual aspects of the armor and the entirety of 6:10–17)

Spiritual Area	Spirit's Part	Ephesians Verses Here	Other Scriptures
Power	"by My Spirit"	3:16–17; 6:10–11, 13	Zech. 4:6; 1 Cor. 2:4
Warfare (weaponry)	Spirit	6:11–17	Matt. 4:1–11; 2 Cor. 10:4–5
Truth ("fruit of light" in Eph. 5:9 is "fruit of the Spirit" in	Spirit of truth	6:14; 5:9	John 14:17, 26; 16:13; 1 John 4:6

Gal. 5:22–23
and "armor
of light in
Rom. 13:12)

Righteousness	Spirit convicts of righteousness	6:14; 5:9	John 16:8–11
Peace	fruit of the Spirit	6:15	Rom. 14:17; Gal. 5:22; cf. John 7:37–39
Faith	strengthened through the Spirit	6:16; 3:16–17	1 Cor. 12:3; Acts 6:5; 11:24
Salvation	rebirth is by the Spirit	6:17	2 Cor. 3:6, the Spirit quickens; John 3:3–7; 6:63
	sealing is by the Spirit or the Father	1:13–14; 4:30	2 Cor. 1:20; cf. 5:5
Word of God, Sword of the Spirit	This word came via human channels, "carried along by the Holy Spirit."	6:17	2 Peter 1:21
	He is the Spirit of truth, righteousness, etc.	6:14	cf. above
	He uses the Word when He leads into testing.		Matt. 4:1–11; Luke 4:1–13, etc.
	He reveals God's truths to men.	3:5	1 Cor. 2:10–11
	He convicts concerning sin, righteousness, judgment, etc.		John 16:8–11

| Prayer in the Spirit | It is in His sphere, purpose, power, etc. | 6:18 | Rom. 8:26–27; Jude 20 |
| Preaching effectively | He gives utterance | 6:19–20 | Luke 4:18; Acts 2:4; 4:8; 6:10; Rom. 15:19; 1 Cor. 2:1–5; 12:8; 1 Thess. 1:5; 1 Peter 4:10–11 |

ENDNOTES

[1] Ἀξιόω in Ephesians 4:1 had the basic root idea based on ancient scales with two arms, "to have equal weight with." It came to have the concept of one thing being a match to the other, appropriate, fitting, consistent, corresponding to. So it became a term for the practical Christian life displaying a resemblance or appropriate reflection of blessings God has given (e.g., 4:1; Col. 1:10; 1 Thess. 2:12).

[2] Scripture emphasizes God's strength in various ways: believers need it (1 Cor. 16:11); God is believers' strength and shield (Ps. 28:7; cf. Ps. 46:1; Isa. 40:29); they are to pray for strength (Ps. 31:2), realizing that God is their strength (Ps. 31:4); God girds them with strength for battle (2 Sam. 22:40; Pss. 18:39; 61:3); He guides men in His strength (Exod. 15:13; Deut. 8:17); they can celebrate His giving of strength (e.g., Ps. 138:3; Phil. 4:13; 2 Tim. 4:17). Strength relates to the main aspects of prayer: praise/thanks (Pss. 59:16–17; 81:28), petition (Pss. 31:2; 86:16; 105:4; 119:28), intercession (Isa. 33:2; Eph. 3:16), affirmation of love or trust (Exod. 15:2; Pss. 18:1; 73:26), and confession (Psalm 51).

[3] Comparisons are also frequent between Psalm 18 and Ephesians 6:10–20, between Jesus' teachings in Matthew 4:1–11 and parallels with Ephesians 6:10–20, and between 2 Corinthians 6:2, 6–7 and Ephesians 6:10–20. In the last passage, Paul draws together salvation, the Spirit, truth, the Word, God's power, weapons, and righteousness. He relates these to the ministry (v. 7), just as he wanted Timothy, a pastor, to "fight a good fight" (1 Tim. 1:18).

[4] Prayer in Ephesians 6:18–20 is not a *seventh* piece of armor, but a *saturation* in all pieces of armor. The reasons for this conclusion are: (1) Paul uses no figure after verse 17; (2) "and" is used before four of the six pieces,

but absent with prayer, and the fourth, though having no "and," has three figures before it and two after it; (3) no genitival form appears with prayer as it does in five of the six figures of speech; (4) no part of the body is used with prayer as with the others; (5) Paul repeats prayer, mentioning it five times (vv. 18–19), which he does with no part of the armor; (6) verbal action is no longer combined with a reference to a part of the body after verse 17. Some say that prayer is a seventh piece, as does E. K. Simpson (*Ephesians* [Grand Rapids: Eerdmans, 1957], 143) but later reverses himself (153). Andrew Lincoln says it is not ("Ephesians," in *Word Biblical Commentary* [Waco, Tex.: Word Books, 1990], 451).

[5] The armor is the "armor of light" (Rom. 13:12), as fruit is "fruit of light" (Eph. 5:9) and "fruit of the Spirit" (Gal. 5:22), light emphasizing the *nature* of it and the Spirit the *Person* (Source). We might well refer to the armor as the "armor of the Spirit," who is prominent in the close context of Ephesians (6:17–18).

[6] It is instructive to check a concordance on the frequent use of "true" and forms of it in the gospel of John.

[7] E.g., Psalm 119:142; Isaiah 48:1; Zechariah 8:8; Ephesians 5:9.

[8] So Markus Barth, "Ephesians," in *The Anchor Bible* (Garden City, N.Y.: Doubleday, 1974), 2:797–99; and much earlier, A. F. Buscarlet, "The 'Preparation' of the Gospel of Peace," *Expository Times* 9 (1897–98): 38–40.

[9] Lincoln, "Ephesians," 448–49: in the OT and other literature, the term nowhere actually denotes "firm footing; its more usual sense is readiness, preparedness, or preparation (LXX Ps. 9:17; Wis. 13:12; Josephus, *Antiq.* 10:1:2 etc.)." Lincoln takes it as "readiness . . . for combat and for standing in the battle," a preparedness in harmony that the gospel of peace bestows. The emphasis is on the stand in battle, not readiness to speak the gospel, as the most effective means of combatting the enemy, as in A. Oepke, "ὑποδέω," *TDNT,* 5:312.

[10] Offensive victories through faith seem evident in Ephesians 1:13, 15; 2:8; 3:12, 17; 6:23; and often in Hebrews 11 (most of the examples at least).

[11] Hudson Taylor celebrated a new joy in his servant life when this con-

cept in a letter by John McCarthy moved him: "How then to have our faith increased? Only by thinking of all that Jesus is and all He is for us; His life, His death, His work, He Himself as revealed to us in the Word, to be the subject of our constant thoughts. Not a striving to have faith . . . but a looking off to the Faithful One seems all we need . . ." (Dr. and Mrs. Howard Taylor, *Hudson Taylor's Spiritual Secret* [Chicago: Moody Press, n.d.], 156).

[12] For a fuller discussion of such prayer, see my "Prayer Relating to Prophecy in Daniel 9" that appears in this volume as Chapter 4. E.g., God has a plan, will fulfil it, and "allows men the privilege of laboring together with Him by yearning and praying for the same wonderful ends (Jer. 29:12)," (ibid., 99).

[13] *Hymns for the Family of God* (Nashville, Tenn.: Paragon Associates, 1976), 616.

[14] Lincoln, "Ephesians," 450–52.

[15] Ibid., 439.

[16] Ibid., 452.

[17] Luke's Gospel, in sensitivity to Jesus' humanity, shows that Jesus prayed before several critical events: before the Spirit's descent (3:21–22), naming the twelve (6:12), the transfiguration (9:18), Peter's trial (22:31–32), and the arrest, trial and crucifixion (22:41–45).

[18] For a discussion of prayer in Acts, see Hermann Wang, "Prayer in the Acts" (Th.M. thesis, Talbot School of Theology, 1987). Wang sums up the essence in most of the references to prayer.

[19] W. Grundmann, "προσκαρτερέω," *TDNT,* 3:618–19.

[20] Barth, "Ephesians," 778.

[21] E.g., morning, noon, and night (Ps. 55:17), seven times a day (Ps. 119:164), midnight (Ps. 119:62), before dawn (Ps. 119:147), day and night (Ps. 22:1–5; Neh. 1:6; 1 Thess. 3:10), three weeks (Dan. 10:2–3), ten days (Acts 1:3, 13; 2:1).

[22] C. H. Spurgeon, *The Treasury of David,* 6 vols. (London: Marshall, Morgan and Scott, 1950), 5:429.

[23] Paul seeks prayer not only for boldness, but for clarity (Col. 4:2–4), rapid spread of the gospel and its being glorified (2 Thess. 3:1), and protection from evil men (2 Thess. 3:2).

1 John 5:16–17

The Sin unto Death

Irvin A. Busenitz

The "sin unto death" in 1 John 5:16 has provoked widespread discussion. The correct meaning revolves around the nature of the sin and the nature of the death referred to. The context and word selection point to the conclusion that the individual "committing a sin not unto death" is an unsaved man who professes to be a believer, but who is, in actuality, in need of salvation. On the one hand, John refers to one who is sinning but is not doing so to the point of the impossibility of being granted eternal life. The apostle encourages intercessory prayer for such an individual, that God may grant to him eternal life. On the other hand, he asserts that if a man does sin to such an extent that repentance and forgiveness are impossible, it would be "unto death," spiritual death in the sense that his condition is irrevocable (cf. Matt. 12:31–32).

* * * * *

Diversity of opinion has abounded concerning the interpretation of the problematic portion found in 1 John 5:16 where the apostle John writes, "If any one sees his brother committing a sin not *leading* to death, he shall ask and God will for him give life to those who commit sin not *leading* to death. There is a sin *leading* to death; I do not say that he should make request for this."[1]

The OT frequently mentions specific sins that merit punishment by death. Numbers 15:30–31 indicates that the one who willfully and defiantly sins "shall be cut off from among his people." The sin of coming near to the tent of meeting was punishable by death (Num. 18:22). Psalm 19:13 suggests the same penalty for presumptuous sins.[2]

The NT has similar examples, the most prominent being that of Ananias and Sapphira (Acts 5:1–10). Other examples include that of Herod (Acts 12) and those who had taken the Lord's Supper unworthily (1 Corinthians 11).

There are two notable differences between the other passages and this one, however. First of all, in the above cases, the sin that led to the punishment is more or less evident; in this instance, it is not revealed. Secondly, the exact nature of the death penalty is ambiguous here, while elsewhere it is not. So the problem encountered here is unique. Two basic questions call for a response in this passage: (1) What is the nature of the sin? and (2) What is the nature of the death? The answers to these will essentially answer a third, namely, can the sin be committed today by Christians?

THE CONTEXT

The entirety of 1 John deals with tests of life, tests designed to give assurance of salvation to believers (cp. 5:13 with 1:4; 2:12–14) and to expose those who are not really believers: "We shall know by this that we are of the truth, and shall assure our heart before Him" (1 John 3:19).[3] The fact that one is or is not a believer is not always obvious; rather, continuation in the truth is a test that will ultimately reflect the validity of the profession.[4]

In the preceding verses (5:14–15), John speaks about prayer and the confidence a believer may have concerning the acceptance of that prayer before God and the granting of the request. In verses 16–17, he gives a specific illustration and limitation within which the prayer of a Christian may be benevolently and effectually employed, namely, in rescuing a brother from death.

> It is not now a case of petition, but of intercession. The assurance of eternal life which the Christian should enjoy (v. 13) ought not to lead him into preoccupation with himself to the neglect of others. On the contrary, he will recognize his duty in love to care for his brother in need. . . . The future tense *he shall ask* expresses not the writer's command but the Christian's inevitable and spontaneous reaction.[5]

Thus it is that when one comes to the throne of God in prayer, the standing of one's brother is immediately brought into focus. This connection has led Cameron to remark, "Our holiest hours of prayer and worship should be marked by benevolence toward our brethren."[6]

THE NATURE OF THE SIN

Various attempts in satisfactorily resolving the difficulties regarding the character of the sin have been made. Some of the many interpretations include (1) the sin against the Holy Spirit, (2) any great sin, such as murder or adultery, (3) rejection of Christ as Messiah, (4) deliberate and willful sins, (5) apostasy, and (6) post-baptismal sins.[7] The most significant of these will be examined.

Mortal Sins

The Church of Rome has consistently maintained that the "sin unto death" is a grave, post-baptismal sin.[8] This sin is commonly referred to as "mortal" sin, as compared with the less significant sin, which is called "venial." Although the designations are not specifically named in Scripture, it is asserted that the distinction between the two types of sin is clearly affirmed. In general, mortal sins are said to be those that exclude the offender from the kingdom (e.g., Eph. 5:5; Gal. 5:19–21) and venial sins are those that do not (e.g., James 3:2; 1 John 1:8; Eccl. 7:21).[9] Additional proof for such distinctions is given by Dens, as quoted by M'Clintock and Strong:

> "It is, moreover, certain," says Dens, "not only from the divine compassion, but from the nature of the thing, that there are venial sins, or such light ones, as in just men may consist with a state of grace and friendship with God; implying that there is a certain kind of sin of which a man may be guilty without offending God."[10]

A more specific basis for these definitions is provided by Aquinas. Describing the distinctiveness of the two types, he explains,

> The difference between venial and mortal sin follows upon a diversity of disorder inherent in the concept of sin itself. This disorder is twofold: the one involves the abandonment of the very source of order, the other only involves departure from secondary elements in that order. . . . Hence, when the soul is so disordered by sin that it turns away from its ultimate goal, God, to whom it is united by charity, then we speak of mortal sin. However, when this disorder stops short of turning away from God, then the sin is venial.[11]

Venial sins, therefore, do not make one the offender of God; they do not cause a diminution of sanctifying grace. Though they constitute a violation of God's law, they are too small and insignificant to divert one from his ultimate goal, God. Mortal sin, on the other hand, constitutes an act in which the offender deliberately chooses "some created good as a final end in preference to the Supreme Good, with a consequent loss of sanctifying grace."[12] The NT does teach that sins differ in magnitude (cf. Matt. 10:15; 11:22, 24; Luke 10:12, 14; 12:47–48). Nevertheless, holding such an interpretation as set forth by the Roman Church entails several difficulties. First, the definition of venial and mortal is imprecise, essentially destroying any real distinction between the two. Because their general definition of sin specifically states that "sin is a deliberate and voluntary act, . . . an act marked by a want of conformity with the law of God,"[13] they are forced to make some fine differentiations and to conclude that venial sin is "imperfectly deliberate" while mortal sin is "fully deliberate."[14] Such terminology makes a distinction virtually imperceptible. Furthermore, the definition is untenable in light of certain scriptural examples. Paul persecuted the first-century Christians in ignorance (1 Tim. 1:13), yet he designates himself as the chief of sinners (1 Tim. 1:15). Eve was deceived by Satan (1 Tim. 2:14) but bore the consequences of mortal sin.

Secondly, Scripture teaches that every offense is deadly and subject to the claims of divine justice. Thus Ezekiel 18:20 declares, "The person who sins will die." Likewise Romans 6:23 asserts, "The wages of sin is death." The malicious motivation behind the sin, or the lack of it, makes no difference, as James 2:10 indicates: "For whoever keeps the whole law and yet stumbles in one point, he has become guilty of all." On the other hand, the Bible explicitly and implicitly declares that no sin is too great to be beyond the scope of God's forgiveness (cf. 1 Tim. 1:15).

Thirdly, that the kind of sin does not determine whether its punishment is temporal or eternal but merely results in greater or lesser punishments is illustrated by the appointed sacrifices of the OT. Different sins demanded different sacrifices; nevertheless, "without the shedding of blood there was no remission" (cf. Heb. 9:22). Though sins differ in degree, the essential character of sin does not vary.

The classification of sins as adumbrated by the Roman Catholic Church has no basis in Scripture, neither in 1 John nor elsewhere. The NT gives no precedent for such a practice nor does it warrant such an arbitrary conclusion.

Apostasy

Some authors have suggested that the "sin unto death" refers to total apostasy, exemplified by the renunciation of the faith. Brooke, a proponent of the view, maintains that the sin is a deliberate rejection of Christ and His claims, for such "was probably the most prominent in the writer's thought."[15] That this is so, it is contended, is evident from

1 John 2:18–19, where the false teachers are reported to have left the fellowship of believers.[16] Brooke further explains that since apostasy exhibits itself apart from any specific act of sin, this conclusion dovetails with the fact that no specific sins are mentioned here. He concludes that "in the author's view any sin which involves a deliberate rejection of the claims of Christ may be described as 'unto death.'"[17] Lenski concurs with this assessment:

> Since ζωή *(zōē)* "life eternal" (v. 13), which, as we now "have" it, is spiritual, "death" must be its opposite, namely the loss of spiritual life, which is spiritual death. Once having been born from God (2:29; 3:9; 4:7; 5:4, 18) into the new life, "death" means that this life has been lost.[18]

The major difficulty with this conclusion, however, is the fact that Scripture nowhere teaches that the genuinely regenerated person can apostasize. This same writer in his gospel contends that the believer is secure (John 10:28–29). Elsewhere in this epistle, he reiterates that the one who is born of God does not habitually sin (1 John 3:9; 5:18). Scholer elaborates,

> There is no reference to apostasy. This is made very clear in 1 John 2:19. . . . After stating that many antichrists, already present and active (2:18; cf. 4:1–5), have come from the Christian community (2:19), the statement is modified in such a way as to negate it. In actuality the antichrists were not from the Christian community, for if they had been they would not have left it. The fact that antichrists left the community was a good thing; it showed conclusively that they were never real members of it in the first place; they had been pretenders only.[19]

The fact that they were never regenerated is also indicated by John' use of the imperfect verb ἦσαν *(ēsan,* "they were") in 2:19:

> The imperfect tense, used twice, indicates that those who depart were not real Christians in the *past.* This agrees with the use of the perfect tense in the epistle to indicate that a man's life reflects evidence whether he has or has not been born of God in the past.[20]

Furthermore, the preposition εἰς *(eis,* "in, into") is usually employed by John when referring to entrance into the new life in Christ (John

5:24; 1 John 3:14). The same preposition could be expected if he had in mind a reversal of that act. Rather, πρὸς (*pros*, "toward, unto") is used here, indicating motion toward. Brooke explains that πρὸς θάνατον (*pros thanaton*, "toward, unto death") must, of course, denote a tendency in the direction of death, and not an attained result.[21]

Passages within the Johannine corpus, as well as many references outside it (cf. Rom. 8:29; Phil. 1:6; Jude 1), lend strong evidence that the Christian will not apostatize, but will persevere in the faith.

Blasphemy Against the Holy Spirit

A third view suggests that John is referring to the "unpardonable sin" spoken of in Matthew 12. Sawtelle explains,

> It is a sin that John has terribly marked again and again in our Epistle, that of willfully rejecting the testimony of the Holy Spirit as to the true nature and Messiahship of Jesus, the denying of Christ in his true nature. That it is a sin which connects itself with one's treatment of Christ is a fair inference from the doctrine of ver. 12.[22]

Stott embraces this view also, contending that the one who is depicted in Matthew 12:31–32 as deliberately and willfully rejecting known truth is also referred to here. "In John's own language he has 'loved darkness rather than light' (Jn. iii.18–21), and in consequence he will 'die in his sins' (Jn. viii. 24). His sin is, in fact, *unto death*."[23]

Support for this conclusion is obtained primarily from the polemic of John which is evident throughout the epistle and especially in the context of the fifth chapter. The apostle frequently expresses the necessity of recognizing and believing that Jesus is God in the flesh (1:1–3; 2:22–24; 4:2–3, 15; 5:1). In chapter five, he specifically notes how the Holy Spirit bears witness to this very fact (5:6–10).[24] Consequently, the argument proceeds, John's comments regarding the witness of the Spirit may have been intended to recall the warning against blaspheming the Holy Spirit recorded in the Synoptics.

This interpretation has much to commend it and is certainly a possible solution. However, the view has some problems. First, the passage really does not connect itself with the "unpardonable sin" of Matthew 12. It contains no concrete evidence that such a connection was intended by the writer.[25]

Second, the one who had committed the "unpardonable sin" would not be considered a "brother" in the local fellowship. Willful and deliberate rejection of the work of the Holy Spirit, as described in the

Gospels, would be difficult to disguise. One guilty of such would hardly be accepted as a brother. Such open antagonism could not be masked and go unnoticed by the others in the fellowship.

Habitual Sinning

A fourth possibility is that the "sin unto death" refers to one who persists in committing sin. One habitually practices sin to the extent that one's character and lifestyle ultimately show others within the local body of believers that one is not a believer.

The main thematic thread of the Epistle supports this contention, for the true believer does not practice sin (2:1; 3:4, 6, 8–9). The immediate context supports this conclusion also, for the following verse reiterates the same fact. This teaching is not limited to the Johannine corpus, for such a teaching is also found in Galatians 5:21; 6:8; and Romans 6:21–23. Although there may be occasional sins, the believer's life will not be characterized by sin as a lifestyle.

The NT elsewhere teaches that those who are immoral, covetous, idolatrous, revilers, drunkards, and swindlers shall not inherit the kingdom (1 Cor. 5:9–13; 6:9–11; Gal. 5:19–21; Eph. 5:5), for their works are the works of the flesh (Gal. 5:19; so also 1 Peter 4:3–5; 1 John 3:15; Rev. 21:7–8; 22:14–15). Continuation in and habitual pursuit of such activity is inconsistent with a believer's life in Christ. An isolated act does not necessarily deny one an inheritance in the kingdom of God, but the constant practice of such things does.

The major difficulty that this view faces is the fact that 1 John 5:16 refers to a sinning "brother." Scholer, for example, asserts that the above argument "breaks down completely because of the use of the present tense of *hamartanein* in 5:16 with reference to the sinning of a believer as well as the use of the present tense in 1:8."[26]

However, neither 1:8 nor 5:16 furnish conclusive evidence that the one sinning is definitely a saved man. In fact, the designation of "brother" may also include one who has only professed but does not actually possess eternal life. This kind of brother is inferred in 2:9, 11, and 3:15, for "the one who hates his brother is in the darkness until now" (cf. 4:20). It is not uncommon for the Scriptures to speak to professing believers when addressing the church, such as in 1 Corinthians 5:11; 2 Corinthians 11:26; and Galatians 2:4. Even the unregenerate of 1 John 2:19 were most probably called brothers.[27]

Furthermore, the use of the present active participle ἁμαρτάνοντα (*hamartanonta,* "sinning"), suggests that John has an unsaved man in view, for he consistently employs the present tense to refer to the sins that characterize the unsaved (3:4, 6, 8; 5:18).[28] Other evidences of an unregenerate heart in 1 John are spoken of in the present tense, such as loving the world (2:15), not keeping the commandments (2:4), hating a brother (2:9, 11; 3:10, 14ff.; 4:8, 20), walking in darkness (1:6; 2:12), lying (1:6), and denying that Jesus is the Christ (2:22ff.).[29] Those who hold to the "believer" view attempt to circumvent this clear indication by attributing a "one time occurrence" to the punctiliar action of the aorist subjunctive ἴδῃ (idē, "sees," 5:16). But the punctiliar action of the aorist does not rule out the idea of continual, ongoing occurrence; it cannot be restricted to a "one time occurrence/once for all" idea. To hide behind the screen of a "particular occasion of practicing sin" greatly obscures and even negates the obvious Johannine practice of employing the present tense to denote continuing, ongoing, characteristic-of-life issues. Furthermore, even if the "seeing" were conceded to be point action, the "sinning" is still clearly habitual and ongoing, a fact demonstrated by John's repeated use of the present active participle to denote durative action. At best, the aorist subjunctive only indicates that the ongoing practice of sin was not actually *observed* on a continual basis.

In light of the above evidence, the most plausible explanation for the sin that leads to death is that it refers to habitual and continual sinning of a professing brother. The apostle probably has no particular sin in mind, for the present participle, *hamartanonta,* denotes not an act of sin but a continuing state.

THE NATURE OF THE DEATH

The second issue that confronts the interpreter in 1 John 5:16 is the nature of the death that results from the sinning described by John. The apostle states that the sin either is not πρὸς θάνατον or is πρὸς θάνατον (*pros thanaton,* "toward, unto death"). Virtually all grammarians and commentators maintain that the πρὸς (*pros,* "toward, unto") does not denote "until," for it nowhere has this meaning in the NT. Rather, it designates that which *eventuates in* or *tends toward* death.

> The Greek (ἁμαρτία πρὸς θάνατον, [*hamartia pros thanaton,* "sin unto death"]) would mean properly a sin which *tends* to death; which would *terminate* in death; of which death was the penalty or would be the result, unless it were arrested; a sin which, if it had its own course, would terminate thus.[30]

Although many different views have been propounded,[31] there are basically two views held by present-day scholars regarding the nature of this death.

Physical Death

Probably the most common interpretation is that the death refers to the physical death of a believer. It is a physical punishment or chastisement that God executes as a result of sin in the believer's life.

> The sin unto death means a case of transgression, particularly of grievous backsliding from the life and power of godliness, which God determines to punish with temporal death, while at the same time he extends mercy to the penitent soul. . . . The sin not unto death is any sin which God does not choose thus to punish.[32]

The major support for this position is the interpretation of "brother." "The text is explicit. It refers to a 'brother,' which term is never used of the unregenerate, and declares definitely that a Christian may sin in such a way that the chastisement of death may fall upon him."[33] Thus it is concluded that since a believer cannot apostatize, John must be speaking of physical death and not spiritual death. However, as was noted earlier, the term "brother" cannot be so restricted; rather, it may be used sometimes to refer to one who is only professing to be a believer, for John does employ the term at times in a more universal sense.

Another proof used for this view is the fact that other passages suggest that sin does sometimes result in the believer's physical death. The most prominent incident is noted in 1 Corinthians 11:30, where Paul indicates that the partaking of the Lord's Supper unworthily (11:27) has been the reason that "many among you sleep."[34]

It is granted that the physical death of a believer may be in view in 1 Corinthians 11. However, this does not prove that physical death of a believer is in view in 1 John 5:16. In addition to the fact that "nothing in this part of 1 John indicates that 'sin leading to death' must be understood as sin punished by fatal bodily illness,"[35] there is significant evidence that suggests otherwise.

Spiritual Death

A second view maintains that the death referred to in 1 John 5:16 is spiritual death. This interpretation hinges primarily upon John's use of ζωήν (zōēn, "life") and, by comparison, θάνατον (thanaton, "death"), for these two are natural opposites and must correspond when in antithesis to each other. If physical death is being referred to, then the life must be physical life; conversely, if spiritual death is in view, then the life must be spiritual life. One cannot "mix-n-match" and still maintain a natural understanding of the death-life antithesis in the passage. If correspondence is maintained, then proponents of the physical death view are faced with the difficulty of explaining why one should pray that God will give the sinning one in 5:16a extended physical life when in fact he is committing sin not leading to premature physical death.

First of all, it should be noted that the apostle significantly employs βιός (*bios*, "life") (2:16) and ψυχή (*psychē*, "life, breath") (3:16, twice) to refer to physical life, but reserves *zōē* to refer to spiritual life elsewhere in the Epistle. The nominal form is used eleven times elsewhere (1:1–2 [twice]; 2:25; 3:14–15; 5:11–12 [twice], 13, 20), *always* meaning eternal or spiritual life. The verbal form, ζάω (*zaō*, "I live"), is used only once (4:9), also with the same meaning. This fact strongly suggests that John has spiritual life in view in 5:16 also. Furthermore, this trend characterizes John's gospel, for *zōē*, the term used in 5:16, always refers to eternal life, and the verb *zaō* designates eternal life in all but three (John 4:50–51, 53) instances. While John does use these terms to refer to physical life in Revelation, the predominant usage is in reference to spiritual life.

Second, John's use of *thanatos* in the Epistle lends additional support. Apart from its use in the phrases under discussion in 5:16–17, the term occurs only in 3:14. In this passage, John employs the term twice to denote spiritual death: "We know that we have passed out of death into life, because we love the brethren. He who does not love abides in death."

Consequently, if physical life had been meant by John in 5:16, it is most likely that he would have used one of the other two terms he employed earlier to refer to physical life. And, since it is likely that *zōē* refers to spiritual life, then *thanatos*, following its usage in 3:14, must have reference to spiritual death. It is conceded that while all persons are born spiritually dead, they certainly are not confirmed in that state. However, following the apostle's teaching here, there may come a time prior to their physical death when their condition becomes irreversible, when divine forgiveness is no longer available to them (cf. Matt. 12:31–32).[36]

Third, the immediate context offers important credence to this conclusion, for both before and after the sixteenth verse, *zōē* is used to refer to eternal, spiritual life (vv. 11–12–13, 20). Says Cameron, "If a different kind of life were meant, it would be natural to expect him to indicate it by the use of a different word, elsewhere used for natural life."[37]

CONCLUSION

The apostle John appears to have in view an unsaved man who professes to be a believer, but who is in actuality in need of salvation. On the one hand, John refers to a man who is sinning but is not doing so to the point of the impossibility of being granted eternal life; he has not yet come to the place where the possibility of divine forgiveness has been revoked. In such cases, as a result of the intercessory prayer of a "brother," God would grant spiritual life. On the other hand, the apostle asserts that if a man does sin to such an extent that repentance and forgiveness are impossible, it would be "unto death"—spiritual death, spiritual death in the sense that his condition is irrevocable (cf. Matt. 12:31–32). Thus the sin *can* be committed by a Christian when "Christian" is used in the broader sense to include *those whose Christianity is merely a matter of profession,* but it cannot if "Christian" means one who has actually been regenerated.

It is clear that "brother" in Scripture normally refers to a saved individual, but John's usage of the term implies that in some cases there will be a difference between what is professed and what is actually true.

Furthermore, experience has vividly illustrated the power of God to regenerate the most reprobate of sinners, and therefore the believer should be careful not to judge the status of another too quickly. Nevertheless, John asserts that the habitual practice of sin does indicate the spiritual state of a man (cf. Gal. 5:21). Consequently, while the believer is to pray for this sinning brother until God reveals otherwise, John reminds him that the efficacy of his prayer may not extend to that person and that the believer's confidence should not be diminished thereby.

This is not an adumbration of the Roman Catholic doctrine regarding mortal sin, for which the consequence is spiritual death (unless it is reversed during this lifetime through confession and penance or after this lifetime while in purgatory through the efforts of relatives still alive). On the contrary, it only maintains that, in keeping with the Johannine theme, persistent sin in the life of anyone who professes to be saved indicates that the person is not saved, and that the ultimate end of such is spiritual death. Although acts of sin do not cause one to die spiritually (man is born spiritually dead), the habitual practice of sin may lead to an irreversible state, a condition in which forgiveness will be no longer available. The limitation has only to do with the unbeliever, however, for the believer's full forgiveness was procured by the death of Christ at Calvary.

ENDNOTES

[1] Scripture quotations in this essay are taken from the *New American Standard Bible* unless otherwise noted. "Sin unto death" in the essay title and used frequently throughout the essay is phraseology derived from 1 John 5:16 in the *King James Version.*

[2] Also cf. Leviticus 4:2; 5:15; Numbers 14:2–4; 20:12; 1 Samuel 2:25. This same philosophy was continued in the Qumran community, as the Manual of Discipline gives evidence (1QS 8:21–9:2). During the first centuries A.D., this concept was taken even further: "Tertullian went a stage further and listed the grosser sins (including murder, adultery, blasphemy and idolatry) as beyond pardon" (John R. W. Stott, *The Epistles of John*, Tyndale's New Testament Commentaries, ed. R. V. G. Tasker [Grand Rapids: Eerdmans, 1976], 187).

[3] See Robert Law, *The Tests of Life* (Edinburgh: T & T Clark, 1914).

[4] Cf. 1 John 2:19 where some who professed Christ and were a part of the local body of believers were ultimately exposed by their departure.

[5] Stott, *Epistles,* 186.

[6] Robert Cameron, *The First Epistle of John* (Philadelphia: A. J. Rowland, 1899), 242.

[7] A list of additional interpretations is given by Barnes, "The First Epistle General of John," *Barnes' Notes on the New Testament,* X (reprint, Grand Rapids: Baker, 1975), 348–49, and Raymond E. Brown, *The Epistles of John,* vol. 30 of *The Anchor Bible* (Garden City, N.Y.: Doubleday, 1982), 611–620.

[8] Deadly sins committed prior to the time of baptism are said to be cleansed at the time of that sacrament (James Gibbons, *Faith of Our Fathers* [Baltimore: John Murphy, 1905], 303ff.). For this reason many have waited until their deathbed to be baptized.

[9] I. McGuiness, "Sin (Theology of)," in *The Catholic Encyclopedia* (New York: McGraw-Hill, 1967), 13:245.

[10] John M'Clintock and James Strong, "Sin," in *Cyclopaedia of Biblical, Theological, and Ecclesiastical Literature* (reprint, Grand Rapids: Baker, 1969), 9:767.

[11] Thomas Aquinas, *Summa Theologiae,* XXV, trans. Timothy McDermott (New York: McGraw-Hill Book Company, 1969), 43.

[12] McGuiness, "Sin," 241.

[13] Ibid.

[14] Ibid.

[15] A. E. Brooke, *A Critical and Exegetical Commentary on the Johannine Epistles,* in *International Critical Commentary,* ed. C. A. Briggs, et al. (Edinburgh: T & T Clark, 1971), 147. Marvin Vincent appears to embrace this view also, for he states that "whatever breaks fellowship between the soul and Christ . . . is unto death for there is no life apart from Christ" (*Word Studies* [New York: Charles Scribner's Sons, 1911], 2:371).

[16] Hebrews 6:4–6; 10:26–29 are usually associated with this view and are frequently employed as proof of its veracity.

[17] Brooke, *Johannine Epistles,* 146–47. Lenski agrees, stating that this sin results in "the loss of spiritual life, which is spiritual death" (R. C. H. Lenski, *The Interpretation of St. Peter, St. John, and St. Jude* [Minneapolis: Augsburg, 1961], 535–36).

[18] Lenski, *St. Peter, St. John, and St. Jude,* 535–36.

[19] David M. Scholer, "Sins Within and Sins Without: An Interpretation of 1 John 5:16–17," *Current Issues in Biblical and Patristic Interpretation* (Grand Rapids: Eerdmans, 1975), 242.

[20] James E. Rosscup, "Paul's Teaching on the Christian's Future Reward With Special Reference to 1 Corinthians 3:10–17" (unpublished Ph.D. dissertation, University of Aberdeen, Scotland, 1976), 448.

[21] Brooke, *Johannine Epistles,* 147.

[22] Henry A. Sawtelle, *Commentary on the Epistles of John,* An American Commentary on the New Testament, ed. Alvah Hovey (Valley Forge: Judson, 1888), 61.

[23] Stott, *Epistles,* 189. Also cf. George G. Findlay, *Fellowship in the Life Eternal* (New York: Hodder & Stoughton, n.d.), 406–7, and Baird Tipson, "A Dark Side of 17th Century English Protestantism: the Sin against the Holy Spirit," *Harvard Theological Review* 77, no. 3–4 (July–October 1984): 301–30.

[24] Stott (*Epistles,* 188ff.) contends that both parties in 5:16 are unbelievers while John Murray maintains that only the one who commits a sin unto death is not a believer, citing John 9:41; 15:22; 1 John 4:2–3; 5:1 as proof. Nevertheless, they both agree as to the nature of the sin unto death, namely, "the denial of Jesus as come in the flesh" (John Murray, "Definitive Sanctification," *Calvin Theological Journal* 2, no. 1 [April 1967]: 11).

[25] Brooke, *Johannine Epistles,* 147.

[26] Scholer, "Sins Within," 231. Scholer, with Murray ("Definitive Sanctification" 11), contends that when John speaks of the believer as not sinning, he is *not* speaking of habitual sinning; rather, such references refer to the fact that the believer does not sin sin unto death, i.e., he does not and cannot deny Jesus as come in the flesh. The believer may, however, sin sin not unto death (246). Also cf. Henry W. Holloman, "The Meaning of 'Sin unto Death' in 1 John 5:16–17" (paper read at Far West Section of the Evangelical Theological Society, April 23, 1982), 1–6.

[27] Cf. Stott, *Epistles,* 189–90, for a helpful discussion.

[28] Scholer ("Sins Within," 246) and Murray ("Definitive Sanctification," 11) seek to answer the Johannine use of the present tense by suggesting that the believer does sin (present tense) not unto death but does not sin (present tense) *unto death.* But 5:18 says nothing of the believer not sinning unto death; it merely says that the believer does not sin (present tense).

[29] Rosscup, "Paul's Teaching," 447–48.

[30] Barnes, *Barnes' Notes,* 249. Lenski concurs: "John says twice that in these cases the sinning is 'not unto death'; πρὸς is used as it was in v. 14 with the meaning not facing death as the inevitable result" (*St. Peter, St. John, and St. Jude,* 535).

[31] Cf. Barnes, *Barnes' Notes,* 348–49, for a list of additional interpretations.

[32] Adam Clarke, *The Holy Bible, Containing the Old and New Testaments With a Commentary and Critical Notes* (New York: Abingdon, n.d.), 6:925.

[33] Lewis Sperry Chafer, *Systematic Theology* (Dallas: Dallas Seminary Press, 1947), 3:310. Cook similarly contends, "The implication is, however, that 'sin unto death' will sometimes lead to untimely physical death

despite our prayers because God knows that chastisement, not forgiveness in this life, is the best thing" (W. Robert Cook, "Hamartiological Problems in First John," *Bibliotheca Sacra* 123, no. 491 [July–September, 1966]: 259).

[34] A number of other biblical examples have been cited, such as Nadab and Abihu (Leviticus 10), Korah and his sons (Numbers 16), Achan (Joshua 7), the disobedient prophet (1 Kings 13), and Ananias and Sapphira (Acts 5). However, these accounts are somewhat ambiguous concerning the actual spiritual standing of the individuals before God.

[35] Stephen S. Smalley, *1, 2, 3 John,* vol. 51 of *Word Biblical Commentary* (Waco, Tex.: Word, 1984), 297.

[36] The difference between the case described in Matthew 12 and the one found in 1 John 5 appears to be that those in the former instance are guilty of open, blatant opposition and rejection of the work of the Holy Spirit, while in the latter instance, the action appears to be more covert and disguised, occurring among those who profess to believe but in reality do not (cf. 1 John 2:19). In both cases, however, the result is the same, an irreversible, confirmed condition in which divine forgiveness is no longer available.

[37] Cameron, *First Epistle,* 243.

Index of Authors

Index of Scriptures

Index of Subjects

adultery 189, 193, 201, 205 n. 24, 249,
    258 n. 2
adulthood
    and homosexuality, 188, 195,
      205 n. 26
    representing maturity, 211–14, 218,
      220 n. 13
Ahab 16–19, 21–22, 27–28, 31, 33–35,
    109, 110, 113 n. 8
all Israel (see Israel)
angel(s) 171, 200
    fallen, 34
    of the LORD, 32
    ruled by Satan, 34
    Satan, 24, 33, 34
    source of false prophecy, 16, 24
apostasy 249–52, 255
armor, Christian 224–25, 227, 231–38,
    241–42, 243–44 n. 4, 244 n. 5
    faith, 229–30
    peace, 229
    righteousness, 229
    salvation, 230
    truth, 228–29
    word of God, 230–31
atonement 66, 76–77, 78 n. 7, 79 n. 13,
    81–82 nn. 22 & 28, 104 n. 55, 200
    and Matthew, 72–73
    and Peter, 73–75
    and sickness, 64–65
    and sin, 69–70, 79 n. 10
authority 65, 87, 88, 89, 105 n. 56, 171,
    176, 177, 201

Baal 16, 109, 110, 115 n. 16

blasphemy 252, 258 n. 2
blessing 90, 100 n. 8, 105 n. 55, 225,
    231–32, 235
    and cursings, 84
    cup of, 49
    formulas, 50
    of Gentiles, 118–20, 123, 137 n. 9,
      142 n. 44, 146 n. 80
    of restoration, 83, 85–89, 92–93,
      96–99
    of salvation, 77
body
    church, 123, 137 n. 9, 173, 174,
      177, 253, 258 n. 4
    of Christ, 65, 66, 72, 74, 77,
      209–10, 212–13, 215–17, 219,
      221 n. 17, 236
    physical or human, 18, 27, 67, 68,
      72, 77, 81 n. 21, 148 n. 85, 152,
      167 n. 15, 172, 176, 178, 179,
      180, 194, 229, 244 n. 4
    resurrection, 79 n. 13
build, building 87
    body, 215, 221 n. 17
    church, 97, 98, 106 nn. 57 & 59, 152,
      154–57, 159–62, 163 nn. 4 & 6,
      164 n. 9, 166 n. 14, 167 n. 17,
      168 n. 29, 169 n. 30, 232, 236
    temple & city, 97–98, 106 nn. 57 & 59

child 93, 226
    and sexual sins, 186, 187, 193
    childless, 48, 52, 53
    Jesus, 72, 73